"Professor Yeh takes us on a tour de force from Ec̶ gathers mission themes and trends that no one e̶ of his unique experiences attending the five major Polycentric Missiology gives us a road map like no o̶t̶h̶e̶r̶.̶ a̶ comprehensive overview of twenty-first century mission. This insightful study will provide signposts for mission leadership and engagement for decades to come. I highly recommend *Polycentric Missiology!*"

Joseph W. Handley Jr., president, Asian Access

"*Polycentric Missiology* not only emerges from everywhere (as indicated by the book's title)—the author being the only one to have personally attended all five of the conferences discussed in the book—but also catapults Allen Yeh from 'up-and-coming' to 'established scholar' status. Here is a historically informed, ecumenically broad, and polyperspectival analysis of missiological trends appropriate to their polymorphic character at the start of the third global millennium, yet one that also characterizes the life-giving generosity of the gospel needed for everyone in a complex and dynamic world."

Amos Yong, professor of theology and mission, Fuller Theological Seminary

"*Polycentric Missiology* traces the history of the five 2010–2012 conferences celebrating the Edinburgh 1910 World Missionary Conference. It is a remarkable book, providing a compelling case for world Christianity. It unpacks the historical, cultural, local, and global themes that shape today's missiological issues. Christian mission is a local and global enterprise. Allen Yeh challenges us to listen to missional voices from all over world Christianity and to embrace mission that is 'from everyone to everywhere.'"

Graham Hill, professor of applied theology, Morling Baptist Theological College, author of *GlobalChurch*

"During 2010 and 2012 five gatherings convened on five continents to commemorate the landmark 1910 Edinburgh World Missionary Conference. Allen Yeh, who attended all five, has helpfully organized and creatively analyzed the main themes, discussions, debates, controversies, and proposals from these conferences. The result is an important report on the state of missionary thinking today, but also a persuasive demonstration of the book's subtitle—that contemporary Christian mission is now 'from everyone to everywhere.' It is an unusually helpful, unusually perceptive study."

Mark Noll, author of *The New Shape of World Christianity*

"In this volume, Allen Yeh provides a creative running commentary on the major international mission conferences held in 2010–2012. This lively and insightful volume is itself a historical milestone—a benchmark for future reflections on the state of mission studies in the age of worldwide Christianity. I commend it with enthusiasm."

Dana L. Robert, Truman Collins Professor of World Christianity and History of Mission, and director of the Center for Global Christianity and Mission, Boston University

"Missiologist Allen Yeh offers a compelling narrative of both continuity and discontinuity for five conferences linking themselves with the centenary of the World Missionary Conference held in Edinburgh in 1910. His reflections, as first-hand accounts coming so soon after these events, will likely prove invaluable for years to come."

Todd Johnson, associate professor of global Christianity,
Gordon-Conwell Theological Seminary

POLYCENTRIC

MISSIOLOGY

TWENTY-FIRST-CENTURY MISSION
FROM EVERYONE TO EVERYWHERE

ALLEN YEH

IVP Academic

An imprint of InterVarsity Press
Downers Grove, Illinois

InterVarsity Press
P.O. Box 1400, Downers Grove, IL 60515-1426
ivpress.com
email@ivpress.com

InterVarsity Press® is the book-publishing division of InterVarsity Christian Fellowship/USA®, a
movement of students and faculty active on campus at hundreds of universities, colleges and schools
of nursing in the United States of America, and a member movement of the International Fellowship
of Evangelical Students. For information about local and regional activities, visit intervarsity.org.

Scripture quotations, unless otherwise noted, are from The Holy Bible, English Standard Version,
copyright © 2001 by Crossway Bibles, a division of Good News Publishers. Used by permission.
All rights reserved.

Table 1: Used by permission of Christianity Today *and Ted Olsen.*
Figure 1: Boston University School of Theology, 2008. Used by permission of Dana Robert.
Appendix D: World Council of Churches, "An Ecumenical Journey." Used by permission.

Cover design: Cindy Kiple
Interior design: Dan van Loon
Images: © Katerina_Andronchik/iStockphoto

ISBN 978-0-8308-4092-2 (print)
ISBN 978-0-8308-9926-5 (digital)

Printed in the United States of America ∞

Library of Congress Cataloging-in-Publication Data
A catalog record for this book is available from the Library of Congress.

P   25   24   23   22   21   20   19   18   17   16   15   14   13   12   11   10   9   8   7   6   5   4   3   2   1

Y   34   33   32   31   30   29   28   27   26   25   24   23   22   21   20   19   18   17   16

Dedicated to my miracle and my muse,

Arianna—

I love you for always

CONTENTS

ACKNOWLEDGMENTS

THANK YOU TO:

Vivian Wu (my mother), Leon Yeh (my father), Shuei-Shih Yeh (my grandfather who financially assisted me through my graduate education), William Lei (my uncle who also financially assisted me through my graduate education), Becky Lei (my aunt whom I admire for her perseverance), Bill and Johanna Molloy (my amazing in-laws), Nancy Davong, Jarrod Keithley, Elizabeth Malott (my research assistants), John Briggs (my DPhil supervisor at Oxford), Brian Stanley (for paving the way with his Edinburgh 1910 book), Ruth Padilla DeBorst (who continues to offer me wise and timely advice from the Two-Thirds World and who has always shown me incredible kindness), Todd Johnson (for encouraging me in this topic), the US Center for World Mission (who thought this project worth pursuing), Tim Tennent (I was his research assistant at Gordon-Conwell), Scott Gibson (my mentor), Lamin Sanneh (I was his research assistant at Yale), Andrew Walls (he is my academic inspiration, and coincidentally, I also read Theology at Exeter College, Oxford, as he did), Margaret Acton (who showed me such hospitality at Edinburgh), Reid Trulson and Reg Mills of American Baptist International Ministries (for giving me release time from the board of directors to do research), Biola's Cook School of Intercultural Studies, and my deans Doug Pennoyer and Bulus Galadima (for giving me a sabbatical to work on this). Most of all, this is done for the mighty and loving God who is the prime mover of mission: *SDG.*

All translations from Spanish are my own, and any errors therein are also my own.

A NOTE ON TERMINOLOGY

IN THE CONTEXT OF WORLD CHRISTIANITY, what term is best to denote the lands of Africa, Asia and Latin America?

Westerners (Europeans and North Americans) will often use "non-Western world," but people often take offense at being defined in opposition to something else. Women would be aghast to be called "non-men," and non-Christians/unbelievers really do not like that label being used for them (though "pagan" is not really a better option)![1] Plus, Latin America is technically in the Western hemisphere, and Australia (a "Western" culture for all intents and purposes) is in the East. Still, the phrase "non-Western world" will be employed in this book when it is specifically used to contrast with the West; otherwise, "Two-Thirds World" will be used when the West is not a reference point.

- "Global South" would work except it excludes Asia, which is an Eastern, not a Southern, continent and is located north of the equator for the most part.

- "Third World" is a passé term from the era of the Cold War—nobody likes to be "third," and "Second World" (communist) countries hardly exist anymore except in Cuba and North Korea.

- Patrick Johnstone coined the phrase "AfAsLa" (Africa/Asia/Latin America) as opposed to "EuNaPa" (Europe/North America/Pacific, "Pacific" meaning Australia and New Zealand), but that has not really caught on.

- "Majority World" refers to population size and thus is more neutral but becomes confusing when simultaneously referring to ethnic minorities in the Western world (are they "majority" or "minority"?).

---

[1]My former pastor, Ken Fong, prefers the term *unconvinced* to show that the onus is on us as Christians.

- "Two-Thirds World" seems to be the preferred option these days, also referring to the size of population in Africa, Asia and Latin America, without any negative or inaccurate meanings associated with it.

INTRODUCTION

THIS BOOK IS A HYBRID. It was initially intended solely to be a history of the four major conferences that celebrated the centenary of the Edinburgh 1910 World Missionary Conference (often dubbed the "Birthplace of the Modern Ecumenical Movement"), namely, Tokyo, Edinburgh, Cape Town and Boston. At my doctoral defense at the University of Oxford in 2008, I had the privilege of having Professor Brian Stanley[1] as the external reader for my thesis. He published a well-researched and well-received book the following year on the history of Edinburgh 1910.[2] I endeavored to write the history of the four 2010 conferences in that vein.

I soon realized that history is nigh impossible to write about with lack of temporal distance. I can report the contemporary facts (which would be more akin to journalism), but I cannot make judgments as to the consequences of those facts, and only time will adequately bear out the results of 2010. However, I am uniquely poised to write this volume as I am only one of two people (as far as I know) who attended all four conferences (the other being Dr. Todd Johnson[3]), and thus I have an advantage in being able to compare and contrast them from an eyewitness's point of view. Another problem with writing contemporary "history" is that just about everyone chronicled here is still alive. Unlike Brian Stanley, who had no risk of offending anyone in his volume about Edinburgh 1910, this book has great

[1]Then he was the director of the Henry Martyn Centre at the University of Cambridge; now he is the director of the Centre for the Study of World Christianity (formerly the Centre for the Study of Christianity in the Non-Western World, founded by Professor Andrew F. Walls) at the University of Edinburgh.

[2]Brian Stanley, *The World Missionary Conference, Edinburgh 1910* (Grand Rapids: Eerdmans, 2009).

[3]Coeditor (with Kenneth Ross) of the *Atlas of Global Christianity 1910–2010* (Edinburgh: Edinburgh University Press, 2009), among other significant works, and the director of the Center for the Study of Global Christianity at Gordon-Conwell Theological Seminary.

potential to offend the people described—and I do not have the luxury of changing the names for the sake of privacy because these are all very public figures! It is my hope that I can balance honesty and charity without sacrificing either.

I also came to another conclusion: one continent was missing. Tokyo is in Asia; Edinburgh is in Europe; Cape Town is in Africa; and Boston is in North America. Stunningly, in a repetition of history (the old adage of "Those who cannot remember the past are condemned to repeat it"[4] comes to mind), Latin America was left off the map. Brian Stanley recounts that this was the great error at Edinburgh 1910, and once again, Latin America was the only continent[5] not to have a major missions conference in 2010.[6] To be fair, this was not the fault of the other conference organizers, as they had nothing to do with the omission, and actually a Latin American conference *was* planned for 2010 but was postponed because the calendar was too full that year and many people would not have had the financial resources to attend more than one conference. That Latin American conference (San José, Costa Rica) was delayed until 2012, and part of the thesis of this book is that it is a necessary addition to the other four, without which the picture would be incomplete. As such, I am the only person to have attended all five conferences.

This book is a hybrid because it is not purely history. In order to serve a larger community (not just ivory-tower academics but also missionaries and lay leaders), and because the proximity of the book to the actual historical events requires me to suspend judgment on a number of issues, this will also be a textbook on contemporary missiology. The thinking behind this is that many controversial issues were discussed and debated at length at these five conferences. Though there was much agreement to be had, not everything reached consensus. As such, instead of me telling you which are the "correct" answers (only time will settle many of these missiological debates), I will report what happened and have follow-up questions at the end of each

---

[4]George Santayana, *Life of Reason, Reason in Common Sense* (New York: Scribner's, 1905), 284.
[5]With apologies to Australia/Oceania and Antarctica.
[6]Even Mark Noll and Carolyn Nystrom's recent book on world Christianity, *Clouds of Witnesses* (Downers Grove, IL: InterVarsity Press, 2011), only highlights Christian voices from Africa and Asia, once again leaving out Latin America, as if Latin America is not legitimately worthy of mention in a book about the Majority World!

chapter, allowing the readers to discuss and respond. It is impossible for me to be completely impartial as author, and I will offer my viewpoints at times, while making it clear that this is merely my perspective. Students of missiology can use this book to learn about the latest issues in missions. These are the issues that were discussed by thousands of the world's Christian leaders and missions experts in practical forums, not in the cloistered halls of universities, so they are real and "live" issues today.

The fact that theology is developed by practitioners makes sense, given the events of history. Most of our greatest Christian doctrines were argued for, and codified at, theological councils and conferences. The Nicene Creed was written at the First Ecumenical Council at Nicaea in AD 325 (and revised into its final form at the Second Ecumenical Council at Constantinople in AD 381), and it was there that a fuller doctrine of the nature of the Trinity was articulated. At the Fourth Ecumenical Council at Chalcedon in AD 451, the concept of the two natures of Christ (fully God and fully man) was established. But these have even older biblical precedents: the Jerusalem Council in Acts 15 (approximately AD 48) was the grandfather of all ecumenical missionary conferences, wrestling with questions about the nature of salvation versus what were merely cultural practices. They ultimately concluded that culture trumps peripheral theology, but core beliefs trump cultural practices.[7] Theological and missiological conferences are far more than esoteric dialogues among eggheads; they have profound implications for the wider umbrella of the church, both vertically (from the clergy to the laity) and horizontally (across time and history). When such decisions are made ecumenically, they become some of our most cherished theological truths and traditions that resonate throughout history.

Regarding the necessity of a book like this: after searching published works, I could not find other textbooks on contemporary missiology of this sort. There are excellent volumes on the history of mission (e.g., Dale Irvin

---

[7]It was decided that Gentiles did not have to be circumcised or follow the laws of Moses and were free to exercise the faith within their own cultural practices. However, they still had to adhere to four major restrictions: "the things polluted by idols, and from sexual immorality, and from what has been strangled, and from blood" (Acts 15:20). These four things all had to do with idolatry in the ancient world (sexual immorality was associated with pagan cultic practices). Essentially the Jerusalem Council decreed that as long as you keep God's holiness and uniqueness, the practice of your Christianity can have a wide interpretation. This was shocking to the Jews in the early church—and, dare I say, it is sadly still shocking to many Christians today!

and Scott Sunquist's *History of the World Christian Movement*, giving a great overview of the expansion of Christianity), biblical theology of mission (e.g., Christopher Wright's *The Mission of God*, comprehensively examining the missional themes found in Scripture), systematic theology of mission (e.g., Timothy Tennent's *Theology in the Context of World Christianity* and Amos Yong's *Renewing Christian Theology: Systematics for a Global Christianity*, both of which consider soteriology, Christology, ecclesiology, eschatology, and so on, through different cultural lenses), but nothing on straight missiology (evangelism, social justice, unreached peoples, contextualization, urbanization, globalization, education and universities, technology/Internet, creation care, other religions, modernism and postmodernism, the arts, HIV/AIDS, short-term missions, post-denominationalism, ecumenism, Pentecostalism, and so on). The closest four I found were Andrew Walls and Cathy Ross's *Mission in the 21st Century*, which has in-depth treatments of five of these issues (evangelism, teaching, service, social justice, creation care) but is limited in scope to only these five; Ralph Winter and Steve Hawthorne's *Perspectives on the World Christian Movement*, which is perhaps the most comprehensive overview of missiology available, though on an introductory lay level; Brian Stanley's history of the Edinburgh 1910 conference; and Norman E. Thomas's *Missions and Unity: Lessons from History, 1792–2010*, which only goes up to, but does not include, 2010. This present volume is intended to be self-consciously timely—written for "such a time as this," if I may be so bold! It is essentially Walls and Ross's book (twenty-first-century missiology) expanded to cover a broader range of topics like Winter and Hawthorne's book, intended to be a historical record of individual conferences like Stanley's book, but covering a broader swath of history like Thomas's book. This is another reason I call this book a hybrid.

The subtitle (*From Everyone to Everywhere*) is similar to some other recent releases. Samuel Escobar's 2003 book *The New Global Mission* has the subtitle *The Gospel from Everywhere to Everyone*, the reverse of my subtitle. The difference is this: I believe that mission starts from people, not places—and the first person with whom it begins, in the concept of the *missio Dei*, is God himself. We are secondary agents of mission. And although mission certainly does spread *to* people as well as originate with people, biblically it is more that places are the intended "targets" as Acts 1:8 suggests: "Jerusalem and in all Judea and Samaria, and to the end of the earth." Mark Noll's *From Every Tribe and Nation* (Baker, 2014) leaves out the recipients, and Carlos F. Cardoza-Orlandi and Justo L. González's *To All Nations from All Nations* (Abingdon, 2013) talks about places but not people.

Anybody who did not go to any of these five missions conferences may have the tendency to dismiss the conferences as irrelevant and only meaningful to those who attended. This book is an attempt to prevent that mentality of exclusivity from undermining the whole purpose of the conferences. They were meant for the world's Christians, and unfortunately it is the reality of such events that only a limited number can attend. This book is a way for everyone to have "attended" and to reap the benefits, so that these expensive, much-publicized events will not have been held in vain and gone down into history as curious inbred clubs and nothing more. If academia does not meet praxis, it is useless, especially in a discipline as obviously practical as missions.

This leads to another question: what is the purpose of anniversary conferences? I see it as similar to a wedding or graduation ceremony. It is a great celebration of the work that has led up to this point, and it marks a significant point in time. However, the work is not done; in fact, it is a "commencement" and thus looks toward the future. To only focus on graduation and not go out into the world to use your education is pointless. To only focus on the wedding day and forget that it only symbolizes the beginning of the real relationship (namely, marriage) is equally missing the point. To those who were not able to attend any of these five conferences, that does not exclude you from participation in the world missionary movement any more than failing to attend a wedding excludes you from later becoming friends of the married couple and being a part of their lives. Think of this book as a photo album of the wedding or graduation. It allows you to "catch up" on what you may have missed in the past so that you may better interact with the present. And conferences are never ends in and of themselves; the legacy they leave motivates and inspires the ongoing daily work, which really matters.

One final major question remains: why are so many conferences needed? And a couple of attendant corollary questions: Which one of these five conferences did the "best" job of following Edinburgh 1910, a hundred years later? Which is worthy to be dubbed the "true" successor? The answer, and the thesis of the book, is that all of them are needed, and together they are the successor to Edinburgh 1910. A century ago, mission was unilateral and unidirectional ("from the West to the rest"). Today, in light of the phenomenon known as world Christianity, mission is polycentric[8] and polydirectional: "from everyone to everywhere." No one conference or continent does mission best. But together, each provides a valuable piece of the puzzle.

I also need to point out an obvious limitation of this book: it is written from an American perspective. Though I am of Asian heritage (my parents are first-generation immigrants to the United States from Taiwan and China), I was born in the Pacific Islands (Guam), I did my later studies in Europe (Scotland and England), my field of research was Latin America, and I have been to over sixty countries on six continents, nevertheless I grew up in a thoroughly American context (Southern California) and was academically trained in the Western world (New England and Great Britain). My worldview is thus formed by my theological education (evangelical), my cultural context (the USA and the English language), and my race/class/gender (Asian American, middle class, male). In reporting the facts of this book, I cannot claim to adequately represent everyone who was involved in these five conferences, much less the missionaries and Christians of the world. I will necessarily have to write through lenses and from categories that I am familiar with, even while acknowledging that many of these issues can be seen from other perspectives. I also cannot include everything that was said and thought in these conferences, unless I were to devote endless volumes to the task. As an editor, I will have to pick and choose certain issues and events to highlight while regrettably omitting some. I apologize in advance for any shortsightedness.

---

[8]That is also the thesis of the festschrift in honor of the dean of Trinity Evangelical Divinity School, Tite Tiénou. In fact, the original title of this book was *Missions in Polycentric Dimensions*. See Casely B. Essamuah and David K. Ngaruiya, eds., *Communities of Faith in Africa and the African Diaspora: In Honor of Dr. Tite Tiénou with Additional Essays on World Christianity* (Eugene, OR: Wipf & Stock, 2013).

FROM 1910 TO 2010

THE LEGACY OF EDINBURGH 1910

The Edinburgh 1910 World Missionary Conference, arguably the most famous missions conference in history and flagged by Mark Noll as the most recent of the twelve "decisive moments" for the church,[1] is burdened with a moniker that it can never fully live up to: "The Birthplace of the Modern Ecumenical Movement." Brian Stanley gives three reasons for this nickname, with reference to the year 1910 itself (past, future and present):

- Past: some scholars connected William Carey's proposal of an ecumenical 1810 conference to its supposed fulfillment at Edinburgh 1910 (see chapter five for a fuller explanation).

- Future: the World Council of Churches (founded in 1948) can directly trace its lineage back to Edinburgh 1910.[2]

---

[1]Mark A. Noll, *Turning Points: Decisive Moments in the History of Christianity* (Grand Rapids: Baker, 2001), 7. The others are (1) the fall of Jerusalem (AD 70), (2) the Council of Nicaea (325), (3) the Council of Chalcedon (451), (4) Benedict's Rule (530), (5) the coronation of Charlemagne (800), (6) the Great Schism (1054), (7) the Diet of Worms (1521), (8) the English Act of Supremacy (1534), (9) the founding of the Jesuits (1540), (10) the conversion of the Wesleys (1738) and (11) the French Revolution (1789).

[2]Brian Stanley, *The World Missionary Conference, Edinburgh 1910* (Grand Rapids: Eerdmans, 2009), 9. Some have even regarded Edinburgh 1910 as an early catalyst for the Second Vatican Council (1968) and as inspiration for the first Lausanne Congress on World Evangelization (1974), thus making Edinburgh the "birthplace" of ecumenism for Catholics and evangelicals, respectively, as well.

- Present: the conference organizers and participants themselves had a sense of self-importance regarding the significance of this conference.[3]

However, Stanley contends that "to a possibly greater extent than any other event in modern Christian history, the conference suffers from the distortions of hindsight."[4] Edinburgh 1910 was not ecumenical because it did not have adequate representations of:

- *denominations*: Aside from Protestants, there were only Anglo-Catholics,[5] but no Roman Catholics or Orthodox, and certainly no Pentecostals as they were just appearing on the world scene historically at the time.[6]

- *nationalities/geographies*: Latin America was infamously excluded, in terms of both delegate representation and being a recipient of missionary work[7] (see chapter seven for further explanation).

- *races/ethnicities*: Though Africa and Asia were represented, only eighteen Asians and one black African were in attendance (the others from Africa were all white expatriate missionaries).[8]

- *gender*: There were very few women compared to men[9] (see chapter four for more).

- *age*: It is debatable whether this was a problem or not; certainly there were no youth representatives at the conference, but if there was one thing that

---

[3]Ibid., 6, 14: "The re-interpretation of Edinburgh 1910 as an event whose significance transcended the foreign mission field began in the minds of some of delegates at the conference itself. . . . They were almost indecently conscious of taking part in an unprecedented event that promised to re-shape the course of Christian history."

[4]Ibid., 9.

[5]Ibid., 9-10.

[6]I also realize the limitations of this threefold Western division of Protestant, Catholic and Orthodox, and that many people in the Two-Thirds World do not classify themselves as any of those three. House churches and independent churches are becoming increasingly common in many parts of the world outside the West.

[7]There was also nobody from the Pacific or Caribbean islands, though many modern geographical classifications tend to lump "Pacific" with Asia and "Caribbean" with Latin America.

[8]Stanley, *World Missionary Conference*, 12-13. It is curious that Latin America's absence from Edinburgh 1910 is historically well known but not black Africa's absence (Mark Christian Hayford, the lone black African at Edinburgh 1910, was not an official delegate). The reasons have to do with the attendance of some twenty white missionaries from Africa and anywhere from six to eight African Americans, and these two groups were regarded as "sufficient" to represent Africa by early twentieth-century standards (ibid., 98-99).

[9]Ibid., 313.

motivated the proceedings, it was young people[10] (see chapter six for a further discussion).

Nevertheless, Stanley himself dedicated several years to penning his centenary commemorative volume of the history of Edinburgh 1910, so this shows the power of a sobriquet: even if it is illegitimately earned, its "myth" still captures the imagination of people. Edinburgh 1910 will always have the historical spotlight shone on it for the simple reason that its nickname perpetuates a certain reputation, whether it be reality or exaggeration.

Edinburgh 1910 is saddled with a second, seemingly contradictory, characteristic: it ended the Great Century of Missions (the nineteenth century), as dubbed by Yale church historian Kenneth Scott Latourette.[11] Keeping in mind that Latourette wrote in the early twentieth century and thus did not have the benefit of knowing the events of the latter twentieth century onward, the reasons he cites for claiming the nineteenth century as the Great Century of Missions are the following:

- *the link between Christianity and imperialism*: "In most of these areas Christianity had been planted by the great missionary movement of the sixteenth, seventeenth, and eighteenth centuries. . . . This expansion was in connexion [*sic*] with phenomenal explorations, commercial enterprises and conquests by Christian Europeans, in themselves also on a scale unprecedented in human history."[12]

- *geographical initiation*: "Not so many continents or major countries were entered for the first time as in the preceding three centuries. . . . What now occurred was the acquisition of fresh footholds in regions and among peoples already touched, an expansion of unprecedented extent from both the newer bases and the older ones, and the entrance of Christianity into the large majority of such countries, islands, peoples, and tribes as had previously not been touched."[13]

---

[10]The organizer of the conference, John R. Mott, was inspired by the SVM (Student Volunteer Movement) and the YMCA, and used this slogan to inspire university students everywhere: "The evangelization of the world in this generation" (for more explanation, see chapters four and six).

[11]Kenneth Scott Latourette, *A History of the Expansion of Christianity*, 8 vols. (New York: Harper, 1937–1945).

[12]Kenneth Scott Latourette, *The Great Century in Europe and the United States of America, A.D. 1800–A.D. 1914*, vol. 4, *A History of the Expansion of Christianity* (New York: Harper, 1941), 2.

[13]Ibid., 3.

- *Christian expansion*: "The scene is no longer confined, as in the first five centuries, solely to the basin of the Mediterranean and to the few peoples outside that basin touched by Mediterranean culture. Nor is it restricted mainly to Europe with a few excursions to Asia and Africa, as in the succeeding thousand years, or chiefly to Europe and America, with some extensions to Asia and Africa, as in the three centuries between A.D. 1500 and A.D. 1800. It is now expanded to include all the globe and all peoples, nations, races, and cultures."[14]

- *Protestantism on the ascendancy*: "It was in Protestantism that the nineteenth century awakening in Christianity was most pronounced. Protestantism became less a political and more a religious movement than any previous time. In many respects the nineteenth century was the Protestant Century. . . . New organizations and new denominations multiplied."[15]

- *mission societies established*: "Within Protestantism arose hundreds of societies for the propagation of Christianity. Many of these were in Europe. A growing number were in the United States, and to a lesser extent, in other regions where Europeans had migrated. Like the corresponding Roman Catholic organizations, they were made possible by the voluntary gifts of thousands. This expansion of Protestantism was even less accomplished by the aid of the state than was that of Roman Catholicism."[16]

- *Protestant Christendom*: "In some respects, the civilization of Western Europe was more profoundly moulded by Christianity than at any previous time. The democracy which was so pronounced a trend in governments in large part had a Christian source, particularly Protestantism."[17]

- *social justice awakening*: "Mainly but by no means exclusively from Anglo-Saxon Protestantism sprang movement after movement to meet the social ills of the day. If, as seems probable, the machine itself was to some degree a product of Christianity (for it was by Christianity that that confidence in an orderly and dependable universe had been bred in the

---

[14]Ibid., 7.
[15]Ibid., 459.
[16]Ibid., 460.
[17]Ibid.

European mind on which was based the scientific attitude out of which came the machine), then Christianity was to that extent responsible for the collective evils which followed it. However, there also issued from Christianity, notably in Great Britain where it had had its earliest extensive application, efforts to remedy the sufferings brought by the machine and so to reconstruct society that it would be a blessing and not a curse. . . . Among the reforms which most clearly caught their inspiration from Christianity were those directed against Negro slavery, for the creation of modern nursing, and for the control and reduction of war and the relief of the sufferings entailed by war."[18]

- *Christianity in the United States*: "In the United States of America the gains made by Christianity were even more striking than in Europe. Here arose the largest of the new nations born of the migration of European peoples. Here Christianity was confronted with a combination of challenges—to follow and mould the population on the westward moving frontier, to hold to their traditional religious allegiance the immigrants from Europe, to reach the non-Christian elements among the immigrants, notably the Jews and the Orientals, to protect the Indian and the Negro from exploitation by the aggressive whites and to win them to its faith, and to shape the rapidly changing culture of the land. In meeting this collection of gigantic problems Christianity made really astounding progress. While at the outset of the nation's independent life only about one in twenty had a formal membership in some church, by 1914 more than four out of ten were on the rolls of the churches, and this in spite of the prodigious growth in population. Not much effort was made to reach the Jews, but numbers from the small Oriental enclaves had been touched, and between a third and a half of the Indians and about half of the Negroes had become professedly Christian. Due largely to impulses issuing from Christianity, Negro slavery had been abolished and the Negroes had made enormous strides in education. From the Christian conscience had come many attempts to protect the Indians and to enable them to achieve a successful adjustment to the strange world created by the white man. From Christianity, too, had come major contributions to

---

[18]Ibid., 460-61.

the ideals of the country, to government, to education, to a different status for women, towards the curbing of the use of alcoholic beverages, to better care of the sick and the insane, to improved prisons, to more tolerable conditions for labourers in mines and factories, and to larger opportunities for the underprivileged in the great cities. As in Europe, most of the programmes for international peace stemmed from Christian idealism. In addition to effecting all these results in the country itself, the Christianity of the United States was increasingly reaching out to other lands and was undertaking a growing share in the world-wide missionary enterprise."[19]

- *world peace*: "The relative peace also assisted the spread of Christianity. Because of it, missionaries could travel with comparative safety, funds could be sent them expeditiously, Christian communities could grow uninterruptedly, and fellowship could be maintained and strengthened between the new churches and those which had founded them."[20]

If one gives at least some validity to Latourette's claim, the question that needs to be asked is, if 1910 was so significant for missions, why did it end, rather than further launch, a great era of missions?

There are at least two reasons for this: one is the traumatic events of world history since 1910, which the Edinburgh participants could not have predicted, and the other is Edinburgh 1910's unanticipated negative effect on world missions in general. With regard to the former (world history), in the last century since Edinburgh 1910 we have had:

- *wars*: two World Wars,[21] the Korean and Vietnam Wars, the Cold War, two Gulf Wars, 9/11 and numerous civil wars globally

- *genocide*: the Holocaust, Cambodia, Rwanda and the Balkans

- *economics*: the Great Depression, the bursting of the Internet bubble, the crash of Freddie Mac and Fannie Mae, the Euro crisis, and other economic downturns

---

[19]Ibid., 461-62.
[20]Ibid., 19.
[21]Stanley, *World Missionary Conference*, 304-5.

- *natural disasters*: four of the world's top ten biggest earthquakes[22] in history have registered in the last decade alone, as well as ecological disasters such as the BP oil spill in the Gulf of Mexico caused by humans

Ruth Tucker observed, "With some forty-five thousand missionaries on the field and the prediction that the number might be tripled in the next thirty years, delegates were optimistic about the prospects for world evangelization. But in the years following Edinburgh, interest in missions waned in most mainline denominations."[23] With regard to the negative effect of Edinburgh 1910 on missions subsequent to the conference, some of the deleterious results were:

- Women's missions declined significantly. Women's missions societies later ceased to be autonomous as they were subsumed under Edinburgh 1910's successors, and women themselves reoriented their attention to domestic issues (such as suffrage) instead of overseas missions.[24]

- Missions was reduced to practical functions and organizational structures, and Edinburgh 1910's successors inherited this way of operating. As Duane Elmer points out, "The missionaries who went out after World War II were committed to bringing the gospel of Jesus Christ to every tribe, tongue and people. Mission was defined in terms of tasks to be accomplished: language study, translation, evangelism, church planting, discipleship, medical work, education and other ministries. While most of these require some relationship with people, the emphasis was on getting the job done. There was a temptation to value relationships only if they contributed to reaching the goals, or so it seemed to people of later generations."[25]

- Theology was brushed aside for the sake of unity. This was a mixed bag because, as Andrew Walls observes, "On theology, Edinburgh 1910 has little to say. The conference ground rules, of course, precluded the introduction of topics known to be controversial among the participants; even

---

[22]Indian Ocean (9.1), 2004; Sumatra (8.6), 2005; Chile (8.8), 2010; Japan (9.0), 2011.

[23]Ruth Tucker, *From Jerusalem to Irian Jaya: A Biographical History of Christian Missions* (Grand Rapids: Zondervan, 2004), 324.

[24]Stanley, *World Missionary Conference*, 315.

[25]Duane Elmer, *Cross-Cultural Connections: Stepping Out and Fitting In Around the World* (Downers Grove, IL: IVP Academic, 2002), 128.

so, it seems remarkable today that so many people, representing such a wide range of theological views, could accept that they were agreed as to what the Gospel was. It seems equally remarkable that they could all accept that evangelism, translation, education, medicine, literature, industrial training and women's work were simply different methods of carrying it. . . . Edinburgh 1910 reflects a certain confidence that, whatever issues may divide Christendom, there is a consensual theological deposit that is the common heritage of Christians."[26]

- Perhaps the most infamous and lasting consequence of unity trumping theological discussion was the exclusion of Latin America. Without Anglo-Catholics in attendance, Edinburgh 1910 would have been completely Protestant in attendance—and mostly *evangelical* Protestants at that. In order to maintain a semblance of ecumenism, the Anglo-Catholic presence was given disproportionate deference.[27] When the question of Latin America as a mission field was raised, the Anglo-Catholics insisted that Latin America was already evangelized because of the heavy Roman Catholic presence there, and any attempt on the part of Protestants to enter that mission field would be tantamount to sheep-stealing.[28] This was a decision that has repercussions to this day, as that mentality still affects a lot of people, including some Protestants who consider "Christendom" as equivalent to "missionized." See chapter three for a further exploration of the definition of missions.

And though these next two afflictions may not have been a consequence of Edinburgh 1910, they are also important to consider: (1) there were more Christian martyrs in the twentieth century than in all previous nineteen centuries combined—specifically, 45.5 million out of the total 70 million (65%)[29]—and (2) the advent of the fundamentalist-modernist controversy in

---

[26]Andrew F. Walls, "The Great Commission 1910–2010" (lecture, University of Edinburgh, 2002), www.towards2010.org/downloads/t2010paper01walls.pdf, 5.

[27]This is similar to how the World Council of Churches regards the Orthodox membership in their midst. Without the Orthodox, the WCC would be only Protestants, and so Orthodox are allowed to exercise disproportionate authority to placate them.

[28]Stanley, *World Missionary Conference*, 13.

[29]Antonio Socci, *The New Persecuted: Inquiries into Anti-Christian Intolerance in the New Century of Martyrs* [*I Nuovi Perseguitati: Indagine Sulla Intolleranza Anticristiana nel Nuovo Secolo del Martirio*] (Casale Monferrato: Edizione Piemmi, 2002).

the United States (with J. Gresham Machen[30] and Harry Emerson Fosdick[31] as representative spokesmen, respectively) caused Western missions to be bifurcated into those focused on evangelism (which became the domain of evangelicals) and those focused on social justice (which became the domain of mainline Protestants).[32] The evangelism and social justice pairing, together always part and parcel of missions, was torn asunder for almost a century as "conservatives" and "liberals" divided the spoils.[33] See chapter five for the history of how Lausanne attempted to bring the two back together and chapter seven for how Latin American *evangélicos* never lost this vision of *misión integral* (holistic mission).

As shown from the above two perspectives, people either have a tendency to run with Edinburgh 1910's nickname uncritically ("It is the birthplace of the modern ecumenical movement!"), or systematically dissect it in order to invalidate it ("It ended the great century of missions!"). Regarding the latter, with all the negatives that have followed the conference, one might ask, in a twist on Nathanael's famous question, "Can anything good come from Edinburgh?"

A third, more tempered perspective may be helpful here. One frequent criticism of Edinburgh 1910 not being worthy of the title of "birthplace" is that it was not the first. In fact it had two predecessors (or six, depending on how one counts). It was seventh in a series of world missionary conferences, predated by New York and London (both 1854), Liverpool (1860), London (1878 and 1888), and New York (1900). Or it can be seen as the third of a series of *ecumenical* missionary conferences if one only considers the Centenary Missionary Conference of London 1888[34] and the Ecumenical

---

[30]He wrote *Christianity and Liberalism* (Grand Rapids: Eerdmans, 1923), arguing that liberalism was not Christianity at all.

[31]He preached a famous sermon, "Shall the Fundamentalists Win?," on May 21, 1922, at Riverside Church in New York City, later published in *Christian Work* 102 (June 10, 1922): 716-72.

[32]The fundamentalist-modernist controversy caused other dichotomies as well, such as in science (creationism vs. evolution) and in educational institutions (Westminster vs. Princeton seminaries).

[33]The loss of a social justice vision by evangelicals in the twentieth century is chronicled in David O. Moberg, *The Great Reversal: Reconciling Evangelism and Social Concern* (Philadelphia: J. B. Lippincott, 1972).

[34]Commemorating the one hundredth anniversary of the beginning of missions from the Anglo-American world. Clearly the penchant for centenary celebrations was just as strong back then as it is now.

Missionary Conference of New York 1900.[35] However, interestingly, the official title of Edinburgh 1910 was changed from "The Third Ecumenical Missionary Conference" to "World Missionary Conference, 1910" because the word *ecumenical* implied a broader swath of denominations than were actually present; thus the name change was an honest attempt to be indicative of reality.[36] So even though the organizers of Edinburgh 1910 tried not to overinflate their title,[37] and though it certainly was not the first missions conference, it still assumed monumental historical importance and outshone its predecessors. This was due to several factors:

- Edinburgh 1910's missions orientation had a wider global scope (deliberately strategizing about targeting the Two-Thirds World) than the previous conferences, the direct result of this being greater ecumenical representation.

- The selection of delegates was done in an unprecedented way. Delegates were limited to those officially appointed by missions agencies, and not by churches, so it was a gathering according to shared vision rather than denominational allegiances.

- The missions agencies that were invited were only those working in the non-Christian world, thus encouraging attendance of Anglo-Catholics and German Lutherans who feared "sheep stealing" (proselytizing by those agencies working within areas where the Christian church was already present; for example, Latin and Orthodox Europe, the Near East where ancient churches still bore their witness, and above all, Latin America, which was deemed to be at least nominally Catholic).

The end result was the most highly inclusive gathering of Christians in history *thus far* (it must be judged by its own temporal standards, not by our present-day criteria), in denominational representation if not in ethnicity/nationality. Regarding the vaunted title of "birthplace," it must also be pointed out that Gustavo Gutiérrez, often called the "father of liberation

---

[35]This was seen as so important that even US President William McKinley attended.

[36]Stanley, *World Missionary Conference*, 36.

[37]Some would say that the word *world* is no less overinflated than *ecumenical*, because clearly the world was not represented. This is akin to American baseball calling its championship the "World Series" (or even the USA calling itself "America" for short even though they are only one nation in the whole of the two continents)! These could either be instances of synecdoche or of great hubris.

theology," was not the first liberation theologian—Rubem Alves was.[38] And William Carey, dubbed the "father of modern missions," was not the first to launch modern missions—Count Nicolaus Ludwig von Zinzendorf and the Moravians were. However, both Gutiérrez and Carey became more famous, influential and popular than their predecessors, are more credited with globalizing these movements, and have more indelibly left their stamp on history (at least in the popular imagination). The same could be said of Edinburgh 1910.

Perhaps more than anything else, the reason why Edinburgh 1910 has the word *ecumenical* associated with it is what resulted from the conference: namely, the Continuation Committee. Of course there are the negative consequences resulting from the conference, as cited above in the second point, but the Continuation Committee was the most significant bright point of the conference proceedings. Stanley said that when this resolution was put to the vote and passed,

> the conference, apparently spontaneously, began to sing the doxology in relief and jubilation. The World Missionary Conference had taken its one and only decision. "This," recalled Oldham fifty years later, "was the turning point in the history of the ecumenical movement." His words were not simply the inflated verdict of hindsight. The report of the conference in the *Missionary Record of the United Free Church of Scotland* claimed that "one of the momentous decisions that make history" had been passed, a decision that would have been impossible ten years previously. The American Congregationalist, Cornelius H. Patton, writing in the Boston *Missionary Herald*, agreed that "the significance of this action can hardly be overstated. It makes international the large measure of comity which has existed for years among the American societies, and is big with promise for a general movement looking to the reunion of Christendom."[39]

The historic nature of this decision was that it spurred an immediate drafting of an ecumenical missionary structure that led to the formation of the International Missionary Council (IMC) in 1921,[40] initiating the framework for modern

---

[38]Alves's *A Theology of Human Hope* (Cleveland: Corpus Books, 1969) was the first book on liberation theology, written two years before Gustavo Gutiérrez's *A Theology of Liberation* (Lima: CEP, 1971).

[39]Stanley, *World Missionary Conference*, 300.

[40]Ibid., 302.

Christian ecumenism henceforth. This, more than anything, is why Edinburgh 1910 is regarded as "the Birthplace of the modern ecumenical movement."

OVERVIEW OF THE MISSIOLOGICAL LANDSCAPE IN 2010

The major issues discussed at Edinburgh 1910 were outlined by eight commissions:

1. Carrying the Gospel to all the world

2. The native church and its workers

3. Education in relation to the Christianisation of national life

4. The missionary message in relation to non-Christian religions

5. The preparation of missionaries

6. The home base of missions

7. Relation of missions to governments

8. Co-operation and the promotion of unity[41]

These were the topics of greatest concern in 1910. What are the issues relevant today? That is the purpose of this book: to unpack this question, with world Christianity being the meta-theme that informs the scope of this book.

Between 1910 and 2010, there have been vast changes in the political, theological, ecclesial and spiritual landscapes. Despite the fact that the world is still one-third Christian, just as it was one hundred years ago, it certainly does not imply that nothing has changed. First and foremost, the center of gravity of Christianity has shifted to the Two-Thirds World (chapter two explains this phenomenon, known as world Christianity, more fully). Just as recently as a decade ago, this was still news. Today, it is fairly common knowledge. It is also worth noting that, though the percentage of Christians is still the same as a century ago, the world's population has more than tripled, from two billion to seven billion.

If more Christians now live in the non-Western world than in the West, it calls into question the older concept of Western missions to the non-Western world being primarily evangelistic. If there are far more Christians in Africa than in Europe, do we really need to keep sending missionaries to

---

[41]Ibid., 33.

Africa to evangelize? Perhaps Africans now need to be going to Europe (and they are)! This is called reverse mission, as we see that the largest church in London is Nigerian and the Chinese are evangelizing westward across the Silk Road with their "Back to Jerusalem movement." Mongolia is the biggest mission-sending nation in the world per capita, Korea has four of the ten largest churches in the world, and Pentecostalism is the fastest-growing form of Christianity around the world (especially in nations like Brazil). Linked with the rapid growth of Two-Thirds World Christianity, however, is the ever-increasing threat of the prosperity, or health-and-wealth, gospel.

On the opposite end of the spectrum from over-enthused Christianity lies rote Christianity. Nominalism is a bigger problem than ever before, demonstrating the ever-increasing need for discipleship—the chief verb in the Great Commission—to be the focus of missions, not evangelism. Continuing to send Western missionaries to Sub-Saharan Africa (the most Christian place on earth) only makes sense if evangelism is not the only or primary way to do mission. Social justice ministries and training/teaching have begun to take priority over evangelism given that Two-Thirds World Christians are so numerous and many are also poor. They lack theological education and equipping more than anything else. They know their own culture better than foreign missionaries do, and they have the human resources; therefore they make much better evangelists to their own people. But it cannot be stressed strongly enough that evangelism is no longer what non-Western Christians need—it is what they do. Gone are the days of Western paternalism; now the new way of mission is partnership.[42] Donating books and starting seminaries are better and more effective uses of mission resources than standing on street corners preaching or planting churches. These are some of the major ways that world Christianity has changed the landscape of mission today.

---

[42]Ralph Winter said that there were three eras of Western Protestant missions from 1800 to 2000: (1) 1800–1910 (coastlands of Africa and Asia), in which William Carey was the chief catalyst; (2) 1865–1980 (penetration inland), in which Hudson Taylor was a prime figure; (3) 1935–present (frontier missions among unreached indigenous peoples), of whom Cameron Townsend was an example par excellence. But according to Tom Steffen, *The Facilitator Era: Beyond Pioneer Church Multiplication* (Eugene, OR: Wipf & Stock, 2011), now we are in the Facilitator Era, from the late 1900s onward. Missions is from the reached to the reached, led by people like Rick Warren. Unlike the first three eras, which were all long-term pioneer mission work, the Facilitator Era is one of partnership, often via short-term missions.

Old paradigms of church and denominations are increasingly irrelevant as we are confronted with African Independent Churches, Latin American base ecclesial communities and Chinese house churches. We have seen the formation of the International Missionary Council, the World Council of Churches and the Lausanne Committee for World Evangelization, and we are now post–Vatican II (signaling a new era in Protestant-Catholic relations). Samuel Huntington's thesis has proved correct in that there are now three major world powers, with the rise of China and Islam in addition to the dominance of the West. Communication, particularly with the advent of the Internet, has revolutionized how we do mission, much as Roman roads contributed to the spread of Christianity in the first century, the printing press helped to further the Protestant Reformation by putting Bibles in the vernacular in the hands of the people, and radio and television helped Billy Graham to become the world's most prolific evangelist. Despite (or maybe because of) globalization, Christianity and wealth are no longer linked; Kenya and Guatemala are two of the most Christian nations on earth, while Japan and Sweden are two of the most secular.

Urbanization is now the reality of this world: as of 2008, more people now live in cities than in rural areas. Short-term missions are now more prevalent than long-term missions. Evangelicals now are more environmentally aware, more social justice–oriented (this is a recovery, not a discovery), and far less triumphalistic (which was characterized in 1910 by the phrase "the evangelization of the world in this generation"). Yet, lest we think that pessimism and cynicism must necessarily pervade our mood due to the horrors of the twentieth century, one of the natural tendencies of humans who travel through dark valleys is a greater reliance on God. As such, there has been a corresponding shift from *missions* to *mission*, as outlined by authors such as David Bosch[43] and Lesslie Newbigin.[44] The focus on the *missio Dei*—that it is God who initiates and we are merely partners in the endeavor—is now widely accepted. With so many new missiological issues, any one missionary conference would be hard-pressed to

---

[43]David Bosch, *Transforming Mission* (Maryknoll, NY: Orbis, 1991), 391.
[44]Lesslie Newbigin, *The Gospel in a Pluralistic Society* (Grand Rapids: Eerdmans, 1989), 121.

address all of them, hence so many attempts to follow in the footsteps of Edinburgh 1910.

In 1910, mission was regarded in geographic and racial terms. It was mostly white Westerners who were firmly entrenched in Christendom, doing missions to the non-white, non-Western, heathen world. Today, culture is the new paradigm.[45] (For a secular parallel to this idea, see the explanation about Samuel Huntington's theory of the remaking of the world order in chapter two.) Political and ideological empires have given way to cultural and religious alliances. The divisions are not so stark, as mission is now "from everyone to everywhere"; however, theology also ought to be from everyone to everywhere, but it still has a long way to go to reach that point.

ECUMENISM AND MISSIONS

Given the fact that the word *ecumenical* is so important to Edinburgh 1910, to the church and to missions, a proper definition ought to be given. Today this word seems to be as fraught with ambiguity as the word *evangelical* (and in fact is often used in opposition to it). What is the definition of *ecumenical*?

As with many words used in Christian theological discourse, the vocabulary is "baptized" from the pagan world. This should not be surprising, as Christians are essentially the same as our theological words: something pagan that has been transformed/translated[46] and appropriated for the cause of God. Words that seem Christian in their origin but actually have pagan roots include *God, church, hell, liturgy, Easter,* even *baptize*! Even in the Greek form, they all originally were pagan words: *theos* (note the similarity with the words Deus and Zeus), *ekklesia* (original pagan meaning: gathering or assembly), *hades* (the Greek mythological reference is obvious), *leitourgia* (originally meaning a public work) and *baptizo* (original pagan meaning: to soak or immerse). *Easter* comes from the ancient Near Eastern fertility goddess *Ishtar* (hence our use of fertility symbols such as eggs and bunnies).[47]

---

[45]Stanley, *World Missionary Conference,* 308.

[46]See Lamin Sanneh, *Translating the Message* (Maryknoll, NY: Orbis, 1989), 1.

[47]For more on this, see Frank Viola and George Barna, *Pagan Christianity? Exploring the Roots of Our Church Practices* (Carol Stream, IL: Tyndale, 2008).

The word *ecumenical* comes from *oikoumene*, which had the pre-Christian meaning of "world" or "empire" (e.g., the Roman Empire).[48] In the early church, the word *ecumenical* was unnecessary because unity was assumed—denominations were a thing of the distant future. At first, the ecumenism was political,[49] under the auspices of the Roman Empire (although the ancient Eastern churches, such as the Armenian, Coptic and Assyrian churches, are certainly not to be forgotten). It was not until later, with the Great Schism of 1054 and then the Protestant Reformation, that ecumenism became a major concern. Willem Visser 't Hooft, the first World Council of Churches general secretary, mentioned a few other definitions: "that which has universal ecclesiastical validity; . . . pertaining to the world-wide missionary outreach of the Church; . . . that quality or attitude which expresses the consciousness of and desire for Christian unity."[50] A later WCC general secretary, Konrad Raiser, reflects on a more modern definition: "the Christ-centric universalism of the classical ecumenical paradigm is rooted in the missionary vision of 'a whole world brought to Christ.'"[51]

Unlike the word *evangelical*, which is often used in secular discourse today (e.g., by the media), the word *ecumenical* seems to be used primarily within ecclesial circles. Why is this word so important? For Christians, historically it brings to mind the original ecumenical councils, which have theological authority (though it does beg the question of how much authority they hold when Christians only accept the ones that cohere with their particular theologies). The church of the East (AKA Nestorians) only accept the first two (Nicaea I and Constantinople I), Oriental Orthodox (i.e., Jacobite Monophysites) only the first three (including Ephesus), Protestants the first four (including Chalcedon), Eastern Orthodox the first seven (including Constantinople II and III and Nicaea II), and all twenty-one are accepted by Roman Catholics. One may also wonder how ecumenical they

---

[48]Willem Adolf Visser 't Hooft, "Appendix I: The Word 'Ecumenical'—Its History and Use," in *A History of the Ecumenical Movement, 1517–1948*, vol. 1, ed. Ruth Rouse and Stephen C. Neill (Geneva: World Council of Churches, 1986), 737.

[49]Calling *ecumenism* political is a bit of a tautology, but that only proves the point of its original meaning and intent.

[50]Visser 't Hooft, "Appendix I."

[51]Konrad Raiser, "Is Ecumenical Apologetics Sufficient? A Response to Lesslie Newbigin's 'Ecumenical Amnesia,'" *International Bulletin of Missionary Research* 18, no. 2 (April 1994): 50.

really are (especially the last fourteen) when only one section of the worldwide church is convening these councils (of course, according to Roman Catholics, they *are* the entire church, so these councils are ecumenical in their own estimation), or when (as in the first seven) the discussions and decisions were only held within the geographical and cultural boundaries of the Roman Empire without regard to other geographical or cultural areas of the world that had flourishing Christian communities too.[52]

Nonetheless, the word *ecumenical* seems to carry weight, and Christians like to use it for that reason, though Vatican II (only accepted by Catholics) was in reality no more "ecumenical" than New York 1900 (only accepted by Protestants).[53] Edinburgh 1910 was a little more ecumenical, as it was mostly Protestants and had a small but influential delegation of Anglo-Catholics. Christians, for all our diversity, all want to use words that connote unity—not that unity and diversity are mutually exclusive by any means. But many Christians use words to connote exclusive claim to being *the* one, for example, *Catholic* ("universal"), *Orthodox* ("right thinking") and *Evangelical* ("gospel people"). By rights, all Christians should be catholic, orthodox *and* evangelical (note the use of the lowercase).

As stated earlier, the word *ecumenical* was dropped from Edinburgh 1910's official title and changed to *world* because the meaning had shifted from its usage at London 1888 and New York 1900 as "global" to its meaning at Edinburgh as "denominational,"[54] which was not accurate to describe the 1910 conference (to them, *world* seemed to mean "global").[55] The two words

---

[52]For more on this, see Philip Jenkins, *The Lost History of Christianity: The Thousand-Year Golden Age of the Church in the Middle East, Africa, and Asia—and How It Died* (New York: HarperCollins, 2008).

[53]In fact, the "oecumenical" conference of London 1888 self-consciously used that word to describe itself in response to the claim of Vatican I (1869–1870) of being ecumenical.

[54]Stanley, *World Missionary Conference*, 19.

[55]Today *world* and *global* do not mean the same thing. There is an ongoing debate between some people over whether the term should be *world* Christianity or *global* Christianity, respectively. According to Craig Ott and Harold Netland, eds., *Globalizing Theology: Belief and Practice in an Era of World Christianity* (Grand Rapids: Baker Academic, 2006), 15n2, "Lamin Sanneh distinguishes between what he calls 'world Christianity' and 'global Christianity.' World Christianity is 'the movement of Christianity as it takes form and shape in societies that previously were not Christian, societies that had no bureaucratic tradition with which to domesticate the gospel' (2003, 23). World Christianity thus reflects the changing demographics of Christianity worldwide and the fact that the Christian faith is now 'at home' in many diverse social and cultural settings, manifesting a variety of local expressions. Global Christianity, by contrast, refers to 'the faithful replication of Christian forms and patterns developed in Europe' (2003, 22). Global Christianity,

ecumenical and *international* are linked, and yet the distinction between the two must be made.

If *ecumenism* changed in definition in the short span between London 1888 and Edinburgh 1910 ("global" to "pan-denominational"),[56] has it changed definition yet again in today's world? When looking at the 2010 conferences, a notable factor is the selection process of who should be represented. All of them seemed to include considerations of race, class and gender.[57] Perhaps these categories are not so modern, as these are the very categories that the apostle Paul uses when he says in Galatians 3:28, "There is neither Jew nor Greek, there is neither slave nor free, there is no male and female, for you are all one in Christ Jesus." If there could be one more biblical category added to the previous three, it would be age. In Ephesians and Colossians, Paul discusses race (Eph 3:6; Col 3:11), gender (Eph 5:22-33; Col 3:18-19), class (Eph 6:5-9; Col 3:22) and then age (Eph 6:1-4; Col 3:20-21), though age is different from the other three in that it is a transitory stage— everyone at some stage is young and then old, whereas the others are immutable. Yet we ought not to forget what ecumenism meant in 1888 and 1900 (worldwide geography) and 1910 (unity among denominations). If we truly wanted to have a snapshot of the worldwide church, ideally we'd have to have every race, class, gender, age, nation and denomination represented.

Let us do the math. For the sake of this (admittedly very unscientific) exercise, let us assume that there are broadly ten races, five different social classes, two genders, five age groups (youth, young adult, middle age, upper middle age, senior), roughly two hundred nations and twenty denominations (Catholics, Orthodox, Anglicans, Lutherans, Presbyterians, Baptists, Methodists, Pentecostals and various independent churches). Multiplying 10 x 5 x 2 x 5 x 200 x 20 = 2 million! Of course in truth there are not that

---

aligned with European Christendom, is closely linked to the economic, political, and cultural dimensions of globalization, which spread the influences of the West worldwide. Global Christianity suggests 'that growing Christian communities of professing Christians around the world are evidence of the economic and political security interests of Europe, that churches everywhere are a religious expression of Europe's political reach, or else a reaction to it' (2003, 23)." Ott and Netland, however, do not see a distinction between the two anymore. Another term that has come up, from more liberal camps, is *Christianities*.

[56]And indeed, the meanings of *world* and *global* have changed too!

[57]Interestingly, these are the same categories of liberation theology: black, Latin American and feminist, respectively.

many permutations, as not every nation has every race and every denomination (though every nation *does* have every class and gender). But consider this: at a worldwide missions conference, it is not sufficient just to invite, for example, one American. One would have to make sure that the United States was represented with black Americans, Asian Americans, white Americans, females, Baptists, Methodists, Presbyterians, Catholics, various age groups and social classes. Now do that kind of diversity for every nation on earth and you begin to see the difficulty. Let us even reduce the two million to 10 percent of that number: 200,000. Even with Cape Town 2010, which had 4,500 people in attendance (and only evangelicals), it was hard to ensure proper worldwide representation, but Edinburgh 2010 had only 290 people— so how ecumenically representative could it be, truly?

Justo and Catherine González acknowledged the multifaceted nature of every person when they wrote:

> Most of us find ourselves in multiple roles. We may be the powerful by race if we are white, yet among the powerless if we are women. We may be part of a powerless group if we are in an ethnic minority, yet if we are well educated and employed, we join the powerful in that category. Even within the family structure, the child is often the last victim of those who have no one else over whom to rule and yet are oppressed themselves. Our tendency is to claim only one part of our identity, to think of ourselves always as part of an oppressed group or to think of ourselves always as the powerful. A much more creative dynamic is possible when we claim both parts of our identity, and the liberation given by the gospel can nurture a constant interior dialogue within our own lives.[58]

They put their finger on the issue: it is one of power (see 1 Cor 4:20—"For the kingdom of God does not consist in talk but in power"). The gospel is, ultimately, about power, but not in the way that one might think. It is the upside-down kingdom where the last are first, those who humble themselves will be exalted, the hungry and poor and the mourners are blessed, the foolish things of the world will shame the wise, and the weak things of the world will shame the strong. As such, unless one is divested of all power

---

[58]Justo and Catherine González, *The Liberating Pulpit* (Nashville: Abingdon, 1994), 28-29. In the secular world, the sociological term for this is called *intersectionality*, but they include sexual orientation in addition to race, class, gender and age.

(such as children, as highlighted in the quote above), we all need to use our power to help the weak, instead of only griping about the areas in which we are powerless. Women with money should help the poor. Men, even if ethnic minorities, should help women. The poor should help children.

This upside-down kingdom, where relinquishing power is the way to gain it,[59] is best expressed in the great christological passage of Philippians 2:5-11:

> Christ Jesus, who, though he was in the form of God, did not count equality
> with God a thing to be grasped, but emptied himself, by taking the form of a
> servant, being born in the likeness of men. And being found in human form,
> he humbled himself by becoming obedient to the point of death, even death
> on a cross. Therefore God has highly exalted him and bestowed on him the
> name that is above every name, so that at the name of Jesus every knee should
> bow, in heaven and on earth and under the earth, and every tongue confess
> that Jesus Christ is Lord, to the glory of God the Father.

That is the gospel. The four-part reconciliation of race (Jew and Gentile), gender (husbands and wives), class (slave and free), age (children and parents) found in Ephesians comprises the second greatest commandment, which is to love your neighbor. That horizontal reconciliation is merely a reflection of the greater vertical reconciliation of sinners to God, the greatest commandment (Eph 2:1-10). Paul uses the word *mystery* in Ephesians seven times to describe both the horizontal and the vertical reconciliations of the gospel. Reconciliation as a synonym for the gospel is also seen in 2 Corinthians 5:17-20, which says,

> Therefore, if anyone is in Christ, he is a new creation. The old has passed away;
> behold, the new has come. All this is from God, who through Christ recon-
> ciled us to himself and gave us the ministry of reconciliation; that is, in Christ
> God was reconciling the world to himself, not counting their trespasses
> against them, and entrusting to us the message of reconciliation. Therefore,
> we are ambassadors for Christ, God making his appeal through us. We im-
> plore you on behalf of Christ, be reconciled to God.

---

[59]Nobel Prize–winning poet T. S. Eliot expressed this gospel ideal when he quoted ancient Greek philosopher Herakleitos at the beginning of his magnum opus *The Four Quartets*: "ὁδὸς ἄνω κάτω μία καὶ ὡυτή" ("The way up and the way down are one and the same"). Eliot echoes this as "in my beginning is my end" ("East Coker" I), which recalls Jesus' injunction, in Matthew 16:24-25, "If anyone would come after me, let him deny himself and take up his cross and follow me. For whoever would save his life will lose it, but whoever loses his life for my sake will find it."

It is natural to ask why ecumenism (which seems to be inward looking) is not opposed to mission (which is outward looking). After all, if so much time is spent reconciling among Christians, it seems to imply that we would neglect the missionary task toward non-Christians. And that would be a logical conclusion if not for the fact that it is a biblical and theological injunction that the two have a symbiotic relationship.

The link between the two is further emphasized in the oft-quoted phrase "mission is the mother of ecumenism."[60] Not only theologically but also pragmatically, missions and ecumenism are inextricably related to each other. Every great missions movement necessitates cooperation between Christians, and conversely, the importance of unity becomes more pronounced as the Christian faith expands worldwide. In addition, the needs of an unevangelized world necessarily pose serious questions about divisions within Western Christendom. If, as Jesus said in John 17:22-23, Christian unity is a missiological sign to the world, then overcoming divisions in Christianity is an urgent priority. If a divided church is an offense, it becomes a missiological necessity to remedy that condition.[61] Attention to the divided state of the church is a precondition to an effective execution of the mission imperative. So perhaps "ecumenism is the mother of missions" is just as accurate, if not more so! Almost every ecumenical movement began as a missions movement, and vice versa.

In ecumenical settings, the horizontal reconciliation found among the various races, classes, genders, ages, denominations and nations (both in Pentecost in Acts 2:1-12 and in heaven in Rev 7:9-10) that compose the church shows unity in diversity, not unity in uniformity.[62] It is the body of Christ as expressed in 1 Corinthians 12:12-31, where every member is

---

[60]See, e.g., Rodney L. Petersen, "The Changing Contours of World Mission and Christianity: Celebrating the Centenary of Edinburgh 1910," Report to the National Council of Churches General Assembly, November 11, 2010, 1, www.bu.edu/cgcm/files/2009/09/2010Boston-Conference-Summary.pdf. This appears to be a variation on Martin Kähler's famous dictum "Mission is the mother of theology" from *Schriften zur Christologie und Mission* (1908), 190.

[61]Martin Luther King Jr. famously said, "11 a.m. on Sunday morning is the most segregated hour of the week." Sadly, that is still true over fifty years later. If the secular world does diversity better than Christians, they will look at us and wonder what Jesus has to offer if the best the church can come up with is visible division.

[62]People from the United States should be able to understand this easily: fifty states united under one federal government but with individualized state laws. So it is with denominational diversity of the nonessentials (like states) amidst unity in the essentials (like the Constitution of the US).

different but all members work together and each is indispensable. Paul again brings up two types of diversity, or reconciliation in power dynamics, in this passage (race and class) when he says: "For just as the body is one and has many members, and all the members of the body, though many, are one body, so it is with Christ. For in one Spirit we were all baptized into one body—Jews or Greeks, slaves or free—and all were made to drink of one Spirit" (1 Cor 12:12-13).

To further emphasize this point about God desiring unity in diversity for his church, John Piper wrote,

> There is a beauty and power of praise that comes from unity in diversity that is greater than that which comes from unity alone. . . . I infer from this that the beauty and power of praise that will come to the Lord from the diversity of the nations are greater than the beauty and power that would come to him if the chorus of the redeemed were culturally uniform. The reason for this can be seen in the analogy of a choir. More depth and beauty is felt from a choir that sings in parts than from a choir that sings only in unison. Unity in diversity is more beautiful and more powerful than the unity of uniformity.[63]

Christianity is the only religion in the world that does not have a geographic center or an ethnic majority. World Christianity validates Christianity much more than a Western-only Christianity does. If there is a real God, it makes sense he would be a global God.

Just as it is ironic to use the words *Catholic* and *Orthodox* and *Evangelical* to define ourselves over against other Christians (because those words in the lowercase form imply unity, not division), it is also ironic that *ecumenical* has been pitted against *evangelical* in modern-day parlance to mean "liberal" as opposed to "conservative." There is an oft-quoted saying that has falsely perpetuated this notion: "Doctrine divides, service unites." Ecumenists are seen as favoring unity at the expense of theology while evangelicals are perceived to do the opposite. But etymologically, Christians ought really to be both ecumenical *and* evangelical, and orthodoxy and orthopraxis should be inseparable from one another.

---

[63]John Piper, *Let the Nations Be Glad!* (Grand Rapids: Baker, 1993), 222.

This, then, was the great legacy of Edinburgh 1910 and the reason this *missionary* conference derived its reputation as the birthplace of the modern *ecumenical* movement: "the work of Commission VIII [Co-operation and the Promotion of Unity] had a far greater impact on subsequent ecumenical history than that of all the other Commissions put together. . . . What broke new ground at Edinburgh was the decision to embody missionary co-operation in a structured form and on a global scale which imposed on wholly autonomous voluntary missionary agencies an obligation to take much more seriously than hitherto a broader ecumenical view of the missionary task."[64]

FROM 1810 TO 1910 TO 2010

Due to Edinburgh 1910's much-vaunted nickname, 2010 was highlighted as the centenary anniversary of Edinburgh 1910, and many organizations were quick to jump on the bandwagon. There were at least *twenty-five* centenary conferences organized in 2010,[65] all of them intentionally hearkening back to Edinburgh 1910. Nevertheless, four in particular were singled out in 2010 as being of prime importance:

- Tokyo 2010 (officially Global Mission Consultation and Celebration: From Edinburgh 1910 to Tokyo 2010), held May 11–14, 2010, at the Nakano Sun Plaza, Tokyo, Japan

- Edinburgh 2010: Witnessing to Christ Today, held June 2–6, 2010, at Pollock Halls and New College, the University of Edinburgh, Scotland

- Cape Town 2010 (officially The Third Lausanne Congress on World Evangelization), held October 16–25, 2010, at the Cape Town International Convention Centre, South Africa

---

[64]Stanley, *World Missionary Conference*, 278.
[65]San Diego, USA (January 7–10); Pune, India (January 13–15); Aarhus, Denmark (January 27–29); Haddington, Scotland (February 6–27); Buenos Aires, Argentina (February 25–26); Oslo, Norway (April 14–15 and September 7–9); New Haven, USA (April 23–24); Munich, Germany (May 13); Patna, India (June 6); Utrecht, The Netherlands (June 10–11); Liverpool, England (June 11–13); Dublin, Ireland (June 16–18); St. Paul, USA (June 17–19); Auckland, New Zealand (June 18–19); Iona, Scotland (June 19–25); Strasbourg, France (July 6–13); Yangon, Myanmar (July 16–17); Neuendettelsau, Germany (September 14–17); Swanwick, England (October 11–12); London, England (October 12–13). The list and full details can be found at www.edinburgh2010.org/en/events/eventsarchive.html.

- 2010Boston: The Changing Contours of World Mission and Christianity, held November 4–7, 2010, at various member schools of the Boston Theological Institute, Massachusetts, USA

The person who highlighted these four was none other than Ralph Winter, perhaps the foremost missiologist in the world at the turn of the millennium (more about him in chapter three). In early 2009, he wrote an article singling out these four centenary celebrations.[66] Like John Mott, the organizer of Edinburgh 1910, Ralph Winter was a visionary and catalyst for missions and ecumenism and had the charismatic power of personality, as well as organizational skills, to bring together many for the cause of mission. It is a testament to how influential he was that *Christianity Today* picked up on this idea of the four centenary conferences of 2010 and published a chart comparing them (see table 1); three of the most prestigious missiological journals (*IBMR*,[67] *EMQ*[68] and *Missiology*[69]) had articles chronicling all four conferences; and indeed this very book is doing the same comparison. Just as Mott popularized Edinburgh 1910, whether it deserves such a place in history as it currently holds in our minds or not, Winter popularized Tokyo, Edinburgh, Cape Town and Boston in 2010, whether *they* deserve such a place in history or not. It does show the power of persuasion by a charismatic thinker, if nothing else.

If Ralph Winter is to 2010 what John Mott was to 1910, then William Carey was the same to 1810. Like the Edinburgh 1910 conference, William Carey possesses a nickname (whether it be accurate or hagiographical) that continues to make him famous: "the father of modern missions."[70] Carey is forever linked to Edinburgh 1910 as the two bookends to the nineteenth century of missions, which professor Kenneth Scott Latourette labeled the "Great Century of Missions." Actually the bookends of the so-called Great Century extend a little more than one hundred years, beginning in the eighteenth century with the publication of the Magna Carta of

---

[66]Ralph D. Winter, "Edinburgh 1910 in the Year 2010," *Mission Frontiers,* January–February 2009, www.missionfrontiers.org/issue/article/edinburgh-1910-in-the-year-2010.

[67]*International Bulletin of Missionary Research* 35, no. 1 (January 2011).

[68]*Evangelical Missions Quarterly* 47, no. 1 (January 2011).

[69]*Missiology: An International Review* 39, no. 2, special electronic edition (April 2011).

[70]Carey is considered the father of modern missions not only because he highlighted the Great Commission as binding on all Christians but because he was the catalyst for the formation of mission societies, and if Latourette is right, he planted the vision for Edinburgh 1910, posthumously.

missions documents, *An Enquiry into the Obligations of Christians to Use Means for the Conversion of the Heathens* by William Carey in 1792, and ending in the twentieth century with the Edinburgh 1910 World Missionary Conference. Thus, in one decisive stroke Latourette forever stamped Carey and Edinburgh on missions history in the popular imagination as the beginning and the end, respectively, of the Great Century of Missions. For the significance of 1810 and the role that Carey indirectly played in the decision of the location of Cape Town 2010, see chapter five.

William Carey's reputation comes from him being the one to popularize the Great Commission as binding for all Christians. Prior to his writing *An Enquiry*, most Protestants believed that Matthew 28:16-20 was binding only for the original eleven disciples. This despite the fact that the Reformation started in 1517—so it was over 250 additional years before missions became a widespread belief among Protestants! With the five hundredth anniversary of the beginning of the Reformation at hand (October 31, 2017), it is concerning that widespread missions has existed for less than half of Protestant history. Carey's advocacy of this Copernican shift in missional thinking caused a spate of voluntary missionary societies (Protestants' answer to Catholic monastic orders, at least as far as an organizational structure for mission was concerned) to spring into existence and the launching of thousands for the task of missions worldwide. Whether the popularizing of the Great Commission[71] is a good or bad thing depends on whom one talks to. But Duane Elmer astutely notes about the Great Commandment:

> This commandment appears in some form in Leviticus 19:18 (cf. Deuteronomy 6:5); Mark 12:28-31; Luke 10:27; John 13:34; 15:12; Romans 13:9; Galatians 5:14; James 2:8; and 1 John 3:23. I list the texts for several reasons: (1) Their frequent occurrence startled me. (2) The powerful witness of loving God and our neighbor is that everyone will know that we are Christ's disciples (John 13:35). (3) Mission is at least as much driven by love as by task. (4) I wonder if the current generation of young people is more motivated by the Great Commandment than by the Great Commission.[72]

---

[71]These two words do not appear in the Bible; neither, however, does *Trinity*, so that is not necessarily an argument for dismissal. In contrast, the words *Great Commandment* are explicitly stated by Jesus himself, so the force of that is undeniable.

[72]Elmer, *Cross-Cultural Connections*, 132.

Table 1. Comparison of the four 2010 conferences

In 1810, English missionary William Carey proposed a World Missionary Conference. In 1910, his dream was realized in Edinburgh, at one of the most influential Christian gatherings in history (Mark Noll's *Turning Points* includes it as one of 12 "decisive moments" for the church). Devoted to "the evangelization of the world in this generation," Edinburgh 1910 marked the culmination of a century of missionary passion, drew attention to Christians outside Europe and North America, and gave birth to the ecumenical movement and the World Council of Churches. This year, four world missionary conferences are celebrating the Edinburgh meeting's centennial, but with distinctly different views of its legacy and future.

	Tokyo, May 11-14	Edinburgh, June 2-5	Cape Town, October 16-25	Boston, November 4-7
Attendance	968 leaders of parachurch missions organizations.	300, mostly clergy. 1,000 attended the closing ceremony.	4,500 evangelical leaders of various stripes. Invitation criteria attempted to ensure that no nationality, ethnicity, age, occupation, or denomination dominates. 10% had to be under 30 (60% under 50), 35% female, 10% not in fulltime ministry, and 65% from the majority world.	TBD. The only conference of the four with open registration (the others had carefully screened invitation lists), Boston's academic focus and light publicity means that only seminary students and professors invested in missions studies are likely to attend the Boston Theological Institute's event.
Hero	Ralph Winter (1924–2009), the missiologist who focused evangelicals' attention on "unreached peoples."	1910 organizer John Mott and V. S. Azariah (1874–1945), the Indian bishop whose 1910 plea, "Give us friends," became a cry for indigenous churches.	John Stott, drafting committee chairman for the 1974 Lausanne Covenant, which emphasized the role of social justice in evangelism.	Brian Stanley, director of the Centre for the Study of World Christianity and author of a landmark history of the 1910 conference.
The Future of Missions Is:	Completing the task of evangelizing and discipling every people group.	"Deconstructing boundaries" in the church: ecclesiological, political, economic, and so on.	Mobilizing Christians for "global solutions" to HIV/AIDS, poverty, Islam, and other global issues.	A fascinating subject that deserves much study.
Sample Text	"God has entrusted this generation with more opportunities and resources to complete the task [of making disciples] than any previous one." (From "Making Disciples of Every People in Our Generation")	"Disturbed by the asymmetries and imbalances of power that divide and trouble us in church and world, we are called to repentance, to critical reflection on systems of power, and to accountable use of power structures." (From "Common Call")	"A concerted and well-reasoned response to . . . global issues and opportunities has been difficult because the church, and evangelicalism in particular, is highly fragmented." (From "Why Cape Town 2010?")	"Apart from intra-Christian and inter-religious critiques of mission, the rise of secular postmodernity challenges the very relevance of Christianity and therefore her impulse to reach out." (From "Call for Papers")
Notable Moment	As the conference ended, Tokyo pastor Reiji Oyama apologized "to countries that Japan invaded and bombed and killed" and to Israel (for Christian anti-Semitism). Global Christian Network head Liz Adleta asked for forgiveness for America's use of nuclear weapons against Japan. More apologies followed.	Days before the conference, Daryl Balia was forced to resign as international director and barred from attending. He had publicly accused other organizers of racism and bullying, and admitted, "They asked me to sound out a homophobic bishop from Uganda to be a keynote speaker, but I never contacted him."	While the conference will stream live online, the Lausanne movement is emphasizing simulcasts at 400 sites in 60 countries. Similarly, it is hosting run-up conversation meetings (in the US, these are called "12 Cities: 12 Conversations"). CT's own Global Conversation series is part of a similar effort.	Promotional materials highlight the introduction of the *Atlas of Global Christianity* (though the volume has been publicly available since October 2009). Meanwhile, conference speakers include Brian McLaren and Ruth Padilla DeBorst (who was on Edinburgh's executive committee and is a keynote speaker at Cape Town).

Source: Ted Olsen, "Spotlight: The Future(s) of Mission," *Christianity Today*, August 2010, 11; www. christianitytoday. com/ct/2010/august/17.11.html.

There should be some sort of link between the Great Commission and the Great Commandment.

If I may be allowed to humbly contribute a suggestion along the lines of what Carey, Mott and Winter have done, I would like to postulate that the addition of the conference in San José, Costa Rica (officially CLADE V, or the Fifth *Congreso Latinoamericano de Evangelización*), held July 9–13, 2012, is necessary to complete the picture. This book is the only publication that includes CLADE V, which makes it unique. Publications such as *Christianity Today*, *Missiology: An International Review*, *International Bulletin of Missionary Research*, *International Journal of Frontier Missiology*, *Evangelical Missions Quarterly* and *Connections* all covered the four 2010 conferences but left out Latin America. Though Latin America may once again seem an afterthought, as the colloquial saying goes, "Better late than never!" Historically the later addition of a Latin American conference had precedence too, as there was a Panamá 1916 meeting held by those who were disgruntled by the omission of Latin America at Edinburgh 1910. So history repeats itself a century later, as Costa Rica 2012[73] remedies the lack of a major Latin American conference in 2010.

Whether or not 1910 and 2010 (or indeed 1810!) deserve to be highlighted as landmark years, it is still useful to use these years to frame and track the changes in mission over the course of the past century. If the nineteenth century was the "Great Century of Missions" and the twentieth century was the "Great Century of Ecumenism," then perhaps the twenty-first century is the "Great Century of World Christianity," as we will see in the next chapter.

QUESTIONS

1. Does Edinburgh 1910 deserve to be known as the birthplace of the modern ecumenical movement? Or does the fact that it ended the Great Century of Missions invalidate its greatness?

2. Does ecumenism necessitate eschewing theology for the sake of unity? Is there any alternative?

---

[73]And in a wry observation, the fact that much ado was made of the so-called Mayan prophecy forecasting the end of the world on December 21, 2012, it seems that the eyes of the secular world were also turned toward Latin America in 2012!

3. Do you agree with the definitions of *ecumenism* as listed in this chapter? Can you come up with your own (better) definition? Does it need to include adequate representation of denominations, nationalities/geography, race, gender, class and age? Is there any category missing?

4. Does the nineteenth century deserve to be known as the Great Century of Missions?

5. Do you think there are more similarities or more differences in missions when comparing 1910 and today? Have the changes been on par with previous centuries, or did the twentieth century see more change than any century prior? Which of the eight commissions from Edinburgh 1910 are still relevant issues?

6. Is evangelism less important than before, given the rise of world Christianity? Or is missions now "evangelism-plus"?

7. Does the word *ecumenical* mean the same thing today as it did a century ago? Does it have such baggage and negative connotations now that it becomes an unhelpful term to employ today? What about the word *evangelical*—does that cause more harm or confusion than help? Are *ecumenical* and *evangelical* really opposites?

8. Think about the categories of power as stated by Justo and Catherine González. In what areas are you powerful? Powerless? How does this affect what your mission in the world looks like?

9. Is reconciliation a good way to express the gospel? Is it sufficient? Is there a more effective way?

10. The Bible states only four categories of reconciliation/power: race, class, gender and age. Are there more? Some people today put sexual orientation as a fifth one, seeking solidarity among ethnic minorities, women and homosexuals. Certainly one point of connection is that all those groups have felt oppression from the majority at some point, but why or why not is sexual orientation a legitimate fifth category? Beyond being historically oppressed, is being gay in the same category as being black or being female?

11. Do you agree that "missions is the mother of ecumenism"? Or should it really be that "ecumenism is the mother of missions"?

12. Does William Carey deserve to be known as the father of modern missions? Are nicknames unhelpful, or do they serve a purpose in history?

13. Do you think the Great Commission is binding on all Christians, not just on the original apostles? Is the Great Commandment a better rallying banner for missions than the Great Commission?

THE CASE FOR WORLD CHRISTIANITY

IT MAY SEEM ODD to use the word *case* in the title of this chapter, as if world Christianity were an argument to be proven. But here the word *case* does not suggest the fact of the existence of world Christianity but the validity of it as a field of study and of its various viewpoints.

The facts of world Christianity are irrefutable. Essentially, it is defined as the shift of the center of gravity of Christianity to the Two-Thirds World in the last half century.[1] However, though the definition may be succinct, the implications are tremendous. This is no less than a seismic reorientation to the Christian landscape, perhaps as important on the map of Christian history as Pentecost or the Protestant Reformation. However, it has been a quiet revolution, in large part because there is not one singular moment causing the shift, such as the Holy Spirit falling on the crowd with tongues of fire or Martin Luther posting the Ninety-Five Theses on the church door at Wittenberg. And world Christianity seems all the more unlikely given the tragic global events that preceded it. But like Isaac emerging from Mount Moriah unscathed, Daniel emerging from the lion's den, or the Israelites in their exodus from Egypt and the Babylonian exile, somehow world Christianity was birthed like a phoenix from the ashes of the horrors of the

---

[1]Philip Jenkins, *The Next Christendom: The Coming of Global Christianity* (New York: Oxford University Press, 2002), 1.

twentieth century. Christianity is thriving *in spite of* the tragedies of the last one hundred years. A few caveats are in order, however.

THE CURRENT STATE OF WORLD CHRISTIANITY

First, it must be said that world Christianity is not a new phenomenon. Christianity started as a world religion, taking root in places like India, Ethiopia and Turkey (Asia Minor) during the first century. It has been indigenous to Asia, Africa and Europe practically since its inception. In addition, for the first thousand years of Christianity's existence, the church thrived in Asia and Africa, but that story is rarely told in the West.[2] So this more *recent* phenomenon of world Christianity is a recovery, not a discovery. And the old idea that Europe *is* the faith—as if the West had some kind of claim of universal primacy on Christianity—was only true during the first half of the second millennium. Not in the beginning, nor now, has that been the case.

Second, it also must be noted that, despite the magnitude of this geographical Christian shift, it has gone relatively unnoticed, both by the secular media and even by the Western Christian world. However, there are glimmers that this is changing. For example, publishers are starting to mine this relatively untapped treasure trove. Journals such as *Studies in World Christianity* (from the University of Edinburgh) and *The Journal of World Christianity* (from New York Theological Seminary) are producing groundbreaking research. Publishers such as Oxford University Press, InterVarsity Press, Eerdmans, Baker and Orbis are all clamoring to put out books in this burgeoning field. A number of universities, such as Princeton Seminary and Duke and Cambridge universities, have recently created new faculty posts in the field of world Christianity. Global centers for the study of world Christianity are becoming increasingly important, such as the Center for the Study of Global Christianity at Gordon-Conwell Theological Seminary, the Oxford Centre for Mission Studies, the Centre for the Study of Christianity in Asia at Trinity Theological College in Singapore, the Nagel Institute at Calvin College, the Akrofi-Christaller Institute in Ghana, the Overseas Ministries Study Center in Connecticut, the Center for the Study of World

---

[2]Philip Jenkins, *The Lost History of Christianity: The Thousand-Year Golden Age of the Church in the Middle East, Africa, and Asia—and How It Died* (New York: HarperOne, 2008).

Christianity[3] at the University of Edinburgh, Centro Evangélico de Misiología Andino-Amazónica (CEMAA) in Peru, and the Center for Global Christianity at Boston University. There are now conferences dedicated exclusively to this field, such as the Yale-Edinburgh Group on the History of the Missionary Movement and World Christianity,[4] and conferences that have world Christianity study groups, such as the American Academy of Religion and the Evangelical Theological Society.[5] Even conferences that have no obvious relationship to world Christianity, such as the Jonathan Edwards Society and the Wheaton Theology Conference, had conference themes in 2011 of "Jonathan Edwards and World Christianity: Ecumenism, Interfaith Dialogue, and Religious Awakening" and "Global Theology in Evangelical Perspective,"[6] respectively. The International Association of Mission Studies (IAMS), perhaps the most distinguished academic missiology society in the world, just published a retrospective of its last forty years that virtually associates the group with world Christianity,[7] even though missions and world Christianity are *not* the same thing, despite having many points of overlap. Groups of theologians from the Two-Thirds World meet regularly, such as the Latin American Theological Fellowship, Partnership-in-Mission Asia, the African Theological Fraternity and the International Fellowship of Mission Theologians (INFEMIT).

Despite all this, world Christianity still remains a relatively unknown field to the secular world, and even to many Christians. The first major impetus for putting this "on the map" was the 2002 publication of Philip Jenkins's *The Next Christendom: The Coming of Global Christianity*.[8] Other scholars had been writing on this subject prior to Jenkins, but he made it accessible to the

---

[3]Initially named the Center for the Study of Christianity in the Non-Western World (CSCNWW) by founder Andrew Walls, it was subsequently renamed to remove the "Non-Western" designation. See the note on terminology at the beginning of the book.

[4]Named thus because it is co-convened by Andrew Walls at Edinburgh and Lamin Sanneh at Yale, and every year the two universities take turns hosting the conference, since 1992.

[5]Regarding the latter, I founded the world Christianity consultation at ETS in 2010 and currently chair the steering committee for it.

[6]The proceedings of the Wheaton conference were published in Jeffrey P. Greenman and Gene L. Green, eds., *Global Theology in Evangelical Perspective* (Downers Grove, IL: InterVarsity Press, 2012).

[7]Gerald H. Anderson, *Witness to World Christianity: The International Association for Mission Studies, 1972–2012* (New Haven, CT: OMSC, 2012).

[8]Jenkins, *Next Christendom*.

layperson. However, Andrew Walls is probably the most eminent scholar in the field, especially with his 1996 publication of *The Missionary Movement in Christian History: Studies in the Transmission of Faith*.[9] In 2008, *Christianity Today* published an article about Walls claiming that he "may be the most important person you don't know."[10] Perhaps analogously one could say that world Christianity may be the most important subject you don't know![11] Thus the "case" must still be made for world Christianity.

This is clear when one considers how few academic experts are writing on the subject in the Western world. Some notable names, in addition to Andrew Walls, are Lamin Sanneh, Dana Robert, Philip Jenkins, Joel Carpenter, Brian Stanley, Todd Johnson, Samuel Escobar, Timothy Tennent, Tite Tiénou and Miriam Adeney. There are a few others, but not many more. It is especially telling that even Mark Noll, the quintessential historian of American Christianity, has thrown his hat into the world Christianity ring with three of his latest books, *The New Shape of World Christianity: How American Experience Reflects Global Faith* (2009); *Clouds of Witnesses: Christian Voices from Africa and Asia* (2011, coauthored with Carolyn Nystrom); and *From Every Tribe and Nation: A Historian's Discovery of the Global Christian Story* (2014).[12] Of course, in the Two-Thirds World there are many scholars of this subject. But they often suffer from lack of exposure and resources so their voices are not as readily heard. Some names in the Two-Thirds World who *have* managed to remain quite prominent in world Christianity include René Padilla from Latin America (as well as his daughter Ruth Padilla DeBorst), the late Kwame Bediako from Africa, and Vinoth Ramachandra and Hwa Yung from Asia. We need new (and younger) scholars to be contributing to this field. To misappropriate Luke 10:2, "The

---

[9]Andrew Walls, *The Missionary Movement in Christian History: Studies in the Transmission of Faith* (Maryknoll, NY: Orbis, 1996).

[10]Tim Stafford, "Historian Ahead of His Time," *Christianity Today,* February 2007, www.christianity today.com/ch/news/2007/ct-mar8.html.

[11]For more on how Walls has had such an impact on the subject, see the festschrift by William R. Burrows, Mark R. Gornik and Janice A. McLean, eds., *Understanding World Christianity: The Vision and Work of Andrew F. Walls* (Maryknoll, NY: Orbis, 2011).

[12]Mark Noll, *The New Shape of World Christianity: How American Experience Reflects Global Faith* (Downers Grove, IL: InterVarsity Press, 2009); Mark Noll and Carolyn Nystrom, *Clouds of Witnesses: Christian Voices from Africa and Asia* (Downers Grove, IL: InterVarsity Press, 2011); and Mark Noll, *From Every Tribe and Nation: A Historian's Discovery of the Global Christian Story* (Grand Rapids: Baker Academic, 2014).

harvest is plentiful, but the laborers are few." It is not enough for the same ten scholars to be producing 90 percent of the material on the subject.

At the inaugural meeting of the ETS world Christianity consultation in November 2010 in Atlanta, Georgia, a question was asked that illustrates the very need for the study and awareness of world Christianity. "African theology. Asian theology. Latin American theology. Aren't all these 'cultural' theologies just relativism? Why can't we just do 'pure' theology?" The question wasn't quite phrased in that way, but that was the intent. The session had four excellent papers about soteriology in China, contextualization in the Arab-Muslim world, missions from Brazil and New Testament studies in Africa. It was the final paper that prompted the cultural theology question. A man in the audience asked, "Why do we need to look at the New Testament from an African perspective? I mean, we don't ask what the African perspective on gravity is, so why do we need to ask what the African perspective on biblical theology is?" This presupposition is all too common: that one's own perspective is normative and unadulterated. One of the main reasons for these personal blind spots is that it is extremely difficult to identify one's own lenses, much as a fish would be hard-pressed to understand what water is (though land creatures would have no problem readily identifying it)!

One member of the audience helpfully addressed the man's question by pointing out that African culture is actually closer to first-century biblical culture than our Western culture is. For example, agrarian metaphors are relatively foreign to Western city-dwellers but quite understandable to much of the Two-Thirds World. The concept of sacrifice is not one that many Westerners understand, but again, it is an integral consideration in life to many outside the West. So Africans (or Asians or Latin Americans) may be able to help Westerners understand some crucial points of the Bible better. This is precisely why we need an African perspective on the New Testament!

Another way to address this question is to think of world Christianity using an analogy with personal relationships. C. S. Lewis, in *The Four Loves*, says that friendship is the greatest of the loves:

> In each of my friends there is something that only some other friend can fully bring out. By myself I am not large enough to call the whole man into activity; I want other lights than my own to show all his facets. . . . Hence true

Friendship is the least jealous of loves. Two friends delight to be joined by a third, and three by a fourth, if only the newcomer is qualified to become a real friend. They can then say, as the blessed souls say in Dante, "Here comes one who will augment our loves." For in this love "to divide is not to take away."[13]

As a personal example, if somebody wants to get to know me, they would of course have to spend time with me. But they could also ask my friends, family and acquaintances about me. My mother would talk about how I was mischievous and naughty as a child. My friends would talk about my love for baseball or playing the violin. My colleagues would talk about my publications and academic work. Many would know me as a world traveler, and some would even have traveled with me. My spouse knows things about me that nobody else would. Are all of them true of me? Definitely. Does anyone have the full picture of me? No—each will emphasize one thing over another or be missing certain pieces of my profile. In order to fully understand me, you would have to ask everyone who knows me, and then slowly the whole picture would come together. Even spending time with me is insufficient because I would only relate to you in the way that is most meaningful and appropriate to you (I would not relate to my mother in the same way I relate with my students, and so forth). So it is with theology, which is the study of God. A European will have one perspective on God based on his or her history and interactions with him, an Asian will say another thing, an African another, and a Latino yet another. Nobody has the full picture of God, and though every perspective might be true, each is incomplete in and of itself, and every cultural perspective is needed to fully understand this global God. This is not relativism, even if two of the perspectives sound quite different from one another, just as my mother and my students offer two very different descriptions of me. Rather than giving us relativistic lenses, culture gives us instruments that help us see our Lord better.

Culture has many technical definitions, but here is a nontechnical definition that works just as well: culture is simply how one does something. How do you eat? With a fork, with chopsticks or with your hands? That is a cultural question. There is no right or wrong way to do it; the point is that you eat. To a large extent, the method matters not; but different people

---

[13]C. S. Lewis, *The Four Loves* (New York: Harcourt, Brace, 1960), 61.

do it differently, and the enjoyment of the food may be enhanced by the method. So it is with theology and culture. In the end, the result is the same (being fed, whether physically or spiritually), but the method may change how one receives it. Andrew Walls makes the analogy of a theater where everyone is watching a play called "the drama of life." Though everyone can see this drama, how you receive it depends on where you are sitting in the auditorium:

> Our seat in the theatre is determined by a complex of conditions: where we were born, where our parents came from, what language we speak at home, what our childhood was like, and so on. People who share broadly similar conditions form culture blocks—rather like blocks of seats in the theatre, from which the view of the stage is very similar. Culture is simply a name for a location in the auditorium where the drama of life is in progress.[14]

Here I must address my fellow Westerners: not only do non-Western perspectives give us insights into God that we in the West could never get on our own; Western theology also has some serious flaws in it. For example, we are often beholden to Platonic dualism, which has filtered down to us through the millennia, and it is so hard for Western Christians to shake this dichotomistic thinking about the spiritual and physical worlds (this is played out in missions in the sense that evangelism is seen as more important than social justice). Another example is the influence of the Enlightenment on Western thought, which all but killed Christianity in Europe. Today, Europe is the most secular continent on earth, thanks to the Enlightenment and rationalism. Yet we unthinkingly and unwittingly export that mindset to the non-Western world because we cannot see past our own cultural lenses. A third example is individualism. Most cultures throughout world history have been communal, but we have reduced salvation to "me and the Jesus prayer." We now have Korean Christians who come to the West to study in our seminaries, imbibe individualistic theology and then take it back to their communal Asian contexts. It is destructive, because the pastors end up doing theology completely wrongly in their native context, but they think this individualism is normative because their Western theology professors told them it was so. One of the dangers of Westerners providing theological

---

[14]Walls, *Missionary Movement in Christian History*, 44.

education to the Two-Thirds World is uncontextualized mechanical mimicry. A fourth example of problematic Western theology is a poverty in our pneumatology. The rest of the world understands spiritual realities far better than the West does;[15] we are effectively "Binitarian" (rather than Trinitarian) in our theology: we have a great theology of God the Father, a wonderful Christocentrism, but very little knowledge or experience with the Holy Spirit. The irony is that the third person of the Trinity is the one who is with us on earth today! Pentecostalism is the fastest-growing segment of Christianity in the non-Western world today, for a good reason; perhaps we in the West can teach the rest of the world about Christology, but the rest of the world can teach us about pneumatology.

A final example from Scripture is in order. The question has often been asked why there are four Gospel accounts.[16] This is because there is a Jewish perspective (Matthew), a Gentile perspective (Luke), an early, succinct perspective to get the word out as quickly as possible (Mark), and an intimate mystical perspective from the one who knew Jesus best (John, the disciple whom Jesus loved). Certainly there could have been more perspectives (each one of the Twelve could have written a Gospel). John said it best in his Gospel when he observed: "Now there are also many other things that Jesus did. Were every one of them to be written, I suppose that the world itself could not contain the books that would be written" (Jn 21:25). It has crossed the minds of many Christians, upon reading that verse, what else Jesus did and why those things were not recorded. But John and the other Gospel writers were selective in their materials, and each only chose the things they deemed important to get across their particular point and perspective. Together, however, the four Gospels provide a fuller picture of Jesus. Any one Gospel by itself would be insufficient.[17] God, in his sovereignty, determined that it should be necessary to have four accounts of the Christ. So it is with world Christianity: if Matthew, Mark, Luke and John could all give

---

[15]Paul G. Hiebert, *Anthropological Reflections on Missiological Issues* (Grand Rapids: Baker, 1994), 189-202.

[16]Thanks to missionary Eduardo Aulie of Mexico for this insight.

[17]However, there have also been some misguided attempts to conflate all four Gospels together into a sort of super-Gospel. This misses the point of four different perspectives. That would be like taking four different ways of making eggs (e.g., scrambled, poached, sunny side-up and hard-boiled) and putting them all into a blender. That actually destroys the joy of each distinct style and instead leads to an incoherent mess.

perspectives on Jesus, so Africa, Asia, Latin America, North America and Europe can give perspectives on God. And collaboratively, the disparate pieces of this beautiful mosaic begin to form into a clear picture.

In short, world Christianity is not relativistic (defining relativism as the perspective that truth is whatever each person perceives it as); culture is needed to more fully see this infinite God whom we worship. We all have true, but incomplete, perspectives—some cultures are good at seeing God as physician; some are good at seeing God as judge; some are good at seeing God as Creator; some are good at seeing God as immanent; but at the present time we all see as through a glass darkly. We need Latinos and Asians and Africans and Europeans and North Americans all bringing their perspective of God to the table like a potluck dinner (or, in the analogy above, like all my friends and family sharing stories about me). Together, all our contributions make up a fabulous cornucopia of stories, images and theologies (perspectives on God) that start to make God a little clearer to us. We would all have blind spots if not for the contributions of our Christian brothers and sisters from around the world who compensate for us in the areas where we are weakest. This is why we all need each other and why culture helps rather than hinders!

It must be said that one can err on the opposite side as well. Two extremes that people often tend toward are either to deny their own lenses or to become beholden to them. Neither Roman Catholicism nor Western evangelicalism (which tend toward the former, as if all their theology is normative and unladen with cultural biases) nor liberation theology[18] (which tends toward the latter by giving oneself wholly over to one's lenses) is a good hermeneutic. In fact, though the two approaches seem to be opposites, they are really operating on the same principle: the idea that "my way is the right way." Whether one denies one's lenses (as in the West) or acknowledges the lenses but decides that this is the only way to view theology (as in liberation theologies), it is a stubborn refusal to consider any other way of viewing God. The answer to this self-centered tendency is world Christianity.

---

[18]Liberation theologies include the Latin American variety, which looks at everything through the lens of class; the black variety, which looks at everything through the lens of race; the feminist variety, which looks at everything from the lens of gender; the womanist variety, which looks through gender and race; and the *mujerista* variety, which looks through gender, race and class.

THE FUTURE OF WORLD CHRISTIANITY

Innovation is a word not often associated with theology, because theology is regarded as eternal and abiding, therefore any "newfangled" theology is suspected of being heresy. But there are more than only two options: not just orthodoxy or heterodoxy but also *undiscovered theology* (which is a subset of orthodoxy).

In order to understand this point, one must distinguish between truth and theology. Though the two have an undeniable relationship with each other, they are not the same thing. *Truth* is eternal and abiding. *Theology* is a human attempt at articulating that truth in limited, fallible language. All language is cultural, that is, laden with semantic baggage. But it is impossible for human beings to articulate truth other than through language (or visual symbols, which is in itself a type of language), so our theology becomes correspondingly fallible and limited by virtue of the medium through which it is conveyed. Thus the need for analogies or caveats to further explain our point when propositional truths are insufficient in and of themselves. For an example of an analogy, take "Jesus is the Lamb of God." Why do we not just use the propositional truth "Jesus is a sacrifice"? There is something lacking in the propositional statement that the illustration makes clearer. Or perhaps it can even further cloud the issue because "lamb" needs to be contextualized in places that do not have lambs as an everyday animal or that do not use lambs as sacrificial offerings. One cannot assume that "lamb" is understood in the same way for all cultures. For an example of a caveat, take "Jesus is the Son of God" with the caveat being "He is eternally begotten." The propositional truth of Jesus being the Son is insufficient because sonship always implies being younger than the father (name a culture in which this is not true!). So the qualifier is necessary lest we make the natural assumption that the Son is not co-eternal with the Father.[19] Language is imperfect, and

---

[19]Two other examples: (1) Even the phrase "Jesus is Lord" is not neutral, because a lord has connotations of a medieval feudal system. "Jesus is King" does not work in places that have monarchies, such as England, because the theocracy in the Bible bears little resemblance to the British monarchy today. Perhaps it is more akin to a benign absolute dictatorship. (2) "God is good" is problematic not only because of the definition of *goodness* (in some cultures, goodness is kind and merciful; in others, goodness is executing justice without mercy) but also because the word *God* is the most notoriously difficult-to-translate word in Scripture. Missionaries Matteo Ricci, James Legge and William Boone all chose different words for "God" (*tian zhu*, *shangdi* and *shen*, respectively) when

language about God (theology) is likewise imperfect. Truth, however, is perfect. But until we get to heaven, theology is the closest we can come to truth, and we are circumscribed by our own limitations.

A second important point about theology is that it is *occasional*—it arises out of specific historical occasions, and usually as a response to heresy. The statement "Heresy is the mother of orthodoxy," though at first shocking, bears itself out in the history of doctrine. The first four ecumenical councils were called specifically to respond to heretics such as Arius and Pelagius. Of course, these men were not considered heretics yet, but the councils decreed them as such after much examination, and then proceeded to codify orthodoxy—thus the articulation of theology. One wonders when (if ever) the orthodoxy would have been codified if not for the heretics being the catalyst. It was not until the fourth century AD that Christians put words to the articulation of the two natures of Christ and to the Trinity, two of the greatest doctrines of the faith. Does this mean that the truth of these doctrines did not exist prior to the fourth century? No, the truth of it always existed; the theology of it, however, was new at the time and was just waiting to be uncovered. Augustine of Hippo was the first to articulate the doctrine of original sin. The same holds true here—the truth of it has always existed, but the theology (the articulation into human language) of it did not exist until Augustine stated it. Martin Luther is another example. *Sola fide* and *sola gratia* were considered new and heretical theologies of the time by the Roman Catholic Church, but today they are widely accepted by many Protestant Christians. Yet another example is William Carey. Christians did not view the Great Commission as binding on them until Carey argued the case for it. And that was only some 250 years ago—quite recent by historical standards! The history of doctrine shows that "new" or "innovative" theology, sometimes known as progressive revelation, continues to enrich Christian thought over the course of the centuries.[20] Martin Luther put it best when he called Christians to be "*reformata et semper reformanda*" ("reformed and always reforming"). Ironically, Protestants now tend to do what they initially accused Catholics of, namely, be beholden to tradition (as if

---

translating the Bible into Chinese, but each word was so laden with external meaning that none proved to be satisfactory in and of themselves. Today the Chinese employ all the terms.

[20]Rob Bell, *Velvet Elvis* (Grand Rapids: Zondervan, 2005), vii-xii.

"reformed" means that we do not need to add or change anything from what was stated in the sixteenth century) instead of the humble awareness of the need for constant course correction implied in the "always reforming" phrase. Linguists understand this well with regard to scholarship; as language evolves with use, so Bible translations need to be constantly updated, and new findings continually shed more light on our understanding of the sacred text.

Of course, when always reforming, one needs to separate the wheat from the chaff because certainly there is much heterodoxy that sprouts among the new orthodoxies. But if one dismisses all "new" theology as heresy, then one would have had to dismiss the theology of Chalcedon, which was "new" at the time, or the writings of Augustine or the writings of Luther. Let us not throw out the proverbial baby with the bathwater. Even in the Bible, the writings of the apostle Paul were a response to heresies. Epistles are, in fact, the most occasional of all genres of the Bible, and yet this is where Christians get some of our most cherished doctrines. John, the beloved disciple, addressed the heresy of Gnosticism in his letters. Paul addressed many false teachings as well. One of the greatest passages about love, 1 Corinthians 13, was not written in a vacuum—it was articulated because Paul was trying to show the Corinthians what a true Christian love looks like as opposed to the false love expressed by the cult of the goddess Aphrodite centered in Corinth.

This is where world Christianity has its place; it's not relativism and not heterodoxy, but the opportunity for "new" and "innovative" orthodoxies, along the lines of Chalcedon and Augustine and Luther (or, for Roman Catholics, Thomas Aquinas)—that is, to help us be always reforming. We should not be so arrogant as to think that we have discovered all truth and that everything about God is already known; otherwise we might as well put down our pens and never write another word about theology. But with this unprecedented phenomenon of world Christianity and globalization, where there are now Christians in every culture who can easily communicate with one another, we are essentially sitting on the cusp of one of the greatest opportunities in world history: the putting together of our collective heads to discover new vistas about God—if we will only accept this mission. But many are still resistant. It is my hope that this book can help change that.

A third point is that creeds are theology, not Scripture, and thus do not hold the same authority. Creeds, though highly cherished, are summaries of Scripture, not Scripture itself, and have the same fallibility as any other theology. One may protest that creeds—specifically the two most widely used, the Apostles' Creed and the Nicene Creed—are universally accepted. This is actually not 100 percent accurate. The Apostles' Creed has the line "He descended into hell," which is highly debated. And if that line is not universally accepted, it throws into doubt the rest of the creed. Not that I actually think the rest of the creed is wrong, but that one particular line shows that the Apostles' Creed is not on the same level of infallibility as Scripture. Not to mention (and this would be the Achilles' heel in claiming universal acceptance of the Apostles' Creed) that it is recited only in the West and not in the East.

The problem with the Nicene Creed is twofold. First, it has been revised once. It was written in the Council of Nicaea in AD 325, then subsequently revised into the Niceno-Constantinopolitan Creed at the Council of Constantinople in AD 381. That is the version widely used today. So the follow-up question is: if it was deemed to be in need of revision once, could it not be deemed such again as we discover more about God? But the second problem with the Nicene Creed (this time let us take the revised form, the Niceno-Constantinopolitan Creed) is that it is not universally accepted either. The debate over the *filioque* clause led to a split between West and East in the Great Schism of 1054. So now there are *three* versions of the Nicene Creed: the original of 325, the revised one of 381 with *filioque* and the revision of 381 without *filioque*. It seems doubtful to make the Nicene Creed the definitive litmus test of orthodoxy when there are three different versions going around, but people do—thus all sides (notably Roman Catholic vs. Eastern Orthodoxy) end up accusing each other of heresy, which again calls into question the universal acceptability of these creeds (again, this is not to suggest that I disagree with these creeds—in fact, I mostly agree with them—but the point is everyone has their own version that they accept). And an even bigger division happened when Chalcedonian Christianity caused the splitting away of a whole Eastern segment of the church, namely the Nestorian and Jacobite (monophysite) churches, sometimes called the Oriental Orthodox Churches. So even Chalcedon was not universally accepted.[21]

If a creed is a summary of Scripture, its purpose is to highlight what the summarizer thinks are the most important points of the Bible. However, everybody summarizes Scripture differently, because theology is occasional. The points people will emphasize parallel the battles they have fought. This is true individually as well as corporately. For example, an individual in destitute poverty will ask different questions about the goodness of God than a rich person would, and she will search the Scriptures to find her answers—probably reading Job, Lamentations, the exilic prophets and the Gospels, rather than Paul.[22] An example of a corporate theological battle is the doctrine of inerrancy, which was never articulated until the fundamentalist-modernist controversy in the United States in the early twentieth century. Nobody else in history or in other geographies ever saw the need to articulate inerrancy until that controversy, and in fact, others look at Americans strangely when they are asked to affirm inerrancy. Yet there is a parallelism here: both the occasional nature of the impoverished person's theology and the occasional nature of the doctrine of inerrancy are obvious.

If theology is occasional, it does not get more occasional than the mission field, where different circumstances require different answers to questions never before considered by the missionaries. In this sense, it should not be surprising that Paul, the greatest missionary in the Bible after Jesus, also wrote half the New Testament, because more intercultural encounters mean more chances to newly theologize. Given this fact, then one must ask: if Christians in a particular geographical region have not fought certain theological battles, do they have to accept the findings of Christians who have fought those battles in other places and times? My answer is yes. Christians in the non-Western world do have to accept the Nicene Creed even if they

---

[21]For a fuller explanation of the issues, see Steve Strauss, "Creeds, Confessions, and Global Theologizing: A Case Study in Comparative Christologies," in *Globalizing Theology: Belief and Practice in an Era of World Christianity*, ed. Craig Ott and Harold Netland (Grand Rapids: Baker Academic, 2006), 140-56. The history of those Oriental Orthodox Churches is detailed in Philip Jenkins's book *The Lost History of Christianity*.

[22]Galatians, which was so important to Luther, would not have been as important to him if he was physically starving.

have not fought those theological battles, because that is the gift of the West to them. Despite the fact that the Nicene Creed is very Greek in its language[23] and is a product of the fourth-century Mediterranean world (thus is very culturally and temporally specific), it is universally applicable. This is exactly what Jesus was: culturally and temporally specific, yet universally applicable. He was a first-century Aramaic-speaking Jew in Roman-occupied Israel who also happened to be the Savior of the world. Theology is also culturally and temporally specific but universally applicable. However, theological exchange must be an equal partnership: Western Christians must also accept the theological findings of non-Western Christians, even if these are not the battles they have fought; otherwise it becomes an issue of power where only one group's viewpoint is considered canonical.

Philip Jenkins points out some of the differences in the theological battles in the Two-Thirds World:

> These newer churches preach deep personal faith and communal orthodoxy, mysticism and Puritanism, all founded on clear scriptural authority. They preach messages that, to a Westerner, appear simplistically charismatic, visionary, and apocalyptic. In this thought-world, prophecy is an everyday reality, while faith-healing, exorcism, and dream-visions are all basic components of religious sensibility. For better or worse, the dominant churches of the future could have much in common with those of medieval or early modern European times. On present evidence, a Southernized Christian future should be distinctly conservative.[24]

In addition, Two-Thirds World theology tends to ask questions about the fate of dead ancestors, spiritual warfare, the relationship between poverty and faith, the acceptability of polygamy, and conversion to Christ in a religiously pluralistic world (e.g., can you be a Messianic Muslim in the same way that someone can be a Messianic Jew?). In the West, however, the questions are regarding the mode of baptism, the status of the papacy, Calvinism vs. Arminianism, egalitarianism vs. complementarianism, denominationalism, and the validity of cessationism and dispensationalism, just to name a few. The questions are often very different but no less valid.

---

[23]For example, the language of this line: "Light of Light, very God of very God."
[24]Jenkins, *Next Christendom*, 8.

A good example of how Western theology is sometimes received in the Two-Thirds World is illustrated in the first chapter of Andrew Walls's book *The Missionary Movement in Christian History*. He writes about a group of Pentecostal Nigerians in the city of Lagos in 1980 who, upon being shown a copy of the Nicene Creed, "accept the creed of Nicea, but display little interest in it: they appear somewhat vague about the relationship of the Divine Son and the Holy Spirit."[25] In contrast, they care very much about "power, as revealed in preaching, healing, and personal vision." This illustrates that Western theology and non-Western theology are not mutually exclusive but in fact can be compatible; it is just that circumstances and occasions dictate what aspects of theology certain people tend to emphasize at any given time. If any Westerners protest that all Christians throughout the world must accept the Nicene Creed regardless of nationality or culture, not only is there the problem of *which* of the three versions of the Nicene Creed to put forth (it seems kind of ironic to make non-Westerners accept it when Westerners cannot even agree among themselves which one to accept) but there is also the issue of reciprocity. What would Westerners think if a group of Africans wrote a creed based on what *they* deemed to be the most important parts of Scripture and insisted that Westerners sign it? Either Western Christians would have to insist that only their creeds are relevant, untainted by culture and universal for all Christians[26]—namely, the insistence on Western superiority—or they would have to likewise accept the creeds of their fellow brothers and sisters in Christ from around the world who see theology through different cultural and occasional lenses. The hyphenation of theology (Asian-theology, African-theology, Latino-theology) is akin to the hyphenation of ethnicities (Asian-American, African-American, Latino-American), where only

---

[25]Walls, *Missionary Movement in Christian History*, 5.

[26]At the Wheaton Theology Conference in 2011, mentioned above, Wheaton professor Gene Green clarified that while Two-Thirds World theology was the focus of that year's theme, "*All* theology is contextual! . . . Are contextual theologies those which come from the Majority World and minority groups within North America? Or are all theologies contextual by their very nature? In other words, do we in North America have an accent, or is it just *them* in Latin America and Africa who have accents and who display this deep interplay between the understanding and display of their faith, and their cultural and social location? . . . All theology is indeed contextual, even Western theology."

the white (those of European descent) are non-hyphenated.[27] African theologian John Mbiti lamented that too many Western Christians can articulate all the Western heresies from ages past but have no clue as to the theological orthodoxies and living faith coming out of the Two-Thirds World today.[28]

Unfortunately, many Western Christians have only two ways of viewing theology: it is either right or wrong. And because Western theology is "right," then Two-Thirds World theology is "wrong."[29] There is no way to see the two as compatible, or that perhaps Western theology is missing something that Two-Thirds World theology may be able to address. Trinity Evangelical Divinity School professor Duane Elmer tackles this mistaken assumption when he writes:

> Many who live in Western cultures see life as rather black and white. They often think in a two-dimensional perspective such as we and they, good and bad, moral and immoral, right and wrong, me and you, church and state, or secular and sacred. Even the proverb "Do you see the glass half full or half empty?" represents a two-dimensional or dichotomistic way of seeing life. . . . By contrast, many Two-Thirds World cultures tend to be more holistic in their view of life. They see life not so much as a timeline but as a tapestry where one sees threads and colors touching, overlapping and reinforcing each other, forming a whole that has its own beauty and integrity. The metaphor of a glass half full or half empty does not work for holistic people. They prefer the metaphor of an onion that gets peeled, layer upon layer. Life is unfolding;

---

[27]One humorous illustration I use in my classes is to recount the times when the assumption is made that we Americans are the only ones who don't have an accent—and we hear someone from England and comment on their "English accent" as if they are the deviant ones! I am quick to point out that the English, not the Americans, invented English, so who really has the accent? Another illustration I use is that people say, "Let us go for ethnic food" by which they mean Mexican or Chinese or Indian. However, every food is "ethnic"! Finally, I use an ice cream illustration: though chocolate and strawberry and butterscotch are all flavors, *vanilla* is a flavor too—it is not tasteless!

[28]John Mbiti, "Theological Impotence and the Universality of the Church," in *Mission Trends No. 3: Third World Theologies*, ed. Gerald H. Anderson and Thomas F. Stransky (Grand Rapids: Eerdmans, 1976), 16-17.

[29]Or maybe it's not stated as strongly as that, but the understanding is that Western theology is normative and that Two-Thirds World theology has a flavor. Ironically, European American theology is labeled by its proponents as "systematic" theology, similar to how the Roman *Catholic* Church has a word in their name that means "universal" (even if they are not). But even the suggestion of being able to systematize theology betrays one's cultural inclination to categorize, a very Western tendency.

each layer is connected to the former and must be understood in relation to the whole and, indeed, part of the whole.[30]

Therefore the reaction of the Nigerian Christians to the Nicene Creed as stated above would trouble Westerners who may feel that to be a true Christian is to do as they do and say as they say. Perhaps we should open our ears and eyes a bit more and see that we can keep our theology while at the same time be enriched by others' theology as well; the two are not mutually exclusive.[31]

In 2010, an exciting and unprecedented publication was introduced to the world. The *Africa Bible Commentary*[32] was published, which proved to be a revolutionary step in the right direction: seventy African scholars commenting on every book of the Bible from an African perspective. This was merely the first of its kind. In 2015, that was followed by the *South Asia Bible Commentary*[33] in the same vein. Currently there are in production two others in the series with potential for more: one for Latin America[34] and one for the Middle East. These commentaries should be de rigueur for Christians in this next century, no matter their geographical location or culture.

Some may protest at the potential danger of this seemingly unrestrained self-theologizing in the Two-Thirds World: if left unchecked, wouldn't there arise all manner of heresy sprouting up everywhere? This is one of the greatest apologetics for theological conferences; they provide checks and balances. Paul Hiebert highlights this as two of the four ways we can guard against syncretism.[35] Number three on his list is the church acting as a hermeneutical community that "extends not only to the church in every culture, but also to the church in all ages," while number four expands it

---

[30]Duane Elmer, *Cross-Cultural Connections: Stepping Out and Fitting In Around the World* (Downers Grove, IL: IVP Academic, 2002), 142-43.

[31]An example of an African creed, though it is written by a white American who was a missionary in Kenya, can be found in Vincent Donovan, *Christianity Rediscovered* (Maryknoll, NY: Orbis, 2003), 148.

[32]Tokunboh Adeyemo, ed., *Africa Bible Commentary* (Grand Rapids: Zondervan, 2010), copublished with Word Alive Publishers in Kenya.

[33]Brian Wintle, ed., *South Asia Bible Commentary* (Grand Rapids: Zondervan, 2015), copublished with Open Door Publications in India.

[34]This will be called the CBC, or *Comentario Bíblico Contemporáneo*.

[35]Number one is to take "the Bible seriously as the rule of faith and life." Number two is recognizing "the work of the Holy Spirit in the lives of all believers open to God's leading."

crossculturally: we need an international hermeneutical community because "one can often see the sins of others better than his or her own, and
theologians can often detect the cultural biases of theologians from other
cultures better than they can critique themselves."[36] Instead of getting rid
of contextualization for fear of syncretism (which would be throwing out
the baby with the bathwater), we need to allow for natural and organic
development of theology in the Two-Thirds World—even if syncretism
does crop up, because that is inevitable (and it is the way that theology
developed in the Western world too). In the end we will be able to separate
the wheat from the weeds, but in the meantime we have to let them grow
up together (Mt 13:24-30) for fear of stunting the growth of the wheat. In
this way, conferences such as the five outlined in this book function as
modern-day versions of the ecumenical councils of early church history.
Missions is the mother of ecumenism; heresy is the mother of orthodoxy;
theology is occasional; therefore missions conferences produce contemporary theological documents that are the creeds of our time, which address occasional topics found not only in the modern world but across
continents and cultures. E. Stanley Jones correctly predicted that we need
to move beyond dependency and independency to interdependency.[37] This
is also an apologetic for physical publishing, and why the Internet is not
adequate for self-theologizing in the Two-Thirds World: editors help to
keep the content under control via peer reviewing, and publishing houses
lend credibility to content. History will judge who ends up as the heretics
or the heroes. For example, will N. T. Wright's "New Perspective" on Paul
make him the new Martin Luther or the new Pelagius? Progressive theology
must be allowed to run its course regardless.

This potential for innovation is one of the most exciting things about
living in the era of world Christianity today. Globalization has many ill effects, but it is not all bad—cross-pollination of ideas can lead to the best of
all worlds. Frans Johansson (a consultant with an MBA from Harvard
Business School) wrote a book called *The Medici Effect*, which outlines why
the Italian Renaissance gained the impetus to influence the European scene

---

[36]Hiebert, *Anthropological Reflections on Missiological Issues*, 91-92.
[37]E. Stanley Jones, *Christian Maturity* (Nashville: Abingdon, 1957), 211.

in the way that it did. It was the wealthy Medici family in Florence who brought together a cross-section of

> sculptors, scientists, poets, philosophers, financiers, painters, and architects . . . [who] found each other, learned from one another, and broke down barriers between disciplines and cultures. Together they forged a new world based on new ideas—what became known as the Renaissance. As a result, the city became the epicenter of a creative explosion, one of the most innovative eras in history.[38]

World Christianity has the potential to become a theological renaissance: the Christian faith meets the Medici Effect. When Christians from every crossroads of life, experience, culture, race, nationality and denomination get together, the productivity can be enormous (yet another argument for the value of theological conferences). In the same way that the world has advanced technologically in the last century faster than it has in the previous two millennia *combined*, perhaps in this next century we will see an explosion of theological production like the world has never seen before—if we are open to the cross-fertilization of theologies and not cloistered in our attitudes that we know better than everyone else.[39]

One may be suspicious of my using a secular book—published by Harvard Business School Press, no less!—to gain insight into how to do theology, but that is precisely the point: foreign ideas, even from the secular world, could open up new vistas to theology like never before. That is the Medici Effect, the intersection and crossroads of different fields of study acting as catalysts on one other. Who knows whether we may see the African Luther[40] or the

---

[38]Frans Johansson, *The Medici Effect: What Elephants and Epidemics Can Teach Us About Innovation* (Boston: Harvard Business School Press, 2006), 2-3.

[39]The hybrid of hitherto nonintersecting ideas can produce unexpected results and great innovation. For example, the iPad came from taking the idea of a computer and the idea of a notepad and putting them together, creating a new product altogether, not simply a better computer or better notepad. In Los Angeles, Kogi tacos are all the rage—celebrity chef Roy Choi decided to put Korean marinated barbeque meat into Mexican food, instead of simply trying to improve on existing Korean or Mexican food. Peter Chao, president of Eagles Communications, uses the metaphor of an estuary where the river runs into the ocean, because the fresh and salt water mixing together is unusual. This explains the tastiness of Maryland crab in the Chesapeake Bay, where the brackish water produces a unique environment for crabs to thrive. If this concept works for technology, food and wildlife, why can it not work for theology?

[40]I purposely did not say "African Augustine" because, though he is thought of as a Western theologian, he was from northern Africa, what is today Algeria. In the first few centuries of the church, Asian, African and European Christians would interact on a regular basis. It is exciting that we are

Asian Augustine or the Latin American Aquinas[41] within our lifetimes as a result of this. There will always be naysayers at the beginning, as every theologian who writes something "new" will face stiff opposition, but history will determine whether the innovation is heresy or a new form of orthodoxy.

One of the goals of missionaries for new Christian communities is to eventually move them toward the three selves: self-sustaining, self-governing and self-propagating.[42] However, Paul Hiebert writes that we should move toward a fourth self: self-theologizing.[43] This fourth self is a sign that the Two-Thirds World churches have grown into maturity and are not merely robotically replicating what has been taught them, but are adapting theology to their own contexts because "one size does not fit all." Some of the worst mistakes in missionary history have been made when Western theologians have tried to take non-Western Christians and fit them into Western cultural molds.

Other innovative ideas from the secular world may help us gain further insight into the potential of world Christianity. Francis Fukuyama, senior fellow at the Center on Democracy, Development and the Rule of Law at Stanford University, wrote a book in 1992 titled *The End of History and the Last Man*, in which he argued that "history"—by which he meant the political and economic development of humankind—had reached the pinnacle of its evolution, namely, democracy and capitalism. In response to Fukuyama's book, Harvard professor Samuel Huntington penned his own book called *The Clash of Civilizations and the Remaking of World Order* the following year, in which he argued that the end of history had not arrived but rather had taken off in a new direction: the world would no longer be defined by ideologies but by culture.[44] This is exemplified by the fact that today the president of the United States is black, the secretary general of the United

---

recovering this dynamism again today. But it is unfortunate that it is still ingrained in the minds of most that Christianity has always been a Western religion. It is Semitic—Eastern—in its origins, let us not forget!

[41]Or perhaps the African Luther, Asian Augustine or Latin American Aquinas already exists, but Westerners just have not paid attention. One person who has taken note is Justo L. González, *The Mestizo Augustine: A Theologian Between Two Cultures* (Downers Grove, IL: IVP Academic, 2016).

[42]This idea was first developed by Henry Venn, general secretary of the Church Missionary Society from 1841 to 1873. See Max Warren, ed., *To Apply the Gospel* (Grand Rapids: Eerdmans, 1971).

[43]Hiebert, *Anthropological Reflections on Missiological Issues*, 97.

[44]For Huntington, instead of First World (democracy and capitalism), Second World (communism), and Third World (developing nations), the world would be split into a new tripartite division of power: the Western world, the Chinese world and the Muslim world. His prediction has become eerily true.

Nations is Asian, and the pope is Latin American. These are three of the most powerful men in the world, and the value of multicultural diversity seems to have had a profound effect on the election of these men in today's world, perhaps more than any other demographic or sociological factor. Johansson explains this with regard to the Medici Effect:

> In field after field, we are finding that our basic understanding of the world is, if not 100 percent accurate, at least good enough. . . . In short, science works, and it works well. However, just as there are a limited number of times that we can discover a continent or a section of human anatomy, we can discover the law of evolution, or a supernova, or thermodynamics, only once. This does *not* mean, however, that science has played out its role. On the contrary, science is becoming increasingly critical to all of our lives. There are more questions to explore than ever before, but a great many of the discoveries will be of a different nature than in the past. Instead of helping us understand the pieces of the world, they will help us understand how those pieces interact.[45]

Essentially he is arguing that we have nearly hit our vertical ceiling with scientific knowledge, but now our world's development is taking a ninety-degree turn by shifting the progress horizontally into a convergence of disciplines: "You will find engineers collaborating with biologists to understand the toughness of the conch shell and applying it to everything from tank armor to auto bodies. Or you will see oceanographers, meteorologists, geologists, physicists, chemists, and biologists collaborating to understand the effects of global warming. New discoveries, world-changing discoveries, will come from the intersections of disciplines, not from within them."[46] This intersection of different disciplines has infinite permutations. Perhaps theology is similar: it could be that we have nearly hit the vertical ceiling with theological development (to rephrase Johansson: "we are finding that our basic understanding of [God] is, if not 100 percent accurate, at least good enough"), but world Christianity affords us the opportunity to branch out horizontally, and this will be the nature of the theological innovation that is to come.[47] It may not be new things that we discover about God, but new

---

[45]Johansson, *Medici Effect*, 26.

[46]Ibid.

[47]Andrew Walls employs similar vocabulary but in a slightly different way in his *Missionary Movement in Christian History*: "Diversity exists not only in a *horizontal* form across the contemporary scene, but also in a *vertical* form across history. Christianity is a generational process, an ongoing dialogue

ways to think about what we already know about God, much as Jesus in the New Testament framed for the Pharisees how to think anew about the Old Testament concept of sabbath.

Much of missions theology in the 1970s and '80s was dominated by Fuller Theological Seminary's Homogeneous Unit Principle (HUP),[48] which states that "people become Christian fastest when least change of race or clan is involved," and "people like to become Christians without crossing racial, linguistic or class barriers." There are two flaws to this principle: first, that pragmatism is the most important thing and therefore speed is of the essence, and second, that the HUP seems racist because it encourages segregation[49] rather than reconciliation with those who are different. World Christianity turns the HUP on its head by encouraging diversity rather than homogeneity. Frans Johansson puts this in secular terms:

> If you wish to generate intersectional ideas, you should seek environments where you will work with people who are different from you. . . . If you are drawn to an organization because everyone there sees the world the same way you do (whether that means left-brained, right-brained, artistically, financially, or by any other measure), consider just how this will help you. Chances are you will end up in a team with people who act and think like you. Your team will get along great and it will get a lot of things done. But will it be innovative? Most likely not. Everyone comes to the table with a similar mindset—and they will leave with the same.[50]

If our goal is to be firm on the essentials but flexible on the nonessentials, then meeting with other Christians who differ on the nonessentials is healthy and helps us freshly engage with our faith and perhaps even humbly correct some errors we may hold (yet another argument for the validity of

---

with culture. Just as diversity of Christian expression and its ultimate coherence combine in the contemporary scene, so they are across the generations. We belong to the ancestors—and to our grandchildren, and this is as true of the Church as a whole as of any local segment of it. The full-grown humanity of Christ requires all the Christian generations, just as it embodies all the cultural variety that six continents can bring. As the writer to the Hebrews puts it, Abraham and the patriarchs have even now not yet reached their goal. They are waiting for 'us' (Heb. 11:39-40)" (xvii).

[48] As initially postulated in Donald McGavran's *Bridges of God* and later expanded in Peter Wagner's *Understanding Church Growth* (Grand Rapids: Eerdmans, 1980).

[49] This seems a not-too-distant echo of "separate but equal" from American racial segregation.

[50] Johansson, *Medici Effect*, 82-83.

theological conferences).[51] If, however, we elevate all nonessentials of doctrine to the same level as essentials, all it does is exacerbate our own theological myopia and breed dogmatism.[52] There are far more nonessential (debatable, nonsalvific) points of theology in Christianity than essentials (points of doctrine that everyone agrees on) in the faith. Diversity keeps us sharp as we engage with other Christian points of view, but it also keeps us humble if we truly listen to others who may correct any errors in our thinking. World Christianity is a far cry from the HUP.

The Bible (the Word) is analogous to Jesus (the Living Word) in that both are fully divine as well as fully human. Scripture is of God and from God and for God. And yet God chose human agents who are locked into culture and time to accomplish his will and write the Bible. World Christianity is often dismissed by those who esteem Christ's divinity over his humanity, which is essentially the ancient heresy known as Docetism. They think culture has no relation to propositional truth and as a result do not take seriously enough the cultural rootedness—essentially the humanness—of the Bible. They end up regarding the Bible as Muslims view the Qu'ran or Mormons view the Book of Mormon—namely, writings handed down from God on high with very little intervention on the part of the human authors like Muhammad or Joseph Smith. But clearly that is not the case with the Bible. Paul and John, for example, have extremely different personalities, which come out in their writings (you do not even need to know Greek; you can sense the differing flavor between their styles of writing immediately, even in English). God did not drop the Scriptures into their laps;[53] rather, the Holy Spirit spoke through the authors and kept their personalities and cultures intact.

This, then, is the difference between systematic theologians and missiologists: the latter know the difference between syncretism and contextualization. The former think only in dualistic black-and-white categories and dismiss any

---

[51]The only exception to this is denominational seminaries, in which their "nonessential" or denominational distinctives are meant to be kept intact. For nondenominational seminaries, however, there should be more openness.

[52]For more on this, see Allen Yeh, "The Road Ahead: Essentials vs. Nonessentials," in Mark Russell, Allen Yeh, Michelle Sanchez, Chelle Stearns and Dwight Friesen, *Routes and Radishes: And Other Things to Talk About at the Evangelical Crossroads* (Grand Rapids: Zondervan, 2010), 33-52.

[53]The only time he did that in the Bible was with Moses and the Ten Commandments, and even then he only wrote it with his divine finger the first time; the second time around, Moses had to write it himself!

other way of thinking as relativism or liberalism.[54] This docetic thinking regards the Word as more divine than human. Missiologists realize that there can be another way besides the extremes of rigid dogmatism (Western conservatism) and liberal relativism, a third way that takes more seriously the human agency of theology and the Bible and even Jesus himself without sacrificing any of the divinity. This third way keeps culture intact and engages it as an indispensable consideration, because that is the way God chooses to communicate with humankind. To be against contextualization for fear of syncretism is like being a teetotaler for fear of alcoholism. It's extremism in the opposite direction and sometimes just as grave an error. It's like riding your bicycle without ever taking off the training wheels for fear of falling. Nineteenth-century Boston preacher Phillips Brooks famously defined preaching as the "communication of truth through personality."[55] Theology can also be defined as truth communicated through personality, which is essentially culture individualized in a person. It is not only nonsensical to deny the human component; it is impossible. What this boils down to, theologically, is an affirmation of the two natures of Christ, divine *and* human, God's truth spoken through culture, both elements of which are present in the Bible and in theology.

Again, diversity—the reconciliation of very different people and their cultures—is not just something nice; it is a reflection of the very gospel itself, as God reconciled himself to sinners. World Christianity is correspondingly not just ideal but is *essential* to Christianity. Unity in diversity is mission because ecumenism is a witness to the world, as Jesus made clear in his high priestly prayer in John 17:22-23, "that they may be one even as we are one, I in them

---

[54]Western conservatives will stigmatize world Christianity by branding it with the scarlet letter *L*, meaning liberal, as they do with anybody who thinks differently from them. What they miss is that Two-Thirds World Christianity tends to be mostly conservative. In 1998 at the Lambeth Conference, it was the African bishops of the Episcopal Church who opposed the measure to ordain homosexual bishops in the Church of England. If it were up to the European bishops, the measure would have passed. (See the quotation from Jenkins, *Next Christendom*, 8, above.) And an African once said to me: "No African would ever attend a church pastored by a homosexual." How ironic that Western evangelicals are so quick to dismiss Two-Thirds World theology as "liberal" when most Two-Thirds World Christians are actually quite conservative and it is the West that brings most of the liberalism to theology.

[55]Phillips Brooks, *Lectures on Preaching* (New York: Dutton, 1877), 5. At the age of forty-two, Brooks delivered the Lyman Beecher Lectures in Preaching at Yale. His published Lectures on Preaching are probably the most widely read of the entire Yale series and still offer tremendous insights and inspiration to the contemporary preacher. It was in those lectures that Brooks offered his now-famous definition of preaching as the "communication of truth through personality."

and you in me, that they may become perfectly one, so that the world may know that you sent me and loved them even as you loved me." And unity in diversity is also the most worshipful honoring of a global God, as we read in Revelation 7:9-10: "behold, a great multitude that no one could number, from every nation, from all tribes and peoples and languages, standing before the throne and before the Lamb, clothed in white robes, with palm branches in their hands, and crying out with a loud voice, 'Salvation belongs to our God who sits on the throne, and to the Lamb!'" Worship and mission are the two greatest human activities we can do, and world Christianity contributes to both. John Piper gives a helpful explanation of their relationship:

> Missions exists because worship doesn't. . . . All of history is moving toward one great goal, the white-hot worship of God and his Son among all the peoples of the earth. Missions is not that goal. It is the means. And for that reason it is the second greatest human activity in the world. . . . Worship, therefore, is the fuel and goal in missions. . . . The goal of missions is the gladness of the peoples in the greatness of God. . . . Missions begins and ends in worship.[56]

In missions conferences, diverse people gather, and the ecumenical unity is not only for strategizing about missions but ultimately for worship as well.

Here is the great danger of world Christianity as a field of study: it could end up being tokenism. A seminary or university could teach systematic theology, Christian education, church history, ethics, pastoral counseling, homiletics, Old Testament, New Testament and exegetical method classes, and then include a world Christianity class to make themselves feel good. This way, all the "normative" theology can be done, with a "cultural" class thrown in for good measure. In actuality, since culture permeates everything, all theology should be considered world Christianity.[57] And we need to teach church history, homiletics, Old and New Testaments, counseling, and theology, all from perspectives of Asia, Africa and Latin America, as well as from Western perspectives. This explosion, or Medici Effect, of new directions in Christian thought and practice may seem overwhelming and, in fact, untenable. But if this is the future of Christianity, to overlook it or to deny it is to hide one's

---

[56]John Piper, *Let the Nations Be Glad!* (Grand Rapids: Baker, 1993), 35.

[57]The same might be said of missiology. Missiology is the intersection of theology with culture. Since all theology ultimately is cultural (because all theology must be articulated with language, which is inherently cultural), really all Christian theology is missiology.

head in the sand. Rather than being overwhelmed by it all, we should find this one of the most exciting times in which to be alive. World Christianity is the "umbrella" or "meta" category that should permeate all of how we think, speak and act. This is why world Christianity is the scope and theme of this book: it is the new way that Christianity should be viewed, because it is the most realistic and accountable to culture, an inescapable fact of life and theology.

Figure 1. The planners of the five conferences on November 3, 2008. From left to right: Ralph and Barbara Winter (Tokyo 2010); Dana Robert (2010Boston); Daryl Balia (Edinburgh 2010); Rodney Petersen (2010Boston); Ruth Padilla DeBorst (Costa Rica 2012); Doug Birdsall (Cape Town 2010); Todd Johnson (2010Boston). This shows that the intention of the planners, from the very beginning, was to link these five conferences.

QUESTIONS

1. What are your own cultural lenses and biases? (This is a difficult exercise as people outside your culture can always see your cultural flaws much clearer than you can.) Is there any way to get beyond them, or do you have to just accept that they're there? If it's the latter, how do you deal healthily with them rather than giving yourself over to them entirely?

2. Do you think that cultural theology is relativism? Why or why not?

3. Is there any such thing as theology free from cultural bias? Stated another way, is the distinction between truth and theology always there? Try stating a propositional truth of theology without using any cultural influence.

4. Is the mother of orthodoxy always heresy? Is it possible (or has it ever happened) that orthodoxy is derived from "thin air," without being a response to error or without being occasional, that is, disconnected from history?

5. How valid are the Apostles' Creed and the Nicene Creed when (1) there is such dispute about certain lines or phrases within them, (2) not every Christian accepts them, and (3) there are multiple versions of them? How do you determine which version is "right"? Do the multiplicity of versions and lack of universal acceptability cast any doubt on them? If not, why? Do these creeds hold the same force as Scripture?

6. How much fourth-century Mediterranean culture do you see in the words of the Apostles' and Nicene Creeds? Would you accept a new Western creed if one were written with nearly universal agreement in the West to address the theological findings since the fourth century AD? Or has revelation stopped since the Nicene Creed and nothing further needs to be added?

7. Would you accept a creed that has been codified by a group of Christians from another culture? Do you have to accept theology that is not relevant to your culture? Would you impose theology on another culture if it is not relevant to them?

8. Is the danger of syncretism "worth it" if it allows for progressive and new discoveries in theology to occur? Do you think we have the capacity today to stem the tide of heresy as the early church did? Do you think modern-day missions conferences (i.e., an international hermeneutical community) have enough authority to do so, or should we seek other, stronger ways of policing orthodoxy?

9. Do you agree that we need to be "always reforming"? What does that mean exactly? Is that a return to the roots or a discovery of something "new" (to us, not to God)?

10. Do you think theology can go in a horizontal, not just vertical, direction when cultures intersect? Do you think that "innovation" is important in theology?

11. What do you think about the Homogeneous Unit Principle? Does it still have validity despite the objections raised?

12. Is diversity just a nice thing to have, or do you think that it is necessary, equivalent to the gospel itself?

13. Should we do all of theological studies and Christian thought through world Christianity perspectives? Is that even possible or feasible?

TOKYO 2010

On May 20, 2009, the world lost a missiological giant: Dr. Ralph Winter,[1] former missionary to Guatemala, professor at Fuller Seminary in California; founder of the American Society of Missiology, the journal *Missiology: An International Review*, the US Center for World Mission,[2] William Carey International University, the Perspectives course, the International Society for Frontier Missiology and the *International Journal of Frontier Missions*; and arguably the greatest missiologist of the latter half of the twentieth century.[3] Before he died, Dr. Winter had singled out four of these numerous 2010 centenary celebrations as being particularly noteworthy: Tokyo, Edinburgh, Cape Town and Boston.[4] It is thus appropriate (conveniently so, given the

---

[1]Much of this was drawn from Allen Yeh, "Tokyo 2010: Global Mission Consultation," *International Bulletin of Missionary Research* 35, no. 1 (January 2011).

[2]Now renamed Frontier Ventures.

[3]For more about his foundational years, see Greg H. Parsons, *Ralph D. Winter: Early Life and Core Missiology* (Pasadena, CA: William Carey International University Press, 2012).

[4]This is the fuller story of how these four conferences were linked, according to my interview with Todd Johnson, who reconstructed the history of the process by looking back at old emails and BTI IMEC (International Mission and Ecumenism Committee) minutes. He related: "December 15, 2005 Dana Robert suggested that we have a 2010 meeting for students. We brainstormed about it in the Spring of 2006. On June 6, 2006 we met and hammered out a document. We began to interact with Edinburgh 2010 folks, then with Doug Birdsall. After Tokyo 2010 was announced our discussions framed our conference in terms of following the other three. As a committee we were talking about 'four conferences' in late 2007. Our interactions with Edinburgh and Cape Town continued and then finally we brought in Tokyo by taking advantage of Ralph and Barb's planned visit in November 2008. Perhaps it is accurate then to say that the four conference idea originated

chronology) that the first overview of one of these conferences is Tokyo 2010, which also happened to be Dr. Winter's brainchild. Unfortunately, he never lived to see it happen, so he suffered the same fate as Moses—leading his people to the brink of the Promised Land but never crossing the Jordan himself. Surely Dr. Winter would have loved to be a part of the centenary celebration(s) of Edinburgh 1910. If he had lived to see Tokyo 2010, my guess is that he would have been proud of many parts of the conference but perhaps disturbed by other parts.

In the *Christianity Today* chart described and reproduced in chapter one, Ted Olsen compared the four 2010 conferences in the following categories:

- Attendance
- Hero
- The Future of Missions Is:
- Sample Text
- Notable Moment

The second category is somewhat controversial because it raises the question of whether "hero" is even one of the five most important things one should be asking about these conferences. Also bear in mind that the chart was published in August 2010—*after* Tokyo and Edinburgh 2010 but *before* Cape Town and Boston, so the assessment of the first two is clearer than the latter two.

FROM EDINBURGH 1910 TO TOKYO 2010

Perhaps this category of hero really is applicable only to Tokyo, which is fitting because in many ways Tokyo bore the most literal resemblance to Edinburgh 1910 (which had its own obvious hero in John Mott) out of all four 2010 conferences. This likeness to Edinburgh 1910 may or may not be a good thing because 1910, though significant, had a mix of the very good and the very bad. Some of the obvious points of resemblance are:

---

in the BTI (since we followed the other three 'global' conferences deliberately). The BTI then hosted the 'four conference' meeting at Boston University in November 2008. Ralph was the first to publish this as a phenomenon a few weeks later. As you know it was then built into our program (at my suggestion) and we received reports from the three other conferences."

- *Theme.* Edinburgh 1910's theme, the famous watchword as pitched by John Mott, was "The Evangelization of the World in This Generation."[5] One can easily detect the note of triumphalism in it. Tokyo 2010 echoed this with a slight tweak: "Making Disciples of Every People in Our Generation." It is obvious that Tokyo was trying to draw the link with 1910[6] with such a similar theme. With the rewording, the triumphalism is toned down, because it does not seem to wholly suggest that we will be the ones to *complete* the task,[7] only that this *is* our task, changing the verb form from a completed noun to a continuing participle. However, the notable change is not just the form of the verb but the verb itself from "Evangelization" to "Making Disciples." This was a conscious choice, based on the widespread realization among evangelicals in the past few decades that "make disciples," not "evangelize," is the main verb of the Matthean Great Commission.

- *Evangelism only.* Unlike Cape Town 2010, which tried to be missiologically comprehensive (though perhaps that could be a mistake, thinking that one conference can cover all the issues), Tokyo decided to stay with what it knows best: frontier missions, that is, proclaiming the gospel to unreached peoples who do not have a missionary or church among them or a Bible in their language. As an example, Tokyo 2010 conspicuously mentioned nothing about social justice, because of this very fact. They were conscious of the other conferences following it, so they did not feel the need to be exhaustive. It is curious that evangelism was its focus, considering how they deviated from the Edinburgh 1910 theme: obviously the Tokyo 2010 planners understood that the Great Commission is about discipleship, unlike an early twentieth-century understanding that saw evangelism as equivalent to mission.

- *Invitees.* Unlike the other four conferences detailed in this book, Tokyo 2010 only invited mission organizations, not individual people, and allowed each mission society to choose its own delegates. This selection

---

[5]Brian Stanley, *The World Missionary Conference, Edinburgh 1910* (Grand Rapids: Eerdmans, 2009), 88.

[6]The first words on the cover of the conference handbook are "From Edinburgh 1910 to Tokyo 2010."

[7]Though that triumphalism *was* evident in another part of the conference, which is detailed later in the chapter.

process was similar to what Edinburgh 1910 did, as Stanley relates: "Delegates represented not churches or denominations but Protestant and Anglican foreign missionary societies, and societies were allocated places strictly on the basis of their annual income. . . . Hence the big battalions of the Anglo-American missionary movement, most of them denominational missions, dominated the field. Thus, of the 1,215 official delegates, 509 were British, 491 were North American, 169 originated from continental Europe, 27 came from the white colonies of South Africa and Australasia, and only 19 were from the non-western or 'majority' world (18 of them from Asia)."[8] When mission societies are the ones represented, conference representation tends to favor Protestants[9] and ones who have the financial means to travel. And it favors the English-speaking world since it was the US and UK who historically came up with the concept of missionary societies.[10] Tokyo was different in this regard. It had a very good international representation, but there still were not enough women.

- *Continuation committee.* As stated in chapter one, what made Edinburgh 1910 the birthplace of the ecumenical movement was not the conference itself; it was the ongoing work of the continuation committee that set a trajectory for ecumenism in the future. Perhaps the same can be said of Tokyo. What makes Tokyo significant is not the conference itself but the ongoing work of their version of the continuation committee, the Global Great Commission Network—Carrying Tokyo 2010 Forward,[11] launched in May 2012. The GGCN is "intended to be a neutral forum where collaboration between networks, agencies, denominations, churches and

---

[8]Stanley, *World Missionary Conference*, 12.

[9]Catholics already had orders that conducted missions, such the Dominicans, Franciscans and Jesuits. Protestants needed to create missionary societies to make up for their lack of built-in organizations that could carry out such a task. See Ruth Tucker, *From Jerusalem to Irian Jaya: A Biographical History of Christian Missions* (Grand Rapids: Zondervan, 2004), 46.

[10]Thanks to William Carey, British Protestants were the first to pioneer this concept, and the early ones included the London Missionary Society (LMS), Baptist Missionary Society (BMS) and Church Missionary Society (CMS). In the United States, it was Adoniram Judson and the American Board of Commissioners for Foreign Missions (ABCFM) who derived from the Haystack Prayer Movement and later birthed the Student Volunteer Movement.

[11]For the latest updates on what the GGCN is doing, see www.ggcn.org. One of the notable projects is the launching of the GC Network (GCn) in early 2013. The GCn is "a social networking site focused on Missions and Great Commission efforts with goals to CONNECT, COMMUNICATE, AND COLLABORATE."

individuals can take place towards the common vision of discipling all peoples."[12] In addition, every few years another conference is held to keep the physical momentum going. The first follow-up to Tokyo 2010 was the Ghana 2013 Global Mission Consultation, held September 25-28 in Accra, and then Peru 2014 and Madrid 2016.

However, there certainly were some notable differences from Edinburgh 1910 as well:

- *Location.* Unlike Edinburgh 1910, which was located in the heartland of Christianity at the time, Tokyo must be considered one of the most non-Christian places on earth in the early twenty-first century, and certainly one of the most resistant to missionary efforts. It is curious that Dr. Winter would choose such a location, but he was a radical enough thinker to perhaps decide that, instead of holding a missions conference in the Christian heartland, they should hold one deep in the middle of non-Christian territory! In fact, this is exactly what happened: Tokyo 2010 drew the attention of Japanese media and onlookers, but it had the additional effect of encouraging Japanese pastors, who often feel they are swimming against the tide in a country that is less than 1 percent Christian, that they are not alone in their faith. Local pastors were invited to attend the conference as guests and observers. The conference itself became a mission to Japan.[13]

- *All evangelicals.* Unlike Edinburgh 1910, which was mostly evangelicals (with the exception of a small group of Anglo-Catholics), there was no attempt at ecumenism here. Tokyo 2010 was all evangelicals, and of the

---

[12]David Taylor, "Introducing the Global Great Commission Network," *Mission Frontiers,* May–June 2012, www.missionfrontiers.org/issue/article/introducing-the-global-great-commission -network.

[13]This is similar to the February 2002 meeting of the house church leaders in China led by Luis Bush, except instead of Bush it was Winter, and instead of China it was Japan. According to David Aikman in *Jesus in Beijing: How Christianity Is Transforming China and Changing the Global Balance of Power* (Washington, DC: Regnery, 2003), 193-95: "By privately meeting with China's major house church network leaders, Luis Bush was in a sense conferring upon them the seal of recognition from global Protestantism. . . . The meeting, later called simply 'The Beijing Forum,' greatly encouraged the Chinese house church leaders. It was the first time they had ever gathered for any conference in Beijing, the very heart of the regime that so often had tried to crush their networks. It was also significant that a top American evangelical, well known in international missionary circles, would be willing to confer with them about not only the continued evangelization of China, but also about Christian missionary outreach to the entire world."

more conservative variety. It was interdenominational, yes, but even that was deemphasized because of mission societies, rather than churches, being invited. Thus Tokyo 2010 in no way would be considered historically to be the birthplace of any kind of ecumenical movement, in contrast to its predecessor.

Let us return to this concept of hero as described in the aforementioned *Christianity Today* chart. Is this a legitimate category in the twenty-first century? Surely in the Great Century of Missions, Latourette could point out people like Adoniram Judson or David Livingstone who returned to their home countries as celebrities after successful missionary endeavors. That romantic Victorian concept of the missionary-cum-adventurer seems anachronistic today; no missionary would be hailed as a hero upon returning home since missions seems to go against the spirit of the age, being viewed suspiciously nowadays through postcolonial lenses. Even among Christians, it seems the most highly regarded people are not missionaries but pastors and theologians like Rick Warren, John Piper or Tim Keller. However, if there truly *was* a hero of Tokyo 2010, Ralph Winter was it. Unlike John Mott at Edinburgh 1910, however, Winter was not present at Tokyo 2010. Yet, because he died a year prior, his spirit pervaded the conference perhaps more than if he were alive.

Who were the heroes of the other three conferences? It is a bit of a stretch to call, as Ted Olsen did, John Mott and V. S. Azariah the heroes of Edinburgh 2010 (they are too far removed historically from most people's memories, except in the minds of scholars), or Brian Stanley the hero of 2010Boston (he may have written the definitive history of Edinburgh 1910, but he was only one of many speakers at 2010Boston). Perhaps John Stott, though still living at the time of Cape Town 2010 but not in attendance due to health issues, would be the equivalent of Winter at Tokyo 2010, but Lausanne can be attributed to so many people whereas Tokyo is undeniably linked to Ralph Winter. For better or for worse, Tokyo 2010 was synonymous with Ralph Winter.

Nonetheless, it is instructive to think about what the idea of hero means to us today. It is interesting that so many titans of the faith have died in the last few years: Ralph Winter, José Míguez Bonino, Elizabeth Isais, Kwame

Bediako, Ogbu Kalu, Chuck Colson and John Stott, to name a few.[14] Some have lamented that there is not a new generation to take over; thus Lausanne has been hosting Younger Leaders Gatherings (YLG)[15] in light of this perceived vacuum. But maybe rather than replicating the generation of heroes, our next generation will be defined differently—not so much by celebrity and individualism and more by collaborative efforts, hearkening back to the Serampore Trio[16] or the Cambridge Seven.[17]

Why is Ralph Winter a hero? Because of his contributions to the field of missiology. The following two are arguably his most important lasting contributions.

First, Ralph Winter believed in sodalities.[18] It is important to recognize the difference between modalities and sodalities. The former is diocesan ecclesial structures doing mission; the latter is missions agencies and parachurch organizations—who can capitalize on missionary specializations such as Scripture translation and jungle aviation—doing mission. Edinburgh 1910 was not like 2010Boston, which was ivory tower academics studying mission. Nor was it like Edinburgh 2010, which was truly ecumenical, including Catholics and Orthodox. It was also not like Cape Town 2010, which was modalities and sodalities doing mission together. But missionaries are the ones on the field doing it, and thus Winter believed that they, not the churches, ought to be the ones in attendance. It was his conviction that the people "on the ground" are more qualified than anyone else to gather together to strategize about mission, and so Tokyo 2010 was a meeting of minds of representatives from nearly every mission organization today. Winter said, "No one will be invited! All participants will be selected and delegated by mission associations and mission agencies. This is what happened in 1910, and that would seem to be one reason why the 1910 meeting has had such an impact across the years—the huge New York meeting ten years earlier that attracted up to

---

[14]Even names whom some are inclined to think less favorably about, such as the head of the Three-Self Patriotic Movement in China, Bishop K. H. Ting.

[15]Singapore 1987, Malaysia 2006, Indonesia 2016.

[16]William Carey, Joshua Marshman and William Ward.

[17]C. T. Studd and his classmates from Cambridge University.

[18]Ralph Winter, "The Two Structures of God's Redemptive Mission," 1973, http://frontiermission fellowship.org/uploads/documents/two-structures.pdf.

200,000 has been almost forgotten."[19] Ever a student of history, he was determined to follow in the legacy of the saints who have come before,[20] even while avoiding past mistakes.

Despite tremendous criticism, Ralph Winter was determined to stand his ground in favoring sodalities over modalities. He protested:

> Thus one reason for the apparent neglect of the subject [mission societies] is the strong feeling on the part of many that the *church* is the central and basic structure, whereas the *mission* is somehow secondary or perhaps merely a temporary aid in establishing churches: the scaffolding must come down when the building is done. But is this an adequate analogy?[21]

When Winter was a faculty member of the School of World Mission at Fuller Seminary, the influential Donald McGavran said that mission used to be understood as proclamation of the good news, but now it is the *missio Dei*,[22] that is, "any activity of the church that God desires."[23] This has led to some confusion about the distinction or relationship between church and mission.

If one takes Winter's approach to sodalities, some negative and positive connotations necessarily arise. One harmful consequence is this: if the church is outsourcing missions to mission agencies, missionaries lose touch and relationship with the churches. Churches thus feel no responsibility for missionary work and have no idea what is even happening on the field. Also, it leads to the professionalization of missions, a job for those who are specially "called" rather than something every lay Christian should be involved in, whether domestically or abroad. However, if church and mission were put back together, would mission positively influence the church, or would the church trump mission?[24] If it is the latter, then Winter's approach would

---

[19]Rick Wood, "Will Tokyo 2010 Be Remembered Like Edinburgh 2010 [*sic*]?," *Mission Frontiers*, July–August 2010, www.missionfrontiers.org/issue/article/will-tokyo-2010-be-remembered -like-edinburgh-2010.

[20]To prove this, look at the names of the buildings on the campus of William Carey International University, which he founded: Speer Hall, Latourette Library, Zwemer Hall, Hudson Taylor Hall, Aylward Hall, Carmichael Classrooms, to name a few.

[21]Parsons, *Ralph D. Winter*, 266, quoting Winter from 1971.

[22]More in chapter four about this.

[23]Parsons, *Ralph D. Winter*, 266.

[24]I once heard the following joke: "What do you get when you combine religion and politics?" Answer: "You get politics." Perhaps, one might analogously say, combining church and mission leads to church only and the subsuming of mission. Similarly, some educational institutions have

be proven correct,[25] at least on a pragmatic level. Surely, the two should not be pitted against each other, but it often is the case that churches operate as inward looking while mission looks outward. A positive outgrowth of mission agencies, however, is the phrase cited in chapter one: "missions is the mother of ecumenism." This means that evangelicalism (not a denomination) can be ecumenical as well when it exhibits interdenominational cooperation. It is no surprise, then, that many mission conferences produce broad statements of faith that can be operating umbrellas for missionary work (the most famous of which is perhaps the Lausanne Covenant).[26] Organizations such as Latin American Mission, Overseas Missionary Fellowship and Africa Inland Mission require their missionaries to sign a statement of faith, but often this is no problem even if their missionaries come from Baptist, Presbyterian, Methodist and Anglican backgrounds, just to name a few major denominations. In this respect, these missionary conferences are essentially producing modern-day creeds. Therefore, it seems that mission organizations today produce more ecumenical theology than anyone else. Theologians do not try to write "umbrella" documents that unite Christians; they often write from their own particular traditions and viewpoints, and the product of their pens seems to divide more than unite. Theologians are out to prove themselves right and others wrong. Missions organizations, on the other hand, write documents to reach consensus and agreement for cooperative work. In most of the five conferences outlined in this book, a document was produced, and they will each be examined in turn.

Moving from praxis to theology, however, is Winter correct in keeping sodalities separate from modalities? Isn't church the main instrument of mission? In the New Testament, we have the example of Paul, who is the

---

deliberately kept their school of world mission (most have changed their name to "School of Intercultural Studies," much as *missions* has been changed to *mission* or the word *crusade* has been largely eradicated from modern usage) separate from their school of theology, such as Fuller Seminary and Biola University. While the separation of Biola's Cook School of Intercultural Studies from Talbot School of Theology may increase Talbot's cloistered way of thinking, it surely is better than Cook losing its independence to think crossculturally outside the box if it were joined with Talbot.

[25]Parsons, *Ralph D. Winter*, 268. If *everything* the church does is mission, the fear is that *nothing* it does will be authentically mission.

[26]See chapter five.

itinerant, constantly on the move; but we also have Apollos and Timothy, the pastors[27] who stay put in one location. Paul is the evangelist, Apollos and Timothy the disciplers. Paul plants the seed; Apollos and Timothy water it (but God makes it grow; 1 Cor 3:6)! But the main verb of the Great Commission, as has already been made clear, is to *make disciples*, not *evangelize*. Tokyo 2010 recognized this by changing the theme of the conference away from Edinburgh 1910's "evangelize" to "disciple," but then proceeded to just focus on evangelism. Far be it from us to say that Paul was not engaged in mission, because obviously mission needs both the Pauls and the Apolloses and Timothys. But are Apollos and Timothy truer missionaries than Paul if he is more of a discipler? An analogy I give in my Theology of Mission classes is that evangelism is like a wedding, and discipleship is like the marriage. One is the initiating act; the other is the ongoing, practical outworking and living relationship that occurs day after day. Which is more important? I think most people would agree it is better to have a great marriage and a bad wedding than a great wedding and a bad marriage. Yet Western missionary efforts have so often concentrated on the wedding (evangelism) over the marriage (discipleship). Have we had a truncated view of mission?

The definition of *disciple* is spelled out on the GGCN website:

> Producing authentic, lifelong followers of Jesus is the goal of making disciples. These individuals evidence their genuineness in the faith by their progress in spiritual maturity that transforms their beliefs, behavior and worldview. Thus an appropriate definition of a disciple is: A consistent lifelong follower of Christ whose life is progressively being transformed into the image of Christ. He joyfully walks with Christ, is constantly being informed by Scripture, prayer, the Holy Spirit and other believers, with the chief end of glorifying God. A former North American mission writer, George Peters, described it this way: "Discipleship is a path rather than an achievement. While there is growth and grading among the disciples, there are no graduated disciples. Discipleship is a perpetual school which may lead from one degree to another but does not graduate its scholars."[28]

---

[27]More properly, bishops (Greek *episkopos*). Apollos was the bishop of Corinth, and Timothy was the bishop of Ephesus.

[28]See "Making Disciples—Defined," http://ggcn.org/pdf/Making_Disciples_Defined.pdf.

Clearly, Tokyo 2010 "gets" discipleship. The question is, does frontier missions do it?

The second most lasting influence of Ralph Winter is his focus on unreached people groups. Prior to 1974, Christians always defined reaching "every nation" as geopolitical countries. Ralph Winter pointed out at Lausanne I that in the book of Revelation the Greek words are *panta ta ethnē*, every ethnic/language group. This dramatically changed the landscape of mission. The task suddenly loomed a lot larger because Christians realized there was still so much work to do.[29] Instead of thinking about evangelizing some 200 political nations, the task was actually to bring the gospel to some 13,000 ethnolinguistic groups on earth. And of the those, only two-thirds of them had any Scriptures in their language (and many of these are only New Testaments). There are 350 million people in unengaged unreached people groups on earth—it's not that they have rejected Jesus, it's that they have not even had a chance to know him![30] Ralph Winter dedicated himself to this task of crosscultural evangelism more than anything else he labored on or researched, and he punctuated this by saying at Lausanne I:

> Nothing must blind us to the immensely important fact that at least *four-fifths* of the non-Christians in the world today will never have any straightforward opportunity to become Christians unless the Christians themselves go more than half way in the specialized task of cross-cultural evangelism. Here is our highest priority.[31]

Frontier Missions became Ralph Winter's passion. This explains why evangelism was the primary focus of Tokyo 2010.

Interestingly, the idea of sodalities and the *panta ta ethnē* were first presented at the original Lausanne Congress on World Evangelization in 1974,[32]

---

[29]There are three different systems for measuring the peoples of the world today and attempting to quantify the task remaining: the Church Planting Progress Indicators from the Southern Baptists' International Mission Board; the Joshua Project (http://joshuaproject.net); and the World Christian Database, according to Jim Haney, "Gathering, Collating and Meshing Information on the Frontiers: Identifying Unreached Peoples," in *Evangelical and Frontier Mission: Perspectives on the Global Progress of the Gospel,* ed. Beth Snodderly and A. Scott Moreau (Oxford: Regnum, 2011), 183-84.

[30]From Paul Eshleman's talk at Tokyo 2010.

[31]Parsons, *Ralph D. Winter,* 297.

[32]Ralph Winter, "The Highest Priority," in *Let the Earth Hear His Voice,* ed. J. D. Douglas (Minneapolis: World Wide Publications, 1975), 225.

thus making Tokyo 2010 a descendent of Lausanne I, in a way, just as Cape Town 2010 (Lausanne III) was.[33] It is curious, then, that Ralph Winter would not include social justice as an integral part of Tokyo 2010. That was arguably the greatest contribution to and reawakening of the evangelical movement that came out of Lausanne I, where he was a key player[34] and a signatory of the Lausanne Covenant, which explicitly reforged the bond between evangelism and social justice as equal partners in mission.[35] But perhaps that is exactly why Ralph Winter did not include social justice: he thought that Lausanne was handling that just fine, and Tokyo existed to address something not adequately covered, much as John the Evangelist wrote his Gospel to cover ground not addressed by the Synoptics.

THE HISTORY OF TOKYO 2010

Since 2003, Ralph Winter had thought about convening a Tokyo 2010 conference.[36] This is what he dubbed the "Third Call." The First Call was Edinburgh 1910 itself. The Second Call was an Edinburgh 1980 meeting called "The World Consultation on Frontier Missions," which eventually led into the AD2000 movement. The problem with that was that it had no continuation committee, so it lost momentum.[37] So he envisioned this Third Call, Tokyo 2010, to address that lack of ongoing structure and propel missions into the future in a sustainable way.

However, the seeds of this conference were being sown long before 2003. Winter was a professor at Fuller Theological Seminary in Pasadena, California, one of two seminaries birthed out of the neo-evangelical movement that characterized much of mid-twentieth-century Christian America with the influence of Billy Graham, Carl F. H. Henry, Harold Lindsell and Harold

---

[33]See appendix B.

[34]He was also present at Lausanne's 2004 Forum in Pattaya, Thailand. I had the privilege of sitting behind him on the arrival bus from the Bangkok airport to the conference site in Pattaya, with some brief interactions.

[35]This reparation was in response to the twentieth century, so often dichotomized by schisms like the fundamentalist-modernist controversy and the creation-evolution debate. Neo-evangelicals called themselves thus to distinguish themselves from what they deemed to be dichotomistic fundamentalists.

[36]For the full history of Ralph Winter's development of this conference, see "Dr. Ralph Winter's Involvement in Tokyo 2010," available online at http://tokyo2010.org/rdw.htm.

[37]See Ralph Winter, "Excerpts from 'The Third Call,'" October 27, 2004, www.tokyo2010.org/Third _Call.pdf.

Ockenga, among others. The educator among that group was Ockenga, the pastor of Boston's famous Park Street Church with a vision to establish not only Fuller but Gordon-Conwell Theological Seminary (one on each coast) in South Hamilton, Massachusetts. Ockenga became the first president of both institutions.[38] Fuller has long been arguably the most well-known evangelical seminary in the United States, if not the world, and it was especially known for its School of World Mission and Institute of Church Growth, founded in 1965.[39]

Winter taught at Fuller's SWM from 1967 to 1976 as one of the first three full-time faculty members along with Donald McGavran and Alan Tippett: "McGavran was very practical and fairly private. He was the diplomat, the activist. Tippett was the scholar, the academic."[40] Winter, however, was the visionary. For example, he did not like to teach "church history" but rather "the expansion of Christianity," after Kenneth Scott Latourette's approach. He was also heavily involved with promoting theological education by extension. He soon realized that the SWM was insufficient because, in his own words, "I was sitting there and realized that I could have 1,000 more missionaries come through my classroom and I would never have a missionary from a place where no missionary had ever gone."[41] This passion for frontier missions caused him to leave Fuller and start the US Center for World Mission (USCWM) and eventually the International Society for Frontier Missiology and its accompanying *International Journal of Frontier Missions*.

The Edinburgh 1980 meeting that Winter referred to as the "Second Call" had the motto "A Church for Every People by the Year 2000!"[42] Contrast this with the Edinburgh 1910 watchword and that of Tokyo 2010. Unlike the other two, Edinburgh 1980 had a time limit as a goal. But this conference was significant because it was the first time they tried the adopt-a-people approach, a perhaps overly optimistic attempt at finishing the task but a

---

[38]See George M. Marsden, *Reforming Fundamentalism: Fuller Seminary and the New Evangelicalism* (Grand Rapids: Eerdmans, 1987).

[39]Parsons, *Ralph D. Winter*, 187.

[40]Ibid., 212.

[41]Ibid., 227.

[42]David Taylor, "The Progress of the Frontier Mission Movement: A Thirty-Year Glance from Edinburgh 1980 Through Tokyo 2010," in *Snodderly and Moreau, Evangelical and Frontier Mission*, 47-48.

concerted effort among mission agencies. What was unusual about it was the spirit of cooperation and coordinated effort involved, which perhaps was made easier with mission structures rather than church denominations. This is why "missions is the mother of ecumenism."

In April 2005, Winter gathered twenty-eight global mission leaders in Amsterdam and formed the Global Network of Mission Structures (GNMS) to address the lack of continuation from the Second Call. That led to the Third Call, the idea that an Edinburgh 1910–style conference would be held in 2010. He presented this idea to the Asia Missions Association meeting in Ephesus, Turkey, in late 2006. He pushed this idea further at the meeting of the Third World Mission Association (TWMA) in 2007 in London, where the commitment was finally made to make this conference happen. "The commitment was made that it would be hosted by the Japanese Church and sponsored jointly by the GNMS, the TWMA, the Asia Mission Association (AMA) and CrossGlobal Link (formerly IFMA). TWMA assumed the primary responsibility to manage the conference under the guidance of a conference planning committee comprised of individuals from several different associations and agencies."[43]

Finally, Winter took a trip to Tokyo (his last overseas trip) where on October 26-27, 2008, he met with the Japanese church leaders and organizers of the conference. On November 10, 2008, he traveled to Boston to meet up with the leaders of the four 2010 meetings, including Edinburgh (Daryl Balia), Cape Town (Doug Birdsall) and Boston (Dana Robert, Todd Johnson and Rodney Petersen). Ruth Padilla DeBorst was also in attendance and drew her inspiration for the Costa Rica (CLADE V) 2012 conference, which was supposed to happen in 2010 as well but ended up being delayed two years. The Tokyo and Boston trips were among Winter's last ever.

TOKYO 2010: CONFERENCE PROCEEDINGS

Tokyo 2010 technically was a project of the US Center for World Mission and had Ralph Winter's fingerprints all over it. However, it was funded by the Koreans and hosted by the Japanese. The conference bag listed Onnuri

---

[43]"Dr. Ralph Winter's Involvement," http://tokyo2010.org/rdw.htm.

Community Church on it as the main sponsor. According to the church's website, *onnuri* means "all nations," and it has over sixty thousand people who attend the nine campuses in Korea as well as twenty-seven church plants around the world.[44]

Why Japan? I have already mentioned how Winter wanted it to be held in one of the *least* Christian countries. And why Tokyo? In light of the global trend toward urbanization, it was appropriate to hold this conference in Tokyo, the largest city in the world by far.

In addition to having this conference in Japan, another strategic move was having this be a partnership between Japan and Korea, like the 2002 World Cup, which helped to bring about reconciliation between these two historically bitter enemies.[45] For Tokyo 2010, Japan hosted it, but Koreans ran it (Yong Cho, a Korean, was the main organizer) and funded it (three Korean megachurches, Yoido and Sarang and Onnuri, largely financially supported the event). Each of the speakers received gifts from the conference organizers, presented by Japanese women in kimonos and Korean women in hanboks, visually highlighting the unity and cooperation between the two nations. It is interesting that Japan usually leads the way in everything in Asia, but when it comes to Christianity, it is Korea who leads. As an example, most songs sung in Japanese churches are either English *or Korean* songs translated into Japanese! The preacher on the first day of the conference, Tsugumichi Okawa, who pastors the largest church in Japan (Yamato Calvary Chapel), was a disciple of Paul Yonggi Cho, the founding pastor of the largest church in Korea (and in the world). The pastors of Onnuri and Yoido also preached during the conference. In light of all this, David Taylor accurately summed up:

> Tokyo 2010 should have the unique privilege of being the first global meeting following the Edinburgh 1910 pattern which was organized, conducted and attended by a majority of non-Western mission leadership. Not only that, the majority of the funding came from the non-Western world as well![46]

---

[44]See www.onnurienglish.org.

[45]The Olympics are also bringing parity by allowing Korea to host the 2018 Winter Games in Pyeongchang and Japan to host the 2020 Summer Games in Tokyo.

[46]David Taylor, "Setting the Pace: Tokyo 2010 Leads the Way in Celebrating Edinburgh 1910," *Mission Frontiers,* July–August 2010, www.missionfrontiers.org/issue/article/setting-the-pace.

Tokyo[47] and Costa Rica were the only two of the five conferences that were primarily organized, led and funded by non-Westerners.

The fact that Two-Thirds World leadership largely ran this event shows that Tokyo 2010 clearly understood what was happening with world Christianity:

> While the largest mission agency in the Western world, the International Mission Board (Southern Baptist Convention), announced they would be cutting back their personnel by 500 this year, the largest foreign mission sending agency in the non-Western world (the Global Mission Society of the Korean Presbyterian Church) announced at Tokyo 2010 that they intend to more than double their mission force in the next decade.[48]

It is a mischaracterization that the West always has more money than the non-Western world. Much of East Asia actually is quite economically developed[49] and in fact is wealthier than the West, as shown by the quote above. It is also a mistake to think that all missions-receiving countries are poor. Japan is one of the wealthiest but least Christian nations on earth, and yet people are not inclined to do missionary work there, either because the stereotype of the missionary is to live in relative poverty or because they are afraid of how much money will need to be given in order to just support one missionary in Japan, whereas the same amount of money could support multiple missionaries in another context.

Thus the Two-Thirds World was well represented among the one-thousand-plus people in attendance as they all gathered in May 2010 at the Nakano Sun Plaza in Tokyo. Tokyo 2010 parallels Edinburgh 1910 and the idea of Cape Town 1810 in that each was the brainchild of one man,

---

[47]Yong Cho and David Taylor, "Making Disciples of Every People in Our Generation: The Vision, Purpose and Objectives of Tokyo 2010," in Snodderly and Moreau, *Evangelical and Frontier Mission*, 203: "Tokyo 2010 became the first-ever global level meeting following the Edinburgh 1910 pattern that was planned, organized, led and funded primarily by the Majority World mission movement. In contrast, the Edinburgh 1910 meeting had just a handful of participants from outside the West, none of which came as representatives of non-western mission agencies, and none of which were part of the leadership team. Similarly, Edinburgh 1980 had just one person from outside the West on its executive team, although its delegation was made up of one-third Majority World mission leaders."

[48]Ibid.

[49]Japan, the so-called Four Little Tigers (South Korea, Taiwan, Hong Kong, Singapore), and the metropolises of China all have gleaming skyscrapers, bullet/maglev trains, and more advanced cell phone technology than the West.

one missiological genius. In the case of the proposed Cape Town conference that never happened in 1810, it was William Carey. In 1910, it was John R. Mott. In 2010, it was Ralph Winter. The leadership of the actual conference, however, was diverse: Obed Álvarez (Peru) was the conference chair; Hisham Kamel (Egypt) was the general coordinator; Minoru Okuyama (Japan) was the chair of the Japanese Host Committee; and Yong Cho (South Korea, but also an employee of the USCWM) was the conference planning committee chairman. Thus Latin America, Africa and Asia were all represented.

Each full day of the conference, there were several plenary speakers during the morning.[50] The afternoons were filled with workshops dedicated to finishing the task (many of them were "task forces"),[51] and each evening had an inspirational celebration time of worship. The tenor of the morning was very different from the evening, as the three evening sessions were led by a Japanese (Talo Sataraka of New Hope International Fellowship) and two Koreans (Yong Jo Ha of Onnuri Community Church in Seoul and Lee Young-Hoon of Yoido Full Gospel Church), so they had more of an Asian feel to them, and not just because of the language, though that was a major issue.[52] The morning plenaries were more informational, as well as being more diverse in their speaker representation.

The conference opened on the first evening with a video that began with the Abrahamic promise from Genesis 15, moving to Edinburgh 1910, and bringing us to the present at Tokyo 2010, all in the context of world Christianity. Some of the most stunning statistics cited included the following:

- There has been a lot of progress since Edinburgh. In 1910, over 90 percent of the world's people groups were still unreached. Now, a century later, less than 25 percent of the world's peoples remain without an indigenous church. In fact, more peoples heard and responded to the gospel in the twentieth century than all previous centuries combined. Just think about it: it took almost 1900 years to reach 10 percent of the world's peoples. But in less than one hundred years an additional

---

[50]See appendix A for the conference schedules.
[51]Divided into two tracks each day: (1) Celebration, New Models, and Coordination and (2) Casting Vision.
[52]See chapter five about the issue of language and translation.

65 percent have been reached—six times as many in almost one-twentieth the time.

- The progress in mission sending from the non-Western world has also been phenomenal over the last century. In 1910, the evangelical church was sending out around 25,000 crosscultural missionaries, 99 percent of which were from the Western world. Today, the evangelical church sends out over 220,000 crosscultural missionaries, 78 percent of which are from the non-Western world.

- But we're not done yet. Our family is not yet complete. There are still 3,700 unreached peoples with no known missionary activity. In addition, there are large unreached groups that are still very under-engaged. Some of the groups will require hundreds of additional missionaries to be sent. Altogether, the task is going to require at least 30,000 missionaries to fully engage all the remaining least-reached peoples with church-planting movement initiatives.[53]

The opening video spelled out the theses and priorities of Tokyo 2010: history (linking Tokyo 2010 with Edinburgh 1910), world Christianity and frontier missions. The last two go together well, because only by mobilizing missionaries from both the West and the non-West will every ethnolinguistic people group be engaged with the gospel.

THE UNENGAGED AND THE POST-CHRISTIAN

Probably the two most notable speakers in plenary sessions at Tokyo 2010 were Paul Eshleman, who gave the keynote address on May 12, and Stefan Gustavsson, who spoke on reaching the secular people of Europe on May 14. It is instructive to compare these two talks because they represent the two extremes of the mission field: those who have never even had the chance to hear and those who have been supersaturated with and have rejected Christianity.[54] For the former, the gospel truly is the good news. It is news because they have never heard it before. For the latter, the gospel is not news at all and, in fact, is not even good. It is notoriously difficult to evangelize people

---

[53]From International Mission Board People Group Database; World Christian Database; USCWM Global Mission Database.

[54]See chapter seven for an explanation of the other two types of missionary engagement: Christianity's encounter with other religions and nominalism.

who have the "been there, done that" mentality and have already made up their minds to reject it.

Paul Eshleman, in his keynote address (the only one of the entire conference that was labeled in such a way, thus highlighting its importance), answered the question of how *discipleship* could be the main verb of the Great Commission and the theme of Tokyo 2010 while at the same time emphasizing frontier missions.[55] He said, "Evangelism is not enough. 'Teaching others to observe all that Jesus has commanded' must be an ongoing process." Then he pointed out ten essential elements, or global evangelization priorities:

1. Scriptures (Mt 4:4)

2. Engaging the unengaged[56] UPGs (unreached people groups) (Rev 5:9)

3. Evangelism (Mt 24:14)

4. Oral learners (Mt 13:34)

5. Church planting and presence (Acts 2:42-47)

6. Prayer and unity (Lk 10:2; Jn 17:20-23)

7. Compassion ministries (Jas 2:14-24)

8. Confession, repentance and Holy Spirit (1 Jn 1:8-10; Eph 5:18)

9. Mobilizing the body of Christ—people and finances (Is 6:8; Lk 6:38)

10. Research, mapping and reporting (Num 13:17-20; Mt 5:14-16)

He drove home the belief that "we may well be living in the generation that will see the fulfillment of Matthew 24:14, 'This gospel of the kingdom will be preached as a witness to all of the nations, and then the end will come.'" But one might wonder: do we want the end to come quickly, when the fates of all of humankind are sealed for eternity? Or do we want more time to see positive responses among people so that they may be saved?

---

[55] According to Cho and Taylor, "Making Disciples of Every People," 201-2, the two foci of Tokyo 2010 were the "breadth" of the Great Commission, which they view as frontier missions, and the "depth" of the Great Commission, which they see as discipleship.

[56] Sometimes called "hidden peoples" (Ralph Winter's term) or "missing peoples," or the "One-Fourth World" (OFW). As opposed to the Two-Thirds World, which is referring to the two-thirds of the world's population who live in Africa, Asia and Latin America, the OFW are the two billion people who currently have no pioneer missionary effort to reach them.

It must be noted that number 7 on the list, also called "Demonstration of the gospel," was one of the few references to social justice in the entire conference, small as it was: "This is an area where we need a lot of work. Though we agree we need to do both proclamation and demonstration, we don't have enough models of doing them together effectively." And number 5 on the list is about modalities, the very thing that was pitted against sodalities. Yet, regarding the relationship between church and discipleship Eshleman said: "It has always been the plan of God that people would be brought to maturity in Christ through the fellowship of a local church." Therefore, frontier missions is not just about evangelism but also church planting, and "I want to call us to do the research together in each country to know which villages, barrios and wards currently have no church. We need several ministries who will mobilize leadership to see a survey taken of where local churches do not exist, in every part of the World." Still, the top four priorities, which Eshleman headlined above all the others, have to do with initial contact and proclamation of the gospel.

Stefan Gustavsson of Sweden gave a Macedonian call ("Come over and help us," an allusion to Acts 16:9) about how to evangelize secular Europeans, the "prodigal sons" of Christianity today. His evidence was that "during the twentieth century, the Latin American Evangelical church increased by over 5,000 percent. The African Evangelical church increased by over 4,000 percent. The Asian Evangelical church increased by over 2,000 percent. . . . [But] the Christian church in Europe is rapidly diminishing." He lamented that his own country, Sweden, is the world's most secularized country. Ultimately, "it is a time of dramatic changes for Europe. The statistics may vary in their details between countries, but the general trend is clear. In Europe the gospel is not viewed as good news—many think it's been tried and found false." He pointed out some of the reasons for this trend: urbanization, secularization, humanism, and the church compromising and withdrawing. Interestingly, he argued that with regard to postmodernism, we ought not think that the best way to minister to it is to become postmodern ourselves. In reality, Europe is a mix of the modern and the postmodern. Universal truth has not been tossed out the window, as science, homosexuality and atheism are all touted as being absolutes that we should accept. And postmodernism cannot be only about deconstruction; at some point, one must construct in order to have something to stand on. His conclusion: "The advent of postmodern thinking has not diminished the need for apologetics; it has doubled it. Now the Christian church has two major challenges to deal with. The concept of truth (that there is such a thing as attainable truth) and the content of truth (that it is the Christian message, not naturalism, which is the truth)." He ended his message with a perhaps unintended affirmation of women: "Acts 16. It tells the amazing story of how the gospel first came to Europe. Paul and his companions were planning to go east, but three times the Holy Spirit redirects them more north and more west, until they reach Philippi. There they can preach the gospel and the first European—a woman called Lydia—becomes a Christian."

Though it was a heavily academic lecture with a lot of statistics, the organizer of the conference, Yong Cho, had a remarkable response. Tearfully, he called for the entire conference to spontaneously pray for Europe to regain its faith, and he invited all the European delegates to come up to the stage. In a remarkable turn, all the Two-Thirds World Christians cried out on behalf of their brothers and sisters in Europe—in particular, two Koreans and two Africans (representing two of the strongest centers of Christianity) who led the prayers. The Holy Spirit was moving; that was the most authentic and unforgettable part of the whole conference. If only the Edinburgh 1910 delegates could have seen this—what a difference a century makes! The Two-Thirds World churches have come of age, while Europe has declined. Who would have believed this a century ago? However, a Korean American delegate said to me after that session, "What a sobering reminder to the Korean church that we should not rest on our laurels. I can already sense that we are going the way of Europe, so we should not become arrogant." As an American, I can say the same thing of the United States.

PENTECOSTALISM

In light of the phenomenon of world Christianity, the interaction between evangelicalism and Pentecostalism is worth noting, since in places like sub-Saharan Africa, China and Brazil Pentecostalism is a major, if not the main, expression of Christianity. Are Pentecostals a subset of evangelicals or not?[57]

---

[57] According to Alan R. Johnson, "Pentecostal Missions and the Influence of Frontier Mission Missiology," in Snodderly and Moreau, *Evangelical and Frontier Mission*, 101: "Pentecostals are typically

A lot of evangelicals have mixed feelings about Pentecostals. On the one hand, Pentecostals are non-Catholics, so evangelicals find resonance with them. Also, if Pentecostals trace their inheritance back to the Azusa Street revival of Los Angeles in 1906,[58] then there is a historical genetic inheritance from America (which is often identified with evangelicalism). But some people were uncomfortable with the opening speaker, who seemed to be preaching a prosperity gospel. It was also interesting that, during the afternoons of the conference while most of the delegates were in seminars, Pentecostal Japanese from all over the country occupied the main auditorium, sometimes with Africans, doing worship services. So what do evangelicals do with them—claim them or disavow them? Seeing as how Pentecostalism is the fastest-growing form of Christianity around the world, evangelicals need to know how to interact properly with it or else risk being unfamiliar with the future of the faith in the Two-Thirds World.

There was good representation numerically of Africans and Latin Americans, but most of the Latin Americans tended to be from Peru or Brazil (and the latter were mostly Brazilians who live in Japan). What has Athens to do with Jerusalem, as Tertullian famously said? Or in this case, what has Japan to do with Brazil? Apparently a lot. Despite the vast cultural differences, Brazil has the largest population of Japanese in the world living outside of Japan, and now it is going the other way too: there are increasing numbers of Brazilians living in Japan. Brazil has a growing Christian (primarily Pentecostal) population, and many Brazilians have started Pentecostal churches in Japan. Historically, this brings the Portuguese influence full circle: Portuguese Jesuits were the first Christian missionaries to evangelize Japan back in the sixteenth century, and now the largest Portuguese-speaking nation in the world, Brazil, is doing it (though Pentecostal, not Catholic). World Christianity is not just about "reverse mission" (non-Westerners evangelizing the West), but it is truly

---

considered separately from evangelicals, even though the theological and missional stance of millions of Pentecostals largely draws from evangelical convictions. Anyone who would understand evangelical engagement in frontier mission must understand the many ways Pentecostals fit into that picture."

[58]It is, however, debatable whether worldwide Pentecostalism really is in such a direct line of descent from Azusa Street, much as many people have disclaimed Baptists as being directly descended from Anabaptists, despite the familial resemblance. See chapter four for more about the origins of Pentecostalism.

"from everyone to everywhere" (Latin Americans evangelizing Asia, Chinese evangelizing the Middle East in the Back-to-Jerusalem movement and so on).

Pentecostalism has resonance with the issue of creeds in chapter two. How do we balance the need for a lot of different theologies in world Christianity with the ability to regulate and check any heresies? In other words, creeds can be helpful, but they can also be stifling—they are meant to codify what we have agreed on thus far, but they are not meant to be the final word on a subject, as if nothing new can ever be said. Pentecostalism is notoriously difficult in this regard because it has no regulatory body to govern it, so one has to be cautious (yet open) when approaching it to discern whether it is truly the Spirit moving in the healings, tongues and prophecies, or if it is a cult or abuse of power in the name of Christianity.[59]

RECONCILIATION

A Japanese delegate delivered a public apology for the atrocities committed by his nation during World War II. It takes a much bigger effort for the Japanese to say something like that than it does for a Westerner! The shame-based culture is one of the reasons Germany has been so publicly repentant about World War II while the Japanese have largely not apologized (to the frustration of Korea and China, among other nations).[60] It was astounding to hear this public apology, and it was followed by many of the Japanese delegates facing many of the US delegates on stage, each apologizing to the other for Pearl Harbor and the atomic bombs. While it was a truly moving moment, it would have been even better to see Japan and Korea face each other on stage. Even more bitter animosity exists between them that needs healing, and some people felt that the United States stole the spotlight in the reconciliation by jumping on stage before the Koreans had the chance to. One of the Egyptian speakers said, "I hope that we can see something similar with

---

[59]See Paul Hiebert's fourfold answer about checks and balances cited in chapter two above.

[60]As an example, see Iris Chang, *The Rape of Nanking* (New York: Penguin, 1997). This event was sometimes called the "Forgotten Holocaust," as more Chinese were killed by Japanese (estimated up to 20 million) during World War II than Jews were killed by Nazis (6 million). The Chinese are still trying to get the Japanese to apologize and to rewrite their history textbooks to acknowledge that this even occurred.

Palestinians and Israelis."[61] Then he called for Christians to pray for Muslims, saying that we must love Muslims because "Muslims are not our enemies; Satan is."

In chapter one, I discussed reconciliation on several levels—race, gender, class, age—as being synonymous with the gospel. As "missions is the mother of ecumenism," it is up to missionaries and mission organizations to lead the way in exemplifying this, and Tokyo 2010 did this well. However, as is inevitable, some types of reconciliation get emphasized less than others. For all the effort in ensuring international and racial representation, there was a lack of female speakers. Whatever the reason, some female delegates felt neglected as a result. It is even more ironic that at many missions conferences the largest missing demographic is white women, given that white women were the bulk of the Protestant missions force for much of history!

Through nobody's fault, there was curiously also a lack of Chinese. Of the five conferences, this was the Asian one, and the Koreans and Japanese were represented in spades. But the Chinese church is a huge force in world missions today, and their omission was startling. However, one main reason why China was left out was that many Chinese Christian leaders were planning on going to the Cape Town (Lausanne III) Congress in October. It is difficult enough for them to get visas to go to one international Christian conference this year; it is nigh impossible to expect that they would be granted permission twice by the Chinese government to leave the country.

IMPACT OF TOKYO 2010

At Tokyo 2010 a list of 632 unengaged peoples, each with a population over 50,000, was presented to mission leaders, and 171 of these peoples were selected by the agency leaders for outreach in the next three years.

At the conference, everyone was asked to fill out a Tokyo 2010 commitment form in the hope that every mission agency would adopt at least one unreached people group, to help complete the task of evangelizing every people group on earth. The form consisted of five categories:

---

[61]Actually there was such a reconciliation on the platform at Cape Town 2010. See Shadia Qubti and Dan Sered, "Testimony: Palestinian-Jewish Reconciliation," in *Christ Our Reconciler: Gospel-Church-World*, ed. Julia E. M. Cameron (Downers Grove, IL: InterVarsity Press, 2012), 53-54.

1. Unengaged Unreached People Groups—fill in the number of groups on the UUPG list I/we will engage within the next 3 years.

2. Evangelism—check one of these three boxes: I/we would like more information on implementing a Short Film strategy; I/we want to be a partner in internet evangelism with Global Media Outreach by recruiting e-missionaries or helping to develop the website in the following languages; I/we will help translate/show the JESUS film in the following new languages (see the list of 865 languages).

3. Orality—list the number of people I/we will send to be equipped as trainers in Orality for our church/org.

4. The Oral Story Bible—write down the number of Oral Bible teams our church/organization will send out in the next 3 years.

5. Church Planting and Research—I am interested in helping to survey my/our country to determine which villages, towns, or city sections have no church. Please contact me when specific plans are developed.

These forms were required to be submitted on May 13, the penultimate day, at the evening session. The reason for the rushed submission was in part due to the desire to have a numbers count by the end of the conference, common at many missions conferences, including Urbana.

The heart and hope behind this adopt-a-people effort is to be commended. It reflects a tremendous sense of optimism and a "can-do" attitude. The implementation, however, was lacking. To reduce finishing the task to a scientific and data-analysis project, with very little time to pray about and commit to adopting these people groups, was difficult at best and disingenuous at worst. Yet, quantification and statistical analyses are necessary, which is why *Operation World* and *The Atlas of Global Christianity* are so helpful.[62] But demographic data can be misleading. For example, one of the biggest questions that must be asked is, who is a Christian? The best we can do right now is self-identification, but groups such as Mormons also self-identify as Christians, as do nominal Christians who do not go to church and who do not live out their faith (an utter lack of discipleship).

---

[62]Jason Mandryk, *Operation World: The Definitive Prayer Guide to Every Nation* (Colorado Springs: Biblica, 2010); Todd M. Johnson and Kenneth R. Ross, eds., *The Atlas of Global Christianity* (Edinburgh: Edinburgh University Press, 2009).

This can give an overly optimistic view of the task, which is why evangelizing other religions and nominal Christians are two additional mission fields to be considered, in addition to frontier missions and reaching post-Christian atheists.[63] On the opposite end, however, "hidden" Christians may still identify as, say, Muslim, and that further skews the data.

Eshleman ended up giving this same call (in the same rushed timeframe) at Cape Town 2010, and it was similarly received with mixed responses. Nobody disputed the need to reach everyone on earth with the gospel, but many were unsure this was the best way to accomplish the task and thought this approach felt forced. Where was the Holy Spirit in this process? This is in stark contrast to Pentecostal missions, which is perhaps *all* about the Holy Spirit but not much about intellectual planning. But we ought to be moved by the Spirit *and* our minds.

TOKYO 2010 DECLARATION

The first document to come out of the 2010 conferences was the Tokyo 2010 Declaration.[64] What is interesting about this document is that, unlike the documents from Edinburgh 2010 and Cape Town 2010, this one was written *prior* to the conference, so there was no input from the conference participants. According to the conference handbook, "The Tokyo Declaration was drafted by a committee made up of representatives from Cross-Global Link, Third World Missions Association, and the Global Network of Mission Structures." It was read by all the missions leaders on the last day, starting with Barbara Winter, Ralph Winter's widow, at the final session of the conference.

One question that must be asked is, what was the unique contribution of the Tokyo 2010 Declaration? Was there anything new said? The document is certainly solidly evangelical and broad enough that everyone present

---

[63]It is interesting, however, that the Tokyo 2010 organizers regarded evangelizing post-Christian atheist Europeans as "frontier missions." But isn't the definition of "frontier missions" to go to people who have no Scripture or missionary or church among them? See Cho and Taylor, "Making Disciples of Every People," 204: "Another unique contribution of Tokyo 2010 to the Edinburgh 2010 tradition was its inclusion and elevation of the 'secular peoples of Europe' as a 'frontier mission' priority for the global church . . . this once Christian continent that is now itself in need of pioneer missionary effort—a phenomenon being referred to as 'reverse mission,' . . . underscoring the reality that the Christian faith is just a generation away from extinction in every society."

[64]For the full text, see appendix C.

could sign it, but was it groundbreaking in any way? Also, this document was written *before* the conference! So what was the point of people gathering there, if not to write the document? The Lausanne movement is rather document-oriented, with their greatest contribution obviously being the Lausanne Covenant. Tokyo 2010 was less document-oriented and more action-oriented, as the call to finish the task of world evangelization was the driving force behind everything.

The declaration, after emphasizing the historic nature of Tokyo 2010 as a centenary celebration of Edinburgh 1910, acknowledged the reality of world Christianity and that mission has changed much since 1910. It then proceeded to outline a four-part declaration:

- mankind's need (because we are sinners)

- God's remedy (Jesus Christ)

- our responsibility (missions—reaching all peoples through discipleship)

- finishing the task[65]

But this is purely gospel, except for the last point. More than this, the document elaborates on the third point by unpacking it via the three sub-verbs of the Great Commission that support "making disciples":

- *Go*: penetration

- *Baptizing*: consolidation

- *Teaching to obey*: transformation

It ends with a pledge to cooperate in the GNMS going forward. But according to the Tokyo 2010 organizers, the most important part of the Tokyo Declaration was

> the transformational dimension of the Great Commission, [which] added an element to the Edinburgh 1910 tradition that many mission leaders felt had been a glaring omission in previous gatherings. For this reason the theme and watchword for Tokyo 2010 was established as "making disciples of every people in our generation." This watchword built on the earlier watchwords of Edinburgh 1910 and Edinburgh 1980: "the evangelization of the world in

---

[65]Kevin S. Higgins, "Missiology and the Measurement of Engagement: Personal Reflections on Tokyo," in Snodderly and Moreau, *Evangelical and Frontier Mission*, 212: "Closure" to finishing the task entails reaching the unreached and engaging the unengaged.

this generation" and "a church for every people by the year 2000." The watchword of Tokyo 2010 thus took the "generation" time frame of Edinburgh 1910, and the people group emphasis of Edinburgh 1980, and added the discipling aspect of Matthew 28:19-20. In doing so, Tokyo 2010 sought to draw attention to an important progression over the last century that has led to greater depth as well as precision in defining how we measure success in fulfilling the Great Commission.[66]

Tokyo 2010 certainly was not the end of the story. Not only did it have its own continuation committee moving forward, but it was one of four 2010 conferences that year. It may have been the vanguard of 2010, but there are others to consider that followed in the path it blazed.

QUESTIONS

1. Is it a good thing that Tokyo 2010 hearkens back to the Edinburgh 1910 theme? If the theme is passé and a relic of a bygone era when Christians were optimistic about the advance of the kingdom and the church throughout the world, is it wise to replicate that today, even in a revised way? Or do you think the revised wording is good and appropriate for today? Does it have the ring of triumphalism to it?

2. If the main verb of the Great Commission is *make disciples*, where does *evangelize* fit in? Do you see evangelism as part of the Great Commission even though that verb does not appear? Should it have priority?

3. Should we have missionary heroes today? The apostle Paul charges us to not follow Paul, Cephas or Apollos (1 Cor 1:10-17; 3:1-9) because that causes divisions in the church, and mission is supposed to be the mother of ecumenical unity. Yet Hebrews 12:1-2 calls us to be spurred on by that "great cloud of witnesses" even as we fix our eyes on Jesus, so acknowledging the historical heroes (saints) that have come before us may be a good encouragement to us. What criteria makes someone a hero—someone we emulate or follow or respect? Should we be more group-oriented instead of individualistic?

---

[66]Cho and Taylor, "Making Disciples of Every People," 202.

4. Are modalities or sodalities the main agent of mission? Why? Which does a better job of "making disciples"? Was the apostle Paul a good missionary by this standard?

5. Do you agree with the definition of discipleship as spelled out on the GGCN website? If not, how would you revise the definition?

6. What does frontier missions have to do with discipleship?

7. Do you agree with Ralph Winter's redefinition of *panta ta ethnē* as meaning ethnolinguistic groups rather than geopolitical nations?

8. Do you think we can finish the task in our generation? Is that something we ought to pursue? How much weight should we give to urgency in the task of missions? Is missiology ultimately about eschatology, since missions is always with a view to future consequences? Or is missions more about the here and now? Or both (already and not yet)?

9. Which should be a greater priority: frontier missions to the unengaged or missions to the post-Christian world that needs to be called back to God? (The latter seems to be more the function of Old Testament prophets like Jonah.) Millions are dying because they have never heard the gospel, and millions of others are dying because they have rejected the gospel and need to be called back to repentance. Are the latter less of a priority than the unengaged? How do we know when to shake the dust off our feet (Mt 10:14) at them and to not throw our pearls before swine (Mt 7:6)? Or should we continue to persevere in post-Christian places like Europe?

10. Should Pentecostals be considered evangelical? How do we discern between the authentic movement of the Holy Spirit and heretical cults? What criteria or checks and balances should we use?

11. Do you agree with the Tokyo 2010 Declaration that "mission is the central theme of Scripture"? Is there anything unique or groundbreaking about the document that contributed something new to the task of global missions? Or do you think it was merely reaffirming what we already know and believe? What is the purpose of such a document?

12. Was this conference a "good" successor to Edinburgh 1910? If so, how? Is it good to *be* a successor to Edinburgh 1910?

EDINBURGH 2010

SCOTLAND WAS ARGUABLY the center of gravity of world Christianity in 1910.[1] Its capital, Edinburgh—at times called the "Athens of the North," as well as less flattering but more affectionate names such as "Auld Reekie"—is not as quintessentially Scottish as one might imagine.[2] It has always been more a city of the world than a city of Scotland. Its international flavor has been quite evident throughout its history, with Holyrood Palace being the seat of power of King James VI (later King James I of England) in the formation of the United Kingdom when the Scottish and English crowns came together; the Gothic architecture of Old Town and the Georgian architecture of New Town forming contrasting styles borrowed from elsewhere; and the seven hills of the city making it resemble Rome more than the typical highlands and islands of Scotland. The city of Stirling possesses far more of the history of the country than Edinburgh—think William Wallace and Robert the Bruce. Perhaps this international flavor made Edinburgh a much better candidate for a

---

[1]There is a surprising similarity between Scotland in 1910 to Korea in 2010. Both are tiny nations that have historically been in the shadow of their larger neighbors (England and Japan, respectively) but that have been among the greatest missionary-sending nations per capita during the height of their influence.

[2]Some of this is based on Allen Yeh, "Tokyo 2010 and Edinburgh 2010: A Comparison of Two Centenary Conferences," *International Journal of Frontier Missiology* 27, no. 3 (July–September 2010).

worldwide ecumenical missions conference than, for example, the country's largest city, Glasgow.

FROM EDINBURGH 1910 TO EDINBURGH 2010

Edinburgh 2010 was the namesake of its predecessor and thus inevitably attracted much attention. However, the most surprising characteristic is that it was the smallest (by far!) of the four 2010 conferences with 290 in attendance.[3] Usually one thinks of the sequel to something grand as necessitating something even grander because of increased expectations; this made the tiny size of Edinburgh 2010 even more jarring. Originally the size was planned to be roughly equal to the first Edinburgh conference (1215), but due to budget constraints and logistical difficulties, it was pared down to the eventual size. The challenge of the small numbers was how ecumenically—and globally—representative it could be when it was nowhere near the size of the other three 2010 conferences nor even its historical predecessor. But, just as Tokyo felt it could focus on frontier missions to the exclusion of almost everything else because there were at least three other conferences that could cover the other issues in 2010, perhaps Edinburgh also felt it did not need to be exhaustive and comprehensive. However, this could only be true if one acknowledged the others. This further emphasizes the need for partnership and humility—truly, missions is the mother of ecumenism.

Despite the small size of this conference, it was among the most ecumenical of the four centenary celebrations in 2010 since it included both Catholic and Orthodox participation, something which not even Edinburgh 1910 had (1910 was mostly Protestant with a few Anglo-Catholics sprinkled in). Even the World Council of Churches has Protestants and Orthodox but no Roman Catholics. So Edinburgh 2010 might rightly be called the most ecumenical missions gathering.[4] However, it must also be said that the meaning of the word *ecumenism* has changed—*ecumenical* concerns the whole church, but there are many ways to slice the church. It

---

[3]The plan was to have 250, but it was increased to nearly 300 when media and staff were accounted for. See table 1.

[4]But see John W. Kennedy, "The Most Diverse Gathering Ever," *Christianity Today*, September 29, 2010, for Cape Town 2010's claim to fame.

could mean all the denominations cooperating together, but it could just as well mean representation of every nationality or ethnic group, regardless of ecclesial affiliation.

J. H. Oldham, John Mott's right-hand man in planning Edinburgh 1910, favored the former definition:

> It is important to bear in mind in this connection the fundamental distinction between "ecumenical" and "international." The term "international" necessarily accepts the division of mankind into separate nations as a natural if not a final state of affairs. The term "ecumenical" refers to the expression within history of the given unity of the church. The one starts from the fact of division and the other from the fact of unity in Christ. The thought and action of the church are international in so far as the church must operate in a world in which the historical Christian bodies share with the rest of mankind the division into national and racial groups. They are ecumenical in so far as they attempt to realize the *una sancta*, the fellowship of Christians who acknowledge the one Lord.[5]

Essentially, Oldham was arguing that the words *ecumenical* and *international* are flip sides of the same coin. But has our priority for ecumenism changed the last one hundred years? Should we be thinking more internationally rather than denominationally now that we have moved into an era of world Christianity where denominational distinctions make less sense today? After all, for example, "Catholic" and "Protestant" are European distinctions that have been imposed on the rest of the world.

If it is the former definition, then Edinburgh 2010 could claim the title of most ecumenical missions conference. If it is the latter definition, then it would be Cape Town 2010. This is not to say that Edinburgh 2010 did not have good ethnic and international representation. In this regard, they clearly outdid 1910 in that the latter had, of the 1215 delegates present, 509 from Britain, 491 from North America, 169 from continental Europe, 27 from South Africa and Australasia (but all were white colonists who lived there), and only 19 from the Two-Thirds World (all from Asia).[6]

---

[5]J. H. Oldham, ed., *The Oxford Conference* (Chicago: Willet, Clark & Co., 1937), 152-53.
[6]Brian Stanley, *The World Missionary Conference, Edinburgh 1910* (Grand Rapids: Eerdmans, 2009), 73, 91.

Edinburgh 2010 was not so skewed toward Westerners and had a much more even representation among the nations.

It must be pointed out, however, that the method of invitation was not the same as 1910. As was mentioned in the last chapter, Edinburgh 1910's criteria for selection was emulated by Tokyo 2010: using the framework of sodalities (mission societies) rather than modalities (church denominations). In this, Edinburgh 2010 parted ways from its forebears. With fewer than three hundred invitees, the selection committee had to focus on individuals, and to be very selective at that. Norman Thomas explained: "Participants came to Edinburgh [1910] not as interested individuals, but as officially accredited delegates of their churches or mission boards, setting a new model for such conferences in the twentieth century. It was unique in that delegates covered the full theological spectrum of Protestantism in North America and Europe";[7] yet this "new model" had regressed back into the old model of "interested individuals" by the time of Edinburgh 2010.

The dates of the conference were also meant to parallel the original: instead of June 14–23 as the 1910 meeting was, the 2010 conference was held June 2–6, being overshadowed by its predecessor not just in attendance but also in duration of time: six days instead of ten. There was an attempt to overlay the dates more precisely, but ironically, the first FIFA World Cup football tournament ever held on the continent of Africa, June 11–July 11, 2010, in South Africa, affected their plans. The organizers of Edinburgh 2010 feared that all attention would be absorbed with football instead of their ecclesiastical proceedings, even if the events were being held half a world away. It just goes to show how times have changed: a century ago, no sporting event would have upstaged a Christian endeavor of such magnitude. In the early twenty-first century, the altar of entertainment and the religion of sport[8] often draw much more attention

---

[7]Norman E. Thomas, *Missions and Unity: Lessons from History, 1792–2010* (Eugene, OR: Cascade, 2010), 49.

[8]Franklin Foer, *How Soccer Explains the World: An Unlikely Theory of Globalization* (New York: HarperCollins, 2004), 198: "Humans crave identifying with a group. It is an unavoidable, immemorial, hardwired instinct. Since modern life has knocked the family and tribe from their central positions, the nation has become the only viable vessel for this impulse. To deny this craving is to deny human nature and human dignity."

than any living faith,[9] especially in post-Christian Europe. No longer are the heroes of the world named William Carey and David Livingstone, but rather Cristiano Ronaldo and David Beckham, and the coffers of stadiums, not cathedrals, are filled to overflowing. It is no wonder that Billy Graham and Pope John Paul II had to regularly resort to places like Yankee Stadium[10] and Wembley Stadium for their venues. It must be said, though, that one could "roll with the punches" and see something like the World Cup as an advantage and not a detriment, as will be seen with Cape Town 2010 in the following chapter.

It is understandable why Edinburgh was chosen as the location for this conference. But does mechanically holding this conference in Edinburgh actually signify a tribute to the past without proper consideration for the future? Having it in Edinburgh seems historically nostalgic but strategically shortsighted, as one of the realities of today's world is the shift in the center of gravity of Christianity to the non-Western world. But perhaps, if we think of it in the same vein as the Tokyo 2010 conference, it is actually more strategic to have it in a non-Christian country. Yet, one has to wonder which of the conference organizers had a tougher time rousing the masses: Edinburgh 2010 in post-Christian Europe or Tokyo 2010 in Christianity-resistant Japan?

In the area of themes, Edinburgh 2010 made a good attempt at being current and relevant. In 1910, the conference was centered on eight themes, as mentioned in chapter one:

1. Carrying the gospel to all the world

2. The native church and its workers

3. Education in relation to the Christianization of national life

4. The missionary message in relation to non-Christian religions

5. The preparation of missionaries

6. The home base of missions

7. Relation of missions to governments

---

[9] Argentina's Pope Francis, elected in 2013, and Brazil's 2014 World Cup and the 2016 Olympics will continue to vie for attention in South America.

[10] The fact that it is commonly called the "Cathedral of Baseball" only proves the point.

8. Co-operation and the promotion of unity

In 2010, there were nine themes:

1. Foundations for mission

2. Christian mission among other faiths

3. Mission and postmodernities

4. Mission and power

5. Forms of missionary engagement

6. Theological education and formation

7. Christian communities in contemporary contexts

8. Mission and unity—ecclesiology and mission

9. Mission spirituality and authentic discipleship

Just looking at this list is instructive: one can get a good picture as to how different mission is today as opposed to a century ago. There are quite a few dissimilarities: the latter is more theological, less Western-centric, more social justice–oriented, and does not assume Christendom as the standard model of Christianity. But notice that interreligious dialogue, education and ecumenism all remain intact as unchanging priorities.

In addition to the above nine themes, there were also seven "transversal" topics, which are common threads that run through all the themes.

1. Women and mission

2. Youth and mission

3. Healing and reconciliation

4. Bible and mission—mission in the Bible

5. Contextualization, inculturation and dialogue of worldviews

6. Subaltern voices

7. Ecological perspectives on mission

So, one might think of it as a grid, with the nine themes on the vertical axis and the seven transversal topics on the horizontal axis for a total of sixty-three different permutations of categories to address. For only 290 people, handling sixty-three different categories was not easy, but this was a working conference, and the attendees were diligent in their efforts. For all the disadvantages of a small size, one advantage is that it is much easier to confer with one another and everyone can easily have a voice.

THE HISTORY OF EDINBURGH 2010

Just as Tokyo 2010 was marked by the charismatic and powerful personality of Ralph Winter, Edinburgh 1910 had the unmistakable handprint of John R. Mott, whose groundbreaking vision for the whole world, amazing intellectual gifts and organizational skills, and submission/obedience to God all helped to shape the conference mightily. Edinburgh 2010 was a tribute to Mott's heart for seeing the whole church reaching the whole world with the gospel, yet 2010 did not really have its own hero. In fact, the story of Mott's successor is one as fraught with controversy as the conference itself was a pale imitation of its illustrious predecessor.

Chapter one of this book describes the formation of the International Missionary Council (IMC) in 1921 from the continuation committee of Edinburgh 1910. Parallel to that were two other streams, also birthed out of Edinburgh 1910: the world conferences on Faith and Order (they held their meetings at Lausanne in 1927 and Edinburgh in 1937) and Life and Work (their meetings were at Stockholm in 1925 and Oxford in 1937). These three "children" of Edinburgh 1910 eventually all remerged into what is now known as the World Council of Churches.

First, Faith and Order and Life and Work coalesced into the first ever General Assembly of the World Council of Churches (WCC) in 1948 at Amsterdam, coming out of the ashes of World War II, which spurred on a need for a worldwide religious organization in parallel to the formation of the political United Nations in 1945. There have since been nine other General Assemblies, held approximately once every seven years, covering every continent.[11] The IMC had meanwhile been holding its own World Mission Conferences.[12] When the IMC eventually got folded into the WCC at the third General Assembly in New Delhi (1961), there was a

---

[11]Evanston 1954; New Delhi 1961; Uppsala 1968; Nairobi 1975; Vancouver 1983; Canberra 1991; Harare 1998; Porto Alegre 2006; Busan 2013.

[12]Lake Mohonk 1921; Oxford 1923; Jerusalem 1928; Tambaram (Madras) 1938; Whitby 1947; Willingen 1952.

decision made to preserve both the WCC's General Assemblies as well as the IMC's World Mission Conferences.[13] It was eventually decided that the two would be held in alternating sequence. Holding the World Mission Conference in Athens in 2005 was a significant step toward ecumenism because that was the first time the conference had been held in an Orthodox country. And the General Assembly had its own groundbreaking event the following year when it hosted its first meeting in the most neglected of the continents, Latin America (the only continent to not have hosted a General Assembly up to that point, while the other continents have all had two each).[14] In some ways, these attempts at diversity are late in coming for a multiethnic organization that claims to have a global scope, much as the United States electing the first black president in 2008, the Southern Baptist Convention installing its first black president in 2012, and the Roman Catholic Church enthroning the first Latin American pope in 2013 are met more with an incredulous "It's about time!" response rather than applause for being progressive. As two counter-examples of being more progressive, the United Nations had a black general secretary from 1997 to 2006, and the country of Peru even had a Japanese president from 1990 to 2000.

Originally Edinburgh 2010 was intended to be a World Mission Conference of the World Council of Churches.[15] When the WCC decided not to take on the task of organizing it, it ultimately ended up being run more locally, jointly organized by the Churches Together in Scotland and the University of Edinburgh.[16] In part this was borne of some national pride as the Scots were keen to show, a century later, that this was their project, as opposed

---

[13]There have since been seven more World Mission Conferences since the IMC merged with the WCC: Achimota (Accra) 1958; New Delhi 1961; Mexico City 1963; Bangkok 1972–1973; Melbourne 1980; San Antonio 1989; Salvador de Bahía 1996; Athens 2005.

[14]If you include Asia and Australia together. See chapter seven for more on why Latin America is often called the neglected/forgotten continent.

[15]See the timeline in appendix D, which shows all the World Mission Conferences and General Assemblies in the history of the WCC. For some reason, they still list Edinburgh 2010 on their chart even though they did not organize or sponsor the event.

[16]Itself a leader in world Christianity and mission, with the Centre for the Study of Christianity in the Non-Western World (CSCNWW) at the divinity school established in 1986 by Prof. Andrew Walls (it was originally founded in Aberdeen in 1982 before its move). Yet, the University of Edinburgh did not appreciate what it had, so most of the unique Two-Thirds World holdings in its library collection have been transferred to Hope Liverpool University, which recognizes its value.

to the Americans and English, who mainly ran things in 1910. The conference organizers started a "Towards 2010" process in 2005, under Prof. Kenneth Ross, with five years of events leading up to the actual conference.

In 2007, they narrowed down the field to five candidates and finally chose as their conference director Methodist minister Dr. Daryl Balia from South Africa.[17] They were attempting to redress the injustice of underrepresentation in 1910—instead of a white man from the northern hemisphere, they selected a brown man from the southern hemisphere for their director.[18] Balia had previously served as an associate professor at the University of KwaZulu-Natal, was chief director of ethics in Nelson Mandela's government and later held the post of the first scholar in residence at the Selly Oak Centre for Mission Studies at the University of Birmingham. However, after three years of preparing for this conference, Balia was unexpectedly forced to resign, just one month prior to the start of the conference! The reasons for this are unclear, as accounts differ, but from the committee's side of the story, there were charges of incompetence, unclear lines of communication, uncertainty about fundraising, and unacceptable comments made privately and publicly by Dr. Balia. From Daryl Balia's own testimony, he was discriminated against because of his color (a charge difficult to believe considering that one of the reasons they chose him in the first place was *because* of his color) and there was a difference in vision: Balia wanted equal representation from all the continents, but the Churches of Scotland wanted the VIPs from the churches to be there. He did make it clear, however, that it was the Churches Together in Scotland, and not the University of Edinburgh, who was to blame.[19]

Regardless of the reasons for the suspension, it did seem a bit heavy-handed of the Edinburgh 2010 committee to completely bar Daryl Balia

---

[17]He related his connection with the Edinburgh conferences, "I was a student participant at the 75th anniversary celebrations which were held in Edinburgh in 1985, but even before that, my grandfather's pastor, the Rev. John Rungiah, was himself a delegate at the 1910 conference and he came to Edinburgh from my home village" (www.edinburgh2010.org/en/news/direct-mail/august-2009.html).

[18]While Edinburgh 2010 could not do what Cape Town 2010 did, namely hold their conference in the Global South to represent the shift of the center of gravity of Christianity there, they could select leadership from that region, which is exactly what they did.

[19]Maria Mackay, "Edinburgh 2010 Director Says Suspension Is 'Human Rights Violation,'" *Christian Today,* June 6, 2010, www.christiantoday.com/article/edinburgh.2010.director.says.suspension .is.human.rights.violation/26048.htm.

from even attending the conference he had developed for several years.[20] Since the suspension was so close to the start of the conference, the issue was not resolved by the time of the conference, and there were ongoing lawsuits and negative media publicity surrounding this incident, all while the conference was going on. Balia was replaced at the last minute by Andrew Anderson, a member of the Churches Together in Scotland executive committee, an ordained minister in the Church of Scotland, and the minister of Greenside Parish Church in Edinburgh. From 2003 to 2006 he also served as the vice convener of the Church of Scotland's World Mission Council. Dr. Kirsteen Kim, director of Programmes in Theology and Religious Studies at Leeds Trinity University College, served as the study process coordinator, and Kirk Sandvig, who was a PhD student at the University of Edinburgh at the time, was the youth and mission coordinator.

Daryl Balia's ouster was not the only controversial incident leading up to the conference. On the first day, as people walked into the venue, there was a group of evangelical Christians protesting outside with a large banner which read: "Cursed be that unity which is bought at the expense of truth!—Martin Luther." Citing the father of the Reformation dredged up a five-hundred-year-old rift between Protestants and Catholics and implied that the unity between the two groups ought not to happen. As evangelicals were certainly part of the planning and attendance of this conference, it is important to note that there are some evangelicals inclined toward ecumenism and others who take the truth-over-unity approach.[21] This shows that evangelicalism has a broad spectrum of beliefs and is not akin to fundamentalism. It is true that unity ought not trump truth, but the trick is to get them to coexist in a way that lends integrity to both.

Edinburgh 2010, as much as 1910, was cognizant of its own self-importance. It was a media event, and the reminders of 1910 never ceased. But it is worth mentioning that Edinburgh 1910 was, ironically, noted as much for whom it left out as much as for whom it included. As an "ecumenical" (the whole church) conference, it was composed mostly of whites,

---

[20]There were great lengths made to bring about reconciliation: the general council (representatives of the Churches) met in emergency meetings; however, there was never any public reconciliation.
[21]See the section titled "Ecumenism and Missions" in chapter one.

males and Westerners, and lacked Catholics, Orthodox, Africans (as a people) and Latin America (as a continent). The question is, did Edinburgh 2010 redress these? Edinburgh 2010 did not think of itself as the sole representative of 2010. They invited the organizers of Tokyo 2010 (Yong Cho) and Cape Town 2010 (Doug Birdsall) as well, thus living up to the billing of fostering an ecumenical spirit.[22]

EDINBURGH 2010: CONFERENCE PROCEEDINGS

Unlike the original 1910 conference, which was held on The Mound (one of the seven hills of Edinburgh) right in the center of the city on the border of Old Town and New Town, the 2010 conference was held in the shadow of Arthur's Seat (another one of the seven hills) in the Old Town at the relatively new dormitories of Pollock Halls, which also houses modern facilities as the John McIntyre Conference Center (JMCC). Though there were logistical reasons for the new location, it also suggested a relegating to the periphery in regard to its importance—no longer was mission symbolically atop the most central hill in Edinburgh, next to the castle, but it was held deep in the old city, off to the side, behind closed walls, where very few people would notice its presence.

Dr. Dana Robert, Truman Collins Professor of World Christianity and History of Mission at Boston University's School of Theology, was the keynote opening speaker. Just as the choice of Daryl Balia was meant to be a divergence from 1910 (he represented the Global South and non-whites), a woman was intentionally chosen to be the opening speaker in an attempt to redress the other major lack of 1910, where there were only about two hundred women out of over twelve hundred delegates.[23] It was a bit surprising that Edinburgh 2010, for all its claim to being the rightful successor to 1910, intentionally tried to diverge from the original significantly more than Tokyo 2010 did.

The mood was also notably different from a century ago. One of the intangible but nonetheless crucial elements that made Edinburgh 1910 different

---

[22]Stanley, *World Missionary Conference*, 14.
[23]It must not be misconstrued that Dr. Robert was chosen solely because of her gender. She is arguably the world's foremost female missiologist alive today, with numerous publications and credentials to her name and a PhD from Yale University, and was eminently worthy of the honor.

from 2010 was the optimism that pervaded it. There was supreme confidence in the efforts of humans to Christianize the whole world, in part because the two World Wars and the Great Depression had not happened yet. At Edinburgh 2010, in addition to the above we have suffered the Korean and Vietnam Wars, the Cold War, 9/11, and further economic recession, leading to more of a sense of pessimism and cynicism; certainly any triumphalism is gone.[24] In light of the dim prospects preceding the 2010 conference, with it having lesser attendance and budget and time and selection criteria and location than the 1910 conference had, Professor Robert humorously and insightfully noted: "A century ago the participants at Edinburgh 1910 *complained* that only one-third of the world was Christian. Today we *rejoice* that one-third of the world are followers of Christ."[25]

Wednesday, June 2, and Sunday, June 6, were the bookends of the conference. Thursday, Friday and Saturday were the heart of the proceedings. Each of those three days had a plenary session (held in the Pentland Suite) and parallel workshop tracks that explored the nine themes listed above and their transversals (in the South Hall Complex). The three plenary sessions were "Mission in Long Perspective," "Mission Worldwide" and "Towards a Common Call."

In plenary one, Dana Robert framed her talk around three historical turning points in mission in the previous century: Edinburgh 1910's contribution to ecumenism; the WCC's 1963 missions conference in Mexico City, redefining mission as from everyone to everywhere; and Edinburgh 2010 ushering in fresh challenges for mission in the twenty-first century and beyond.

Plenary two featured four speakers: Rev. Dr. Lee Young-Hoon, senior pastor of the Yoido Full Gospel Church in South Korea; Dr. Antonios Kireopoulos, associate general secretary for faith and order and interfaith relations at the National Council of Churches of Christ in the USA; Dr. Prof. Teresa Francesca Rossi, associate director of the Centro Pro Unione in Rome

---

[24]This is also true of the secular world: just a couple of decades ago, the assumption was that by now we would have jet-powered flying cars and that the future lay in power and progress. Rather, the reality is that our fuel resources are running low and power has given way to efficiency: hybrid and electric cars.

[25]Kirsteen Kim and Andrew Anderson, eds., *Mission Today and Tomorrow* (Oxford: Regnum, 2011), 67-68, italics mine.

(Franciscan Friars of the Atonement); and Rev. Dr. Fidon Mwombeki, general secretary of United Evangelical Mission. Each discussed his or her respective ministry with regard to mission and ecumenism. They provided a variety of multidenominational and international perspectives: from Pentecostal to Mainline Protestant to Roman Catholic to evangelical, and from Asia to the Americas to Europe to Africa.

Plenary three is discussed below under "Edinburgh 2010 Common Call."

The parallel workshop tracks are where the real work was done. The advantage of having such a small conference is that everyone could truly contribute and collaborate. Cape Town 2010 may have called itself a congress and not a conference with the aspiration that every attendee had a voice, but that was merely styling and not reality. At Edinburgh 2010, whether intentionally or merely a result of the tiny size, there was full participation from all. For example, I was assigned to be in charge of transversal 4 for theme 1—that is, "Contextualization, inculturation and dialogue of worldviews" within the "Foundations for mission" theme. In no other of the 2010 conferences was I given such a responsibility.

DIVERSITY

If there was one thing that Edinburgh 2010 did well (though not perfectly), it was in the area of diversity. It was perhaps the most diverse among the 2010 conferences—in every way possible except in international representation (Cape Town excelled at that)—despite the fact that it was the smallest. Denominationally and in terms of gender, age and culture it strove for equivalent representation across the board, even if it did not always succeed.

The conference commenced with greetings by the stakeholders of the conference: Rev. Dr. Olav Fykse Tveit, general secretary of the World Council of Churches;[26] Rev. Dr. Geoff Tunnicliffe, secretary general of the World Evangelical Alliance;[27] and Cardinal Keith O'Brien, archbishop and metropolitan of the Archdiocese of St Andrews and Edinburgh.[28] This shows that the conference was intended to be thoroughly ecumenical, encompassing the mainline Protestant, evangelical Protestant and Roman

---

[26]Ibid., 7-9.
[27]Ibid., 10-11.
[28]Ibid., 11-13.

Catholic sectors of Christianity. Not directly represented by stakeholders were the Orthodox and Pentecostals, though they were acknowledged as two more of the five main groups. Though these categories of Catholic, Orthodox, evangelicals, mainline Protestants and Pentecostals seem to be overly general (or perhaps overly Western) in terms of denominational criteria for invitees, perhaps it was necessary to reduce it to these five when there were fewer than three hundred people in attendance, so in this way they could claim to represent the world's denominations. Nonetheless, at least they acknowledged the Pentecostals on equal footing with the other older, established traditions, which is more than can be said for the other conferences except Tokyo. Part of the lack of recognition for Pentecostals does have to do with the fact that Pentecostalism is still a fairly new phenomenon, historically speaking.

Depending on what theory one subscribes to, there were three possible origins of Pentecostalism: (1) Bethel Bible College and Charles Fox Parham in Topeka, Kansas, in 1901. This had its origins in the Holiness movement and Wesleyan Methodism and was largely a white movement. (2) The Azusa Street Revival and William J. Seymour in Los Angeles in 1906. This was largely a black and multiethnic movement.[29] (3) Walter Hollenweger, who posited a polycentric thesis. The origins of this are outside the United States, in places like Wales (1904), India (1905), Chile (1906) and Korea (1907); had no connection with North America or its missionaries; and are indigenous/

---

[29]Seymour was actually Parham's disciple. Harvey Cox, *Fire from Heaven: The Rise of Pentecostal Spirituality and the Reshaping of Religion in the Twenty-First Century* (Cambridge, MA: Da Capo Press, 1995), 149: "No responsible historian of religion now disputes that pentecostalism was conceived when essentially African and African American religious practices began to mingle with the poor white southern Christianity that sprang from a Wesleyan lineage. But it was a long gestation, and a fierce debate still simmers about when and where the birth actually took place. Some trace it to New Year's Eve, 1900, when a white woman named Agnes Ozman is said to have spoken in tongues at Charles Parham's Bethel Bible School in Topeka. Others locate it at the Azusa Street Revival in Los Angeles, led by William Seymour. Those who hold that tongue speaking is *the* defining characteristic of pentecostalism insist on the Topeka advent. But the dispute will probably never be settled since both Topeka and Azusa Street have now achieved a certain mythic quality. Those who take a broader view of what the pentecostal movement is, and who underline the power of the Spirit to break down racial and ethnic walls, claim that the former stable on Azusa Street is the real manger scene. I personally find it hard to accept the case for Topeka, since glossolalia has been documented in virtually every period of religious enthusiasm since Paul both commended it and warned about its excesses in the first century A.D. Emissaries from Azusa Street, on the other hand, fanned out all over America and into several foreign countries sowing the seeds for what became 'the pentecostal movement' of the following decades."

homegrown revivals. Regardless of which one is correct, they all occurred right around the same time as Edinburgh 1910, and Pentecostalism was still nascent, so it makes sense that 1910 did not address it. Today, one hundred years later, it is *the* form of Christianity to be reckoned with. This makes sense, considering that the Holy Spirit is the person of the Trinity who is with us today—the Father and the Son are both enthroned in heaven, but the Holy Spirit is our current Immanuel ("God with us") now that the Son is seated at the right hand of the Father. And if you take Pentecostalism back to its primogenitor, from which it draws its name, that is where the church was born. Pentecostalism has ecumenical effect: it transcends denomination (there are Catholic Pentecostals as well as Protestant Pentecostals) and nationality; it can be found in places as diverse as China, Brazil, Nigeria and Canada (cf. Acts 2:1-11). It must also be said that Pentecostalism is growing in part because of postmodernity, as the role of experience (which was also strongly emphasized by Wesley and thus has heavily influenced evangelicals) is becoming increasingly emphasized in today's world.

Perhaps the one area of diversity where Edinburgh 2010 fell short was with regard to youth. When it came to denominational and cultural and international diversity, they were excellent, and far outstripped 1910. With regard to gender, and notably with Dana Robert, they were conscious about redressing the previous lack of representation a century ago.[30] As for youth, though there were plenty of young people present, they were the only ones who did not really have a voice, and they complained about not being heard. They mostly worked as stewards of the conference, much as they often do in WCC General Assemblies and as they did at Cape Town 2010. This was the one area where 1910 did better than 2010. Even though youth were not delegates in 1910, it was they who inspired the whole conference. It was good that women and youth were the first two transversal categories listed, but it was not realized as well as it was envisioned: the intention was to have 50 percent women, though it fell a little short, and 30 percent youth—but the 3 percent representation did not even come close! Though a youth coordinator was intentionally put into place (Kirk Sandvig), and Jec Borlado gave an excellent paper on youth that was unfortunately not published in

---

[30]Stanley, *World Missionary Conference*, 312-13.

the final book compiling the conference papers, there was hardly any mention of students at the 2010 event, in contrast to a conference like Urbana, which is geared specifically toward students. I suspect that Mott would have been happier with Urbana than Edinburgh 2010 in this regard. In fact, Edinburgh 1985 (sponsored by the Student Christian Movement), the seventy-fifth anniversary of the 1910 conference, was 100 percent for students.

One of the most delightful parts of this conference was the worship music, which outdid all the other conferences in its diversity. The music was led by John Bell of the Iona community in Scotland, and the songs were drawn from over twenty countries—mostly smaller nations, such as El Salvador, Rwanda, Taiwan, Malawi, New Zealand, Nicaragua, Malaysia, Ghana, Paraguay, Cameroon, Vietnam, Zimbabwe and Singapore. And in a non-ecclesial category of music, on Friday night of the conference they hosted a ceilidh, a celebration of Scottish song and dance, for all the conference attendees.

The English language dominated, as it must for pragmatic reasons. Though they had a unique trio of liturgical leaders using English (spoken by a Pakistani), French (spoken by a Scot) and Spanish (spoken by a Brazilian), English was the operative language, and the others seemed a bit token. Anybody who did not speak English well had difficulty really participating in the conference, because translators and headphones will always remain unwieldy. As one Latin American delegate remarked, "People whose mother tongue is not English are just observers, not really participants." And it must be acknowledged that though Spanish is prevalent in Latin America and French is prevalent in Africa, these are colonial European languages that will always have a hegemony over international gatherings for pragmatic reasons.

CONTROVERSIES AND PERILS OF ECUMENISM

Denominations were established for a reason: to disagree on nonessentials of the faith.[31] Christians should all, at least as a starting point, agree on the nonexhaustive list of the essentials of the faith as outlined in the Apostles' Creed and the Nicene Creed; those are what bind Christians together. The

---

[31]Allen Yeh, "The Road Ahead: Essentials vs. Nonessentials," in Mark Russell, Allen Yeh, Michelle Sanchez, Chelle Stearns and Dwight Friesen, *Routes and Radishes: And Other Things to Talk About at the Evangelical Crossroads* (Grand Rapids: Zondervan, 2010), 33-50.

difficulty arises when Christians start making nonessentials into essentials, thus invalidating each other's claim to the faith (Paul addresses this problem in Romans 14 and how to deal with it). And in an ecumenical conference, sometimes even the nonessentials become points of contention because different people are meeting in the same room to discuss missional strategies and cannot agree on how to proceed.[32] It often felt that way at Edinburgh 2010—so much diversity, but most of the time we were just working on coming to a common starting point so we hardly even got to the task of practical strategy! At Tokyo 2010 and Cape Town 2010, it was already assumed that everyone was evangelical so we could just move forward with strategy. As such, Edinburgh 2010 probably had more points of controversy than any of the other 2010 conferences—mainly because the other conferences were more homogeneous in their representation and thus naturally would have a greater degree of agreement on issues. And yet, there was something necessary about the dialogue of differences and coming to a final consensus. It was evocative of the ancient ecumenical councils and the lasting legacy they have left for the church worldwide. The councils have paved a theological way for us all.

One example of a controversial moment was a Greek Orthodox representative from the United States representing the WCC, Tony Kireopoulos,[33] who spoke on the second day with a thinly veiled criticism of the dominance of American evangelicals and their representative televangelists, especially with regard to the upcoming Lausanne Congress in Cape Town. This raised the hackles of some in the audience, and later Doug Birdsall, the chairman of the Lausanne movement, spoke from the platform describing the upcoming Cape Town 2010 Congress, saying jokingly, "And there may even be some televangelists there!"

Another example of a controversy was during the request for additions/modifications to the Common Call document. One young woman said that there was not enough diversity represented among male and female (implying that there be mention of transgender as well). The older generation

---

[32]See chapter seven for more explanation of how Latin America was "left off the map" at Edinburgh 1910 due to the disagreement of how to proceed missionally.

[33]Antonios Kireopoulos, "Case Study 2: Ecumenical Charity as Christian Witness," in Kim and Anderson, *Mission Today and Tomorrow*, 98-103.

largely dismissed her while there was a smattering of applause from the youth. This illustrates the crucial need for communication between generations and for dialogue about issues that were not even discussed a decade ago.

It was not only the Catholics and Orthodox who criticized the evangelicals; it went the other way too. And it was not just Westerners criticizing non-Westerners; that also went the other way. In 1910, V. S. Azariah, the first bishop of the southern Indian diocese of Dornakal and one of only seventeen Asians present at that conference, spoke boldly about the condescending attitude of Western missionaries toward non-Western Christians. He said, "Too often you promise us thrones in heaven, but will not offer us chairs in your drawing rooms," clearly wanting equal partnership that goes beyond paternalism. He concluded with his famous quote, "You have given your goods to feed the poor. You have given your bodies to be burned. We also ask for *love*. Give us FRIENDS!"[34] In the 2010 conference, Azariah's name was mentioned more than any other 1910 figure, including John Mott's. I'm sure most people must have thought, *Who is going to be 2010's V. S. Azariah?*

It turned out to be another South Asian, Dr. Vinoth Ramachandra,[35] of International Fellowship of Evangelical Students (IFES), who was one of the speakers offering reflections on the last day. He offered the following critique: though this may be the most inclusive conference of the last one hundred years with regard to ecclesiastical traditions (in itself a very complimentary statement), there were still not enough women and not enough youth. He also decried the lack of evangelistic fervor: "Except for Dana Robert's opening address, I confess I haven't sensed the passion for the gospel and the deep sense of accountability to God for the nations that resonates through much of the 1910 reports." In addition, Westerners are so beholden to their titles, vestments and degrees, while there really needed to be a breaking down of barriers between clergy and laity toward the priesthood of all believers. (This statement really made the Catholics, Orthodox, Methodists and Anglicans uncomfortable or upset!) He also called out the hypocrisy of non-Westerners who criticize Westerners for

---

[34]Stanley, *World Missionary Conference*, 125.
[35]Vinoth Ramachandra, "Reflections," in Kim and Anderson, *Mission Today and Tomorrow*, 334-36.

these things, yet do these things themselves! Plus, most of the non-Westerners at the conference were Global South people who now reside in the Global North. And Westerners often define non-Westerners in religious terms, but there are many more who are technologically driven today more than anything else.[36] Finally, he criticized the division of Christians into "ecumenical," "evangelical" and "charismatic" (which were some of the categories in how Edinburgh 2010 defined itself). Ramachandra received much applause for his speech, but some might question if such statements are even appropriate for an ecumenical conference. Some would say no, because the point is to have unity and consensus. Others say yes, because we ought to be sharpening one another and, as a Catholic said to me, we sometimes need to learn to give and take some hits, though gently. Unity does not mean uniformity.

Ramachandra, a Sri Lankan evangelical, was also joined by Mrs. Anastasia Vassiliadou, a Greek Orthodox, and finally Rev. Dr. Stephen B. Bevans,[37] of the Catholic Theological Union in Chicago. These three speakers further showed the intentionality of Edinburgh 2010 to have diversity of denominations, gender and continents represented on the platform. Bevans offered a hope: for more youth and the future leadership of world Christianity. But he also offered this lament: that missiologist Andrew Walls, arguably the most prominent missiologist of the past quarter century, was not honored in his own country. Also, Bevans noted that despite all our diversity, Oceania was left out of the conference.

MISSIO DEI

Though the previous section recounted the controversies and disagreements inevitable with such a diverse gathering, that belies the fact that there actually was a remarkable amount of civility and consensus. The spirit of the conference was largely gracious, and the major consensus lay in the universal

---

[36]Ibid., 335. Ramanchandra's exact quote was, "China and India together produce more science and engineering graduates every year than North America and Europe combined. But Asian mission studies dissertations and the bulk of articles in mission studies journals focus on historical studies of religious sects and denominations, traditional tribal cultures or exotic new religious movements." Perhaps instead of thinking of Asia as simply premodern, we need to think of Asia as thoroughly modern at the same time, and becoming increasingly postmodern too.
[37]Ibid., 337-38.

agreement about the *missio Dei* (the mission of God—that all mission must start from the Trinity and not from humans), as well as the emphases on social justice, prayer and creation care. There was no need to convince people of the validity of these issues.

The idea behind the *missio Dei* is that it is God, and not us, who is the initiator of mission. Anthropocentrism tends to dissolve in the face of suffering, and our belief in the unlimited potential of humanity makes way for a healthy reliance on God when we are confronted with the inability to do it on our own strength. This is the idea behind the phrase "There are no atheists in foxholes": when one is in the trenches of war with bullets flying over head and bombs exploding all around, everyone—rich and poor, black and white, old and young, male and female—is equalized. Everyone prays, because anyone could die at any time. As the optimistic modernism of the twentieth century gave way to cynicism about human beings' ability to save the world (after all, after the great experiment of atheistic Marxism, and science producing weapons like the atomic bomb, and the inability of humans to cure AIDS and cancer), there is little wonder that people have decided that perhaps the answer is in God and not in humanity. We have great potential for achievement, but that is matched by an equally depraved appetite for destruction.

Actually, the *missio Dei* is not a new theology: at the IMC's World Mission Conference at Willingen 1952, there was a reaction against the perceived church-centric view of missions present in the assembly. The result was the affirmation of mission as the *missio Dei*, and it ended up being an enduring contribution of Willingen, spearheaded by the efforts of Lutheran theologian Georg Vicedom. They made the statement "There is no participation in Christ without participation in His mission to the world."[38]

If God, and not humans, is the initiator of mission, this has profound impact for defining what mission is. One question that must be asked is, is a missionary the equivalent of "apostle" in the Bible? Because *apostle* means "one who is sent." This is why the twelve disciples (students) in the Gospels had their designation changed to the twelve apostles (sent out) in Acts. It

---

[38]Lesslie Newbigin, "Mission to Six Continents," in *A History of the Ecumenical Movement*, vol. 2, ed. Harold E. Fey (Geneva: World Council of Churches, 1970), 178-79.

seems that, by biblical example, one goes from learner to doer. The twelve apostles were sent out by the Trinity. The Father is clearly the initiator of mission, but the Son also has a part to play as he commissioned the Eleven in Matthew 28:18-20. And the Holy Spirit empowers the apostles as well, as we see in Acts 1:8.

The debate over who the first American missionary was is a good illustration of this question of whether God or humans are the initiator of missions. Popularly the Judsons (Adoniram and Ann), who went from America to Burma in 1812–1813, have been regarded as the first missionaries. Thirty years prior to them, however, was a freed black slave named George Leile (sometimes spelled Lisle) who went to Jamaica to do evangelistic work. Many scholars of late have called for a revision of history to emphasize Leile over the Judsons. Though Leile had the advantage of chronology, he was not sent per se. He had no sending body or church or missionary society. In contrast, the Judsons were definitely sent by the American Board of Commissioners for Foreign Missions (ABCFM).

Shifting from the plural to the singular version of *mission* has affected missiological labels and definitions in twentieth-century missiology onward, so that organizations like the US Center for World Mission and the Oxford Centre for Mission Studies use the singular version of the word. David Bosch articulated this shift when he wrote:

> For the *missiones ecclesiae* (the missionary activities of the church) the *missio Dei* has important consequences. "Mission," singular, remains primary; "missions," in the plural, constitutes a derivative. With reference to the post-Willingen period, Neill (1966a:572) boldly proclaims, "The age of missions is at an end; the age of mission has begun." It follows that we have to distinguish between mission and missions. We cannot without ado claim that what we do is identical to the *missio Dei*; our missionary activities are only authentic insofar as they reflect participation in the mission of God. . . . The primary purpose of the *missiones ecclesiae* can therefore not simply be the planting of churches or the saving of souls; rather, it has to be service to the *missio Dei*, representing God in and over against the world, pointing to God, holding up the God-child before the eyes of the world in a ceaseless celebration of the Feast of the Epiphany. In its mission, the church witnesses to the fullness of

the promise of God's reign and participates in the ongoing struggle between that reign and the powers of darkness and evil.[39]

Rev. Dr. John Kaoma, of St. John's Anglican Seminary in Zambia, contributed a paper from the parallel sessions in which he highlighted the broader implications of the *missio Dei*, especially with regard to another pressing contemporary issue: creation care. He wrote:

> The shift from an ecclesiocentric to a theocentric (*missio Dei*) conception of Christian mission should redirect missiological thinking to ecological liberation. Although it is tempting to consider humanity (*imago Dei*) as the sole beneficiary of *missio Dei*, God's mission is holistic. . . . Witnessing to Christ would mean addressing population growth, pollution, species extinction, climate change and human responsibility towards future generations. In other words, the instrumental view of the natural world, which dominated early missionary activities and still influences our economic theories, should be replaced with "holistic approaches" that honour the interconnectedness of creation. In this case, the *missio Dei* should be understood as the mission of the Creator (*missio Creator*) revealed in the cosmic Christ, under whose authority, care and influence Earth and heaven now exist. Thus, all environmental issues are subjects of mission studies.[40]

A CELEBRATION OF HISTORICAL PROPORTIONS

The Scottish Parliament, for most of its history, met in the great Assembly Hall of the Church of Scotland, now part of New College of the University of Edinburgh's Divinity School on the Mound, next to Edinburgh Castle. This was the same location for the Edinburgh 1910 World Missionary Conference. In 2010, both settings had changed: the Parliament now meets at the bottom of the Royal Mile instead of the top of the Mound, and the missionary conference took place at Pollock Halls in the Old Town instead of the Mound as well. It seemed strange to hold the conference in the same city

---

[39]David Bosch, *Transforming Mission* (Maryknoll, NY: Orbis, 1991), 391. Also see Lesslie Newbigin, *The Gospel in a Pluralistic Society* (Grand Rapids: Eerdmans, 1989), 121.

[40]Kapya John Kaoma, "*Missio Dei* or *Missio Creator Dei*? Witnessing to Christ in the Face of the Current Ecological Crisis," in Kim and Anderson, *Mission Today and Tomorrow*, 296-303.

but not in the same location—and yet the dates of the conference were slightly off too.

Still, in a nod to history, neither the Parliament nor the Assembly Hall were forgotten. On the second night of the conference (Thursday, June 3), participants were treated to an evening drinks reception at the Scottish Parliament, hosted by MPs. The new building, right across the street from the Queen's Edinburgh residence, Holyrood Palace, opened in 2004 to some controversy due to its abstract postmodern design by Spanish architect Enric Miralles. Still, it represented a move into the future, with the crown and the state being literally side by side at the bottom of the Royal Mile, instead of Parliament being paired with the ancient castle at the top of the Mound. But there were also pragmatic reasons for the move of Parliament and the conference site, and perhaps this was appropriate since steps forward into the future are not motivated as much by nostalgia as by innovation or necessity.

On the final day of the conference (Sunday, June 6), delegates dispersed temporarily in the morning to attend various churches throughout the city for worship services. While this move was indeed appropriate given the fact that Edinburgh 1910 enlisted the involvement of local churches, there was some criticism that only "high church" (Orthodox, Catholic, Methodist and Church of Scotland) churches were included in the ten official Sunday visitations—which means the two largest churches in the city, Morningside Baptist and Charlotte Chapel, were not on the list. It is a reality of countries that do not have separation of church and state that churches not officially sanctioned by the state, such as the Baptists in the United Kingdom, are considered "nonconformists."

The archbishop of York, John Sentamu, spoke at one of the officially sanctioned Sunday morning worship services, namely, St. Mary's Cathedral, the mother church of the Diocese of Edinburgh. Sentamu is notable as the highest-ranking Anglican clergyman from an ethnic minority background in history. Originally from Uganda, he was installed as the second in command of the Church of England (the archbishop of Canterbury would be the highest-ranking clergyman) in 2005. His enthronement was not without controversy, as he encountered many threats due to racism, but he has proven resilient and faithful. He paralleled Daryl Balia as both are from Africa and called to major leadership positions in the United Kingdom, showing the face of world Christianity today. Sentamu's sermon focused on the trinitarian *missio Dei*: he stated that God is always the director of mission, but we've wrongly turned the divine initiative into our enterprise. Jesus Christ *is* the message, and worship and witness are done by the power of the Holy Spirit. Human activity only begets human activity, but we need renewal and liberation by the Spirit, just as God breathed life into the valley of dry bones in Ezekiel.

After church, all the conference delegates convened from 3:00 to 5:30 p.m. at the historic Assembly Hall on the Mound for the closing celebration. The highlight of that final session was the joyful pan-African choir, and the archbishop of York delivered the keynote sermon. With Dana Robert and John Sentamu as the opening and closing speakers, respectively, Edinburgh 2010 sent a strong message that it was rectifying the mistakes of the past (with not just more representation by women and the Majority World but also more leadership) while still paying homage to tradition by keeping the conference in Edinburgh. Speaking of tradition, they highlighted three special guests who had historical predecessors from 1910: (1) B. S. Devamani,[41] the bishop of Dornakal, V. S. Azariah's modern-day successor in the Church of South India, who reread Azariah's speech from a century ago; (2) Samuel and Eunice Min, the latter of whom is the granddaughter of the younger brother of Yun Ch'iho, the only Korean in attendance at Edinburgh 1910; and (3) Noah Moses Israel from KwaZulu-Natal in South Africa, whose wife was the granddaughter of Rev. John Rangiah, the first Indian Baptist missionary to minister in Natal. These nods to Africa, women and Asia were welcome, but Latin American presence, which was the great omission of 1910, was still conspicuously missing.

Despite the vivid spectacle of the closing celebration, there were still some criticisms. There were, visibly, many empty seats, especially in the balcony. Of course Edinburgh 2010 was a lot smaller than its predecessor a century ago, but those seats could have been filled by locals and from

---

[41]The Rt. Rev. Dr. Bachu Satyanandam Devamani died in April 2013.

churches in the area. Did this signify a lack of engagement with the city of Edinburgh itself, even while purporting to be a worldwide conference? If nothing else, it showed either disinterest or an ignorance of the conference's existence by the locals.

IMPACT OF EDINBURGH 2010

What made Edinburgh 1910 famous was being the birthplace of the modern ecumenical movement. And what made it the birthplace of the modern ecumenical movement was the continuation committee, not the conference itself. And this is what made the lack of a continuation committee at Edinburgh 2010 such a surprise.

Yet 2010 was not solely present-minded. They decided to take a different tack altogether by looking toward the future both before and after the conference. For several years in the run-up to 2010, they had a process called "Toward Edinburgh 2010," by which they sought worldwide input of scholars and planners, often via the Internet[42] but sometimes through pre-conference meetings. And after the conference ended, they continued to publish a book series as the legacy and follow-up to 2010. The Edinburgh 2010 series was published by Regnum (the publishing arm of the Oxford Centre for Mission Studies in the UK) and continues to thrive, with thirty-three volumes as the final goal.[43] Balia was the coeditor of one of the two volumes in the Edinburgh 2010 book series leading up to the conference.

Looking back at the conference itself, there were numerous things lacking. There was nothing that looked toward the state of mission in the

---

[42]As an example, see www.edinburgh2010.org/en/resources/papersdocuments.html.

[43]Two of them were published prior to the Edinburgh 2010 conference: vol. 1, *Mission Then and Now*, ed. David A. Kerr and Kenneth R. Ross; and vol. 2, *Witnessing to Christ Today*, ed. Daryl Balia and Kirsteen Kim. Vol. 3, *Mission Today and Tomorrow*, ed. Kirsteen Kim and Andrew Anderson, was published after the conference as a compilation of the documents of Edinburgh 2010. The subsequent volumes address a variety of topics, including vol. 5, *Holistic Mission*; vol. 9, *Evangelical and Frontier Mission*; vol. 15, *A Century of Catholic Mission*; vol. 17, *Orthodox Perspectives on Mission*; vol. 20, *Pentecostal Perspectives on Global Mission*; and volumes about Korean perspectives, African perspectives and Latin American perspectives on mission. The full list of volumes can be obtained at www.ocms.ac.uk/regnum/list.php?cat=3. There were also four smaller paperback books published by William Carey International University Press, the publishing arm of the US Center for World Mission (which cosponsored the Tokyo 2010 conference, showing yet more ecumenical cooperation with Edinburgh): *Edinburgh 2010: Springboard for Mission*; *New Directions for Church in Mission*; *Fresh Perspectives on Christian Mission*; and *Youth Perspectives*.

next century. It did not even deal well with trends of this century, such as business as mission or the emergent church. While Edinburgh 2010 produced the Common Call document, that was neither a creed nor a call to action (like the Lausanne Covenant). The problem with the World Council of Churches (which Edinburgh 2010 was based on) is that it cannot account for non-ecclesial structures like Latin American Base Ecclesial Communities, African Independent Churches and Chinese house churches.

All of the above is not to suggest that the conference was not a success; in fact, Edinburgh 1910 probably had many more problems, and it was still deemed a landmark event. Whether Edinburgh 2010 will actually go down in history the same way as 1910 remains to be seen, however.

EDINBURGH 2010 COMMON CALL

The subject of the third and final plenary session (the day before the closing ceremony) was a presentation of the findings and conclusions of the nine themes, followed by the Common Call.[44] The latter was Edinburgh 2010's equivalent of the Tokyo Declaration or the Cape Town Commitment. As with the conference size itself, the Common Call document was much smaller than the others in 2010. It was drafted by five people representing the conference's stakeholders[45] and presented to the conference delegates (hot off the press at the time of the last plenary!), and then the audience gave input in its penultimate form. As mentioned previously, this is the beauty of a small conference (not to mention a small document): everyone can offer input and help to mold and shape it.

Audience input proved necessary, as reflected by some of the comments. One young man said that there was no talk of evangelism, to much applause. A young woman suggested that transgender be included, to a small smattering of applause (mostly from youth). A woman suggested that we include a prohibition of sheep stealing or cross-proselytizing—to no

---

[44]For the full text, see appendix C.

[45]Doug Birdsall (the chairman of Lausanne, representing evangelicals), Mario Conti (archbishop of Glasgow, representing Catholics), Julie Ma (from Korea and the Oxford Centre for Mission Studies, representing Pentecostals), Setri Nyomi (from Ghana and the Alliance of Reformed Churches, representing mainline Protestants) and Vitros Vasiliadis (from Aristotle University in Greece, representing Orthodox).

applause! This is interesting and shocking because that was the hot-button issue of Edinburgh 1910: whether or not Protestants/evangelicals evangelizing in Latin America is tantamount to sheep stealing (converting Catholics to Protestantism).

Perhaps the most problematic issue about the Common Call was highlighted by a comment from a participant[46] that it had very little forward movement as to predicting or planning for mission in the next ten years. As mentioned above, Edinburgh 1910's great strength was not the conference itself; it was the fact that the conference launched a whole century of ecumenical mission. It may be difficult to say the same thing about Edinburgh 2010, especially since there was no continuation committee or its equivalent—ironic, considering all the other 2010 conferences have one! The one area where Edinburgh 2010 continues its theological reflection is in its Edinburgh Centenary Series published by Regnum, which has produced some landmark missiology over the course of its thirty-three-book run. It closed with a celebration of all its authors at the Oxford Centre for Mission Studies on September 4, 2015, where Dana Robert also gave the keynote address.[47] But the question remains: how will the impact of Edinburgh 2010 sustain itself in an ongoing way after this?

To further emphasize this limited future-oriented mentality, the theme of the conference was "Witnessing to Christ Today." It is a bit strange that, given this theme, there was hardly any mention of evangelism. Is there significance to the language of "witness" instead of "evangelize"? This may have been an attempt to show that witnessing goes beyond the verbal, à la St. Francis of Assisi's famous dictum (though apocryphally attributed): "Preach the gospel, and if necessary, use words." Or it may have been an attempt to shy away from language that is no longer politically correct, such as *crusade* (Campus Crusade for Christ rebranded its college ministry in 2011 simply as "Cru" in an attempt to be non-offensive). This is in contrast to Edinburgh 1910, as Brian Stanley noted: "Crusading language was often implicit and occasionally explicit at Edinburgh."[48] Some feel that the word *mission* seems to be headed in the same direction as *crusade*; will it soon

---

[46]Dr. Josias "Sas" Conradie from South Africa, head of the Global Mission Fund, which is a partnership between the Church Mission Society in the UK and the World Evangelical Alliance Mission Commission.

[47]Dana Robert, "One Christ—Many Witnesses: Visions of Mission and Unity, Edinburgh and Beyond," *Transformation*, May 16, 2016, 1-12.

[48]Stanley, *World Missionary Conference*, 2.

become antiquated, obsolete and offensive? The US Center for World Mission renamed itself Frontier Ventures in 2015, and both Biola University and Fuller Seminary renamed their School of World Missions as School of Intercultural Studies, so perhaps this is the direction we are headed.

QUESTIONS

1. Which is more "ecumenical" (representing the whole church): Edinburgh 2010, which had the most diverse denominational representation, or Cape Town 2010, which had the most diverse international representation? What do you think about Edinburgh 2010 using the five categories of Catholic, Orthodox, evangelical Protestant, mainline Protestant and Pentecostal in order to show sufficient denominational diversity?

2. What is a better location for a missions conference—in the center of power of Christianity or in the least Christian lands? Look at chapter one, note 65 for the list of the other 2010 conferences. Notice that almost all were held in the West (only 6 out of 25 were held in the Two-Thirds World!), though much of the West is now post-Christian. So we might ask: can a rich country in the West that is now post-Christian be considered a "center of power" if it still controls the publishing and the seminaries and the grand buildings but lacks the numbers of Christians?

3. Most younger Christians today do not choose a church based on its denomination, and in fact most do not define themselves in terms of denominational loyalties. Are denominational distinctions passé today? Are they an invention of the West? Do we still need them? Are they helpful identifiers?

4. Are the Edinburgh 2010 themes a good update of the 1910 themes? What would you have changed/added? What do you think of the transversals? What issues are "timeless" and will always be relevant in world missions?

5. What place does criticism and controversy have in an ecumenical conference? Should the emphasis be on consensus or correcting one another's unhealthy tendencies? What do you think about the comments

made by Kieropoulos and Ramachandra, for example? Were they out of line or healthy?

6. Should we just give up meeting in ecumenical circles and only meet with like-minded believers (evangelicals with other evangelicals, for example) in order to actually get work done? Or is there something necessary in having Catholics, Orthodox, evangelicals, mainline Protestants and Pentecostals all gathered together to discuss?

7. Was George Leile the first missionary from America, or was it Adoniram and Ann Judson? Does it matter that Leile was not sent by other people? Is being sent by God sufficient, or do you need a church or missionary board as a sending body (both financially and in prayer) to truly be considered a missionary? Is it legitimate to be a "lone ranger" missionary? Though God is the initiator of mission, can mission be done without the church?

8. Vinoth Ramachandra controversially raised the question of how bad it is if people from the Global South end up migrating to the Global North to do all their ministry and scholarship. Should the fact that Daryl Balia and John Sentamu both did this be considered a Christian "brain drain" that needs to be rectified if the non-Western world is to truly thrive when it comes to the four selves: self-governing, self-propagating, self-sustaining and self-theologizing?

9. The words *conservative* and *liberal* have been so politicized today, but at their core they signify either keeping the status quo or changing it. Uncritically doing only one or the other is not realistic. How would you judge Edinburgh 2010's efforts at keeping some things the same while changing others? Did they pay proper tribute to the past while moving properly into the future?

10. The word *mission* is not in the Bible (though, to be fair, neither is *Trinity*). Do you feel that the word *mission* will soon become offensive language? Do you think it already is? Should we put a moratorium on the word? Is the word worth preserving despite having some negative baggage associated with it? (This is a question that some people are asking about the word *evangelical*.) Is there another word that we can use?

CAPE TOWN 2010 (AKA LAUSANNE III)

PERHAPS THE "JEWEL IN THE CROWN" of the 2010 conferences was Cape Town 2010, because it was not only the largest one (4,500 participants) and the longest one (ten days) but also the one that garnered the most worldwide publicity.[1] It also bore the name Lausanne, which could have been a liability or a strength depending on whether it relied on its historical memory or modern-day reputation. The Lausanne movement was strong in the 1970s and '80s but had largely fallen by the wayside in the 1990s and as such was nearly an unrecognizable name to the majority of millennials. The question was, after almost fifteen years of dormancy, could this sleeping giant be awakened? Or was it better to start anew with something fresh for a new century of missions?

Just after the turn of the twenty-first century, a strong push was made to revitalize Lausanne under the leadership of Doug Birdsall, its new executive chairman. This culminated in the grand spectacle that was Cape Town 2010, or the Third Lausanne Congress on World Evangelization. The World Evangelical Alliance (WEA) cosponsored this congress along with Lausanne, so it was truly a joint effort and as "ecumenical" as one could be while still being firmly evangelical—the ecumenism coming from its 4,200 delegates hearkening from 198 nations and hundreds of (Protestant) denominations.

---

[1]Some of this was drawn from Allen Yeh, "A Participant's Account of Lausanne III," *Evangelical Missions Quarterly* 47, no. 1 (January 2011).

The WEA alone claims to serve 600 million evangelicals worldwide, with 150 member organizations from 129 different nations. In addition, there were 350 observers from Roman Catholic, Orthodox and other traditions. This was diversity on a scale that none of the other conferences could claim, and caused *Christianity Today* to call this "The Most Diverse Gathering Ever."[2] Evangelicalism is often criticized for its lack of denominational unity, but Timothy George insisted: "Perhaps evangelical catholicity today is best seen in its worldwide missionary vision. Indeed, what ecumenism is to post-Vatican II Catholicism, world evangelization is for evangelicalism: not an added appendix, but an organic part of its life and work."[3]

Evangelicalism[4] is self-consciously *not* a denomination but a set of principles and commitments around which many different denominations can unite and agree.[5] The classic academic definition is given by David Bebbington, professor at the University of Stirling in Scotland. This fourfold descriptor, dubbed the "Bebbington Quadrilateral," includes biblicism, crucicentrism, conversionism and activism.[6] This framework allows for a wide variety of expressions of the Christian faith and thus reveals evangelicalism's genius: it is firm enough to have footholds of "trust" among its constituents, and yet it is flexible enough to contain many Christians of varied international and denominational backgrounds within its midst. This serves to preserve the integrity and distinct identity of its various factions while also allowing enough commonality to ensure the willingness of its people to enter into partnership with others of their kind. As such, "evangelical catholicity" is not an oxymoron. If the size of Cape Town 2010 was any indication, evangelicalism seems to be a greater unifying factor than

---

[2]John W. Kennedy, "The Most Diverse Gathering Ever," *Christianity Today*, September 29, 2010.

[3]Timothy George, "What I'd Like to Tell the Pope About the Church," *Christianity Today*, June 15, 1998, www.christianitytoday.com/ct/1998/june15/8t7041.html.

[4]See Karen Stiller, "The World Behind 'Evangelicals Around the World,'" *Lausanne Global Analysis* 4, no. 5 (September 2015), who discussed the disagreement over whether *evangelical* should be capitalized. The final consensus is that if it is a noun, yes; if it is an adjective, no.

[5]For more on this, see Allen Yeh, "The Road We Travel: A Loaded Word: A Brief History of Evangelicalism," in Allen Yeh et al., *Routes and Radishes: And Other Things to Talk About at the Evangelical Crossroads* (Grand Rapids: Zondervan, 2010), 13-32. This book was written by five young evangelicals who met at the Lausanne Younger Leaders' Gathering in Malaysia in 2006 and birthed out of conversations and ideas generated there, and it was coincidentally released for publication at the same time that Cape Town 2010 was happening.

[6]David Bebbington, *Evangelicalism in Modern Britain* (London: Unwin Hyman, 1989), 2-3.

many other attempts at ecumenism throughout history.[7] Even if evangelicalism does not survive into the future in this form or with this name, it is
this sort of thing that is necessary for the younger generation of Christians
who are increasingly post-denominational and distrust formal ecclesial
structures or who, at the very least, have no heart identification with any
particular modality.

FROM EDINBURGH 1910 TO CAPE TOWN 2010

Distinct from the other three 2010 conferences, Cape Town 2010 can trace
its inspiration back a century further, not to Edinburgh 1910 but to Cape
Town 1810. No, there was not a Cape Town 1810 conference, but it existed
in concept in the mind of William Carey, "the father of modern missions."
As was explained in chapter one, Carey wrote *An Enquiry*, the document
that launched the Great Century of Missions in 1792. Part one of this work
unpacked the Great Commission as binding on all Christians.[8] But part
five was a call for the establishment of mission societies.[9] After part one,
part five was perhaps the most important in serving to shape the way
mission was done during the Great Century. Mission societies existed not
only for the sake of collaboration among denominations but also for work
such as prayer, for social action such as abolition of the slave trade, and for
the raising of funds.

Though Carey may not have been "ecumenical" in the sense of embracing
Catholics and Orthodox, he was ecumenical among Protestants in working
for interdenominational cooperation. In 1806, Carey proposed that there be
a gathering of Christians to discuss working together for worldwide missions.

---

[7]The breadth of worldwide evangelicalism can be seen in Brian C. Stiller, Todd M. Johnson, Karen
Stiller and Mark Hutchinson, eds., *Evangelicals Around the World: A Global Handbook for the
21st Century* (Nashville: Thomas Nelson, 2015). Not only is evangelicalism the second biggest Christian community in the world at 600 million (after Roman Catholics at 1.2 billion but before the
WCC at 550 million, which includes Orthodox), it is one of the world's most diverse in terms of
culture, nationality and denomination.

[8]Though this may be surprising for evangelicals today, the Great Commission for most of Protestant
history was not regarded as a missionary passage. It was seen as a proof-text for the Trinity, however. The Protestant Reformers saw it as a command only binding on the original eleven disciples.
William Carey was the one who insisted that if the Great Commission was Jesus' command to his
disciples, then all Christians (who are also disciples) ought to have this command binding on them
as well!

[9]A. H. Oussoren, *William Carey, Especially His Missionary Principles* (Leiden: A. W. Sijthoff's Uit-
geversmaatschappi, 1945), 129-58.

He wrote to his theologian friend Andrew Fuller (his "rope holder") in England from Calcutta:

> The Cape of Good Hope is now in the hands of the English; should it continue so, would it be possible to have a general association of all denominations of Christians, from the four corners of the world, kept there once in about ten years? I earnestly recommend this plan, let the first meeting be in the Year 1810, or 1812 at furthest. I have no doubt but it would be attended with very important effects; we could understand one another better, and more entirely enter into one another's views by two hour conversation than by two or three years epistolary correspondence.[10]

This was dismissed by Fuller, among others, as unfeasible. Fuller objected:

> I consider this as one of bro'r Carey's pleasing dreams. Seriously I see no important object to be obtained by such a meeting, which might not be quite as well attained without it. And in a meeting of all denominations, there would be no unity, without which we had better stay at home.[11]

Although Carey's dream never came to fruition in his lifetime, one hundred years later the Edinburgh 1910 World Missionary Conference was convened in Scotland, and Carey's "pleasing dream" can be considered the catalyst for this event, though a century later. However, was it really? Latourette wrote: "There is no evidence that the memory of Carey's proposal survived in such fashion as to contribute to Edinburgh 1910. National and regional conferences of missionaries from 1854 onwards made more direct contributions to the ideas from which the Edinburgh Conference developed, and some of them did more to suggest patterns and methods of work than the series of conferences held in the West."[12]

---

[10] William Carey to Andrew Fuller, Calcutta, May 15, 1806, cited by Kenneth Scott Latourette, "Ecumenical Bearings of the Missionary Movement and the International Missionary Council," in *A History of the Ecumenical Movement*, vol. 1, ed. Ruth Rouse and Stephen C. Neill (Geneva: World Council of Churches, 1954), 355, n. 2.

[11] Andrew Fuller to William Ward, Serampore, December 2, 1806, cited by Ruth Rouse, "William Carey's 'Pleasing Dream,'" *International Review of Mission* 38 (April 1949): 181.

[12] Kenneth Scott Latourette, "Ecumenical Bearings of the Missionary Movement and the International Missionary Council," in *A History of the Ecumenical Movement 1517–1948*, vol. 1, ed. Ruth Rouse and Stephen C. Neill (Geneva: World Council of Churches, 1954), 355. Brian Stanley also makes this case in *The World Missionary Conference, Edinburgh 1910* (Grand Rapids: Eerdmans, 2009), 9.

If Carey's Cape Town 1810 suggestion did not lead to the establishment of Edinburgh 1910, did it at least lead to another bicentenary of his suggestion for an ecumenical missions conference? The Tokyo 2010 conference also purported to be the centenary of the Edinburgh 1910 World Missionary Conference. However, it can be argued that it also received its cue from Carey, albeit less directly. Winter, being a firm believer in the efficacy of sodalities over against modalities, thus invited mission societies and not denominational representatives in keeping with Carey's vision in *An Enquiry*.

Still, the one most directly in line of Carey's influence was obviously Cape Town 2010. It was inspired not only by the date—the bicentenary of Carey's suggestion—but the location as well. Finally Carey's "pleasing dream" was able to come alive, even if two hundred years after the fact.

The location served another purpose: it was the only one of the four 2010 conferences literally in the Global South,[13] so it was more reflective of the state of world Christianity.[14] Edinburgh 2010 tried to consciously address this by having its director be a Global South representative (who just happened to be from South Africa as well). While Tokyo 2010 could claim a certain cutting-edge radicalism by holding its conference in one of the most non-Christian places on earth, and while Edinburgh 2010 could follow the namesake of its predecessor Edinburgh 1910, Cape Town kept the spirit of Edinburgh 1910 by locating itself in the center of gravity of Christianity in the world in its time: namely, sub-Saharan Africa. Certainly there is something very admirable about that. However, while much was made of the location, in some sense Cape Town was a very unlikely candidate because it surely is *not* representative of the typical sub-Saharan African nation, at least culturally. In almost every way of measuring it, South Africa (and especially Cape Town) is thoroughly European, similar to how Argentina is European in nature but located within to Latin America.[15] But perhaps the symbolism

---

[13]A literal reading of "Global South" would be anything south of the equator—therefore Costa Rica, China, India, and so on, do not qualify geographically, though they qualify culturally.

[14]The other prime location under consideration for this Congress was Beijing, China, but it was deemed to be too difficult to organize a conference of this size with such governmental and visa restrictions.

[15]It is a bit like claiming that Pope Francis is the first Latin American Pope. While that may be true by his birth, his parents are actually Italian and his birth name bears that out: Jorge Mario Bergoglio. He does not have any indigenous Latin American blood in him; he is ethnically white Euro-

of the place, more than the functional reality, made it an ideal location. And, unlike northern Africa, which is steeped in Islam, it still is representative of the Global South in the sense that it is part of the historically recent world Christian rise.

All this is not to suggest that Cape Town 2010 only looked to 1810 and not to 1910. William Carey's 1810 suggestion can claim to have been the first seed of an idea planted, but it never saw the light of day. Certainly Edinburgh 1910 was the predecessor that all the 2010 conferences followed, and Cape Town 2010 was no exception. However, Kenneth Ross of Edinburgh said that Lausanne has more claim on Edinburgh 1910 than may at first be evident, because it is the spiritual progeny:

> Though in strictly institutional terms it is the World Council of Churches that is the heir of Edinburgh 1910, in terms of promoting the agenda of world evangelization, the Lausanne movement might be seen as standing in direct continuity. . . . As Andrew Walls suggests: "Both 'ecumenical' and 'evangelical' today have their roots in Edinburgh 1910. If each will go back to the pit whence both were dug, each may understand both themselves and the other better."[16]

Lausanne and the WCC are both needed as balancing counterparts, much as John Stott saw missions as comprising both evangelism and social justice. And by the same token, both Edinburgh 2010 and Cape Town 2010 were needed, for missions is most healthy when balanced by ecumenism and evangelicalism.

THE HISTORY OF CAPE TOWN 2010

It may seem logical to start telling the story of the Lausanne movement from the first International Congress on World Evangelization (AKA Lausanne I) in Lausanne, Switzerland, in 1974, from which it earned its name. However, the roots of Lausanne can be traced further back than that. In 1966 (October 26–November 1), Billy Graham convened a conference in Berlin called the

---

pean. Yet he was born and raised in Argentina so he is Argentine in his nationality and outlook, even if he is bicultural. In this way the Vatican can have its cake and eat it too (have a Global South representative who is still the closest thing to Italian); and so could Lausanne (have a Global South location that is still the closest thing to being European).

[16]Kenneth R. Ross, "The Centenary of Edinburgh 1910: Its Possibilities," *International Bulletin of Missionary Research* 30, no. 4 (October 2006): 178.

World Congress on Evangelism[17] under the theme of "One Race, One Gospel, One Task," with twelve hundred participants. Though in historical hindsight this ended up serving as more of a prequel to Lausanne I, Graham actually intended Berlin to be the first missions congress in a series, and for Lausanne to be the second. Why did Berlin never achieve the significance of its successor, despite being the first of its kind (a truly international gathering of evangelical missions leaders in the spirit of Edinburgh 1910)? Unlike Edinburgh 1910 overtaking its predecessors (London 1888 and New York 1900) in historical memory because of its continuation committee, Berlin 1966 never achieved the fame of Lausanne 1974 because it did not produce a major document.

Lausanne never was intended to be a worldwide movement. Its initial conception was just a one-time congress held July 16–25, 1974, at the Palais de Beaulieu in the city of Lausanne with the theme "Let the Earth Hear His Voice!" But what a groundbreaking congress it was! It was the most international gathering of missionary leaders up to that point in time. *Time Magazine* called it "a formidable forum, possibly the widest-ranging meeting of Christians ever held."[18] Though world Christianity was not yet a reality in 1974 as we know it today, nevertheless the scope of 2,473 leaders from 150 nations and 135 denominations[19] was unprecedented. V. S. Azariah's cry of "Give us friends!" seemed to ring true at Lausanne I. The efforts were spearheaded by Billy Graham and John Stott, in some ways reflective of the dynamic pair (also an American and a Briton, coincidentally) who led Edinburgh 1910: John R. Mott and J. H. Oldham. In both cases the American was the public face of the conference, but the Brit was the architectural genius behind it all.[20] Lausanne I certainly had its share of groundbreaking speeches and moments, and two of the most notable were Ralph Winter redefining *panta ta ethnē* ("all the nations") as ethnolinguistic groups instead

---

[17]Carl F. H. Henry, "Good News for a World in Need," *Christianity Today*, October 1966, 34.

[18]"Religion: A Challenge from Evangelicals," *Time* 104, no. 6 (August 1974).

[19]Al Tizon, *Transformation After Lausanne: Radical Evangelical Mission in Global-Local Perspective* (Eugene, OR: Wipf & Stock, 2008), 37.

[20]Alister Chapman, *Godly Ambition: John Stott and the Evangelical Movement* (Oxford: Oxford University Press, 2012), 50: "[Billy] Graham brought him [Stott] to . . . Berlin and Lausanne to give keynote addresses at major global conferences on evangelism. Graham was not exactly a patron, but as in the geopolitical special relationship between America and Britain it was clear who was the senior partner."

of political nations[21] and C. René Padilla trying to redress the North American "Great Reversal" by advocating for *misión integral* (holistic mission).[22] But the most influential part of Lausanne I was not actually any talk from the congress itself, but the document *The Lausanne Covenant*, which has become a de facto definition for what it means to be evangelical today. It was not intended to serve that purpose—and yet, because missions is the mother of ecumenism, and Lausanne was a missions conference, *The Lausanne Covenant* provided that overarching unifying framework that ties evangelicals together and in doing so actually ended up being *the* modern-day creed for evangelicals, if there is such a thing. Many evangelical missions organizations require affirmation of *The Lausanne Covenant* for anyone wanting to come on board with the organization.

The second International Congress on World Evangelization (Lausanne II) was held in Manila, The Philippines, July 11–20, 1989,[23] with the theme "Proclaim Christ Until He Comes: Calling the Whole Church to Take the Whole Gospel to the Whole World." This congress was even more international than the first: with 4,300 people from 173 countries, it seemed that this gathering was full of potential. The world had changed drastically since 1974: the Tiananmen Square protests in China had just happened a month prior (June 4, 1989), the iron curtain was on the brink of collapsing (August–November 1989), Europe was becoming increasingly secular and postmodern, global Pentecostalism was on the rise, and the twentieth-century missiological great Lesslie Newbigin had just penned his landmark *The Gospel in a Pluralist Society* in response. Unfortunately, Lausanne II did not have the impact of its predecessor. Even the document that came out of the congress, *The Manila Manifesto*, is rarely cited or used outside of Lausanne circles. One of the criticisms is that, despite the changing times, there was not much in the 1989 congress notably different from what was said in 1974. The theme was a phrase out of the *Lausanne Covenant*, and the emphasis of

---

[21]Ralph Winter, "The Highest Priority: Cross-Cultural Evangelism," in *Let the Earth Hear His Voice*, ed. J. D. Douglas (Minneapolis: World Wide Publications, 1975), 213-41.

[22]René Padilla, "Evangelism and the World," in Douglas, *Let the Earth Hear His Voice*, 116-46.

[23]It was not until March 24–28, 2015, when the Lausanne Global Diaspora Forum was held in Pasig City, The Philippines, that the Lausanne movement returned to metro Manila to hold an official worldwide gathering.

the congress was a deepening understanding of *misión integral*. This is not to say that there were no innovations that came from Lausanne II. The famous idea of the 10/40 Window[24] was first coined at that congress by Luis Bush, who initially called it the "resistant window."

Unfortunately, one of the most notable things to come out of Lausanne II was actually a negative consequence: a split within the ranks. Thomas Wang, the international director of Lausanne, came with his AD2000 and Beyond agenda, desiring to see the completion of the evangelistic task in the world by the year 2000 as the main focus of Lausanne II.[25] There were some who did not want to follow this agenda, so the Lausanne movement split. It also lost momentum due to financial debt and the loss of interest of its founder Billy Graham,[26] and essentially went into a coma for a decade and a half—the same length of time between Lausanne I and II. In many ways, this irony is reminiscent of Edinburgh 1910—it *ended* the Great Century of Missions rather than continuing it or revitalizing it. Similarly, Lausanne II, for all its energy, ended up being almost a death knell to a concerted worldwide missionary movement.

This is not to suggest that the Lausanne movement wholly died or that only the three international congresses mattered. Lausanne also has sponsored, and continues to sponsor, other smaller gatherings, such as the Younger Leaders Gathering,[27] the Researchers' Conference[28] and the Theology Working Group, among others.[29]

At the 2004 Forum for World Evangelization in Pattaya, Thailand, the Lausanne movement took on new life. Faced with the question of "Does the world still need Lausanne?" the president of Asian Access at the time,[30]

---

[24]The continents outside the Americas from 10 degrees latitude north to 40 degrees latitude north that comprise the most resistant areas of the world to Christianity, in large part because of its demographic containing most of the other major religions in the world: Islam, Hinduism, Buddhism, Jainism, Sikhism, Baháʼí, etc. This area is basically north Africa, the Middle East, and South and Southeast Asia, with parts of China included.

[25]Chapman, *Godly Ambition*, 149.

[26]Ibid. Graham's interest was more in on-the-ground evangelism rather than convening missionary leaders for ecumenical unity.

[27]Singapore 1987; Malaysia 2006; Indonesia 2016.

[28]Holland 1987; UK 1996; Thailand 2001; Cyprus 2005; Australia 2008; Brazil 2011; Malaysia 2015.

[29]For a complete flowchart of all Lausanne gatherings, see https://www.lausanne.org/wp-content/uploads/2009/12/Flowchart_of_Lausanne_Gatherings.pdf.

[30]Due to the ever-increasing workload of shouldering two leadership positions, Birdsall chose to give up the presidency of Asian Access in order to fully devote himself to the Lausanne movement. He was succeeded by Joseph Handley Jr.

Douglas Birdsall, was elected as the new executive chair of the Lausanne movement. A relative unknown without the international recognition of Billy Graham or John Stott, he nonetheless shouldered the responsibility as Lausanne's fifth executive chairman.[31] Not only did he revitalize Lausanne and restore it as a household name among missionaries worldwide, but his work culminated in historic events such as the Consultation on Global Theological Education held at Gordon-Conwell Seminary near Boston from May 29 to June 1, 2012, where sixty-three seminary presidents and senior academics from more than thirty countries met to talk about the future of theological education. A follow-up Consultation on Global Theological Education took place June 2–6, 2014, in São Paulo, Brazil, thus ensuring that the Majority World was fairly represented along with the West. But his most notable achievement was organizing and convening the third International Congress on World Evangelization, also known as Lausanne III, or Cape Town 2010. Birdsall spent the next decade[32] spreading the good news of the "Spirit of Lausanne,"[33] where he provided strong leadership and also gave talks in which he made the movement memorable: not only was it a tongue-twister to say the name (he joked it was *not* pronounced "lasagna" or "lamaze"!), but he cleared up the confusion by differentiating Lausanne as an alliterative series of *C*'s: it is known as a city, a congress and a continuing movement,[34] all of which were relevant to the movement. Lausanne once again became a relevant piece of the worldwide missions movement, and Cape Town 2010 became *the* landmark missions conference of 2010, if not the twenty-first century.

CAPE TOWN 2010: CONFERENCE PROCEEDINGS

Lausanne III was held at the Cape Town International Convention Centre, and the timing, October 18–24, 2010, was no accident. It was intentionally planned to follow the (June 11–July 11) 2010 World Cup, the first World Cup held in

---

[31]The previous chairmen were John Stott, Leighton Ford, Fergus MacDonald and Paul Cedar.

[32]Until he retired from the chair position and became the new president and CEO of the American Bible Society in 2013.

[33]This phrase was coined at Lausanne I in 1974, and it embodied "dedication to prayer, and to the study of God's Word; a desire to work in unity and partnership; a clear reflection of the hope of the gospel; and humility in service." See Julia E. M. Cameron, ed., *Christ Our Reconciler: Gospel-Church-World* (Downers Grove, IL: InterVarsity Press, 2012), 10.

[34]One might add that it is also a covenant.

Africa.[35] The main reason for this was to ride its infrastructural coattails: the city, in particular the Convention Centre, was outfitted with the upgrades that typically accompany a major global gathering: improved public transportation and hotels, and the latest communication technology. A joint venture with the World Evangelical Alliance, it had a double pool of people to draw from, and it showed in its diversity. Unlike Tokyo 2010, whose attendees were limited to sodalities who chose their own representatives, or Edinburgh 2010, which wanted denominational representation, anybody who was an evangelical missions leader was eligible to apply to be part of Cape Town 2010, and with over four thousand spots available they were able to generate diversity across nationality, race, denomination, age and vocation—there were pastors, missionaries, theologians, missions executives, students, businesspeople, media representatives and people from a wide cross-section of the church. They were able to generate international youth participation by having them there as stewards helping out and serving to facilitate the logistics of the smooth running of the congress in exchange for reduced-cost attendance at this landmark event. Who knows whether some of these four hundred young people will be the future leaders of Lausanne, having been spurred on by the memory of having been physically present—this may have as profound an effect, if not more, than having them attend a Younger Leaders Gathering.

Cape Town 2010 was self-consciously a congress, not a conference. This meant that the people who attended were not simply audience members witnessing what went on, but they theoretically had a voice and a vote in the proceedings. This does not mean, however, that everyone contributed. First of all, *The Cape Town Commitment* (*CTC*)—the document that came out of Cape Town 2010—was already half-written when the congress began. Every delegate received a copy of the first half of the *CTC*.[36] One of the major purposes of Lausanne III was to have the delegates read it and contribute to the formation of the second half of *The Cape Town Commitment*. With over

---

[35]It would have been nice to say that it was the first major global sports event held in the Global South, but that is not true, because the Sydney Olympics in 2000 was the first to hold that honor, even if Australia is culturally Western. Nor was it the first major global sports event held in the Two-Thirds World, because the Mexico City Olympics of 1968 and the Japan and South Korea World Cup of 2002 were the first of their kind in this regard.

[36]The phrase "the Whole Church taking the Whole Gospel to the Whole World" actually does not come from Lausanne! It was coined in the document produced at the first World Council of Churches CWME (Conference on World Mission and Evangelism) in 1963, "Witness in Six Continents."

four thousand people in attendance, however, hearing everybody's voice was a bit of a tall order. In order to facilitate this, everybody sat in preset table groups (cleverly marketed as taking place under the shadow of Table Mountain) of six people with a leader; this way everybody had the opportunity to be a presenter. The membership of each table was intentionally composed of diverse representation from as many continents as possible. While this idea was great, unfortunately due to the necessity of conversing with people of the same language, most Latinos ended up with other Spanish speakers and were not able to be in as diverse table groups as the English speakers, for example.[37]

All this being said, there were still plenary sessions that acted as the "pillars" of the congress. Over the course of seven days (October 17–24, 2010, with Thursday the 21st being a free day), each day had two morning plenary sessions and an evening plenary. The early morning plenaries were led by representatives from six different continents. In chronological order, they were: Asia (Ajith Fernando of Sri Lanka); Latin America (Ruth Padilla De-Borst from Costa Rica); North America (John Piper from the US); Europe (Vaughan Roberts from the UK); Africa (Calisto Odede from Kenya); and the Middle East (Ramez and Rebecca Atallah from Egypt). Like good evangelicals, the first speakers each day were Bible expositors, asked to unpack the six chapters of Ephesians, which served as the theme of the congress.[38] The primacy of the Bible remains one of the hallmarks of evangelicals.

The later morning plenaries were dedicated to various topics, namely, making the case for the truth of Christ in a pluralistic, globalized world; building the peace of Christ in our divided and broken world; bearing witness to the love of Christ with people of other faiths; discerning the will of Christ for twenty-first century world evangelization; calling the church of Christ back to humility, integrity and simplicity; and partnering in the body of Christ toward a new global equilibrium. This shows another

---

[37]I was a table leader and we had one Latino (Uruguayan) at our table who wanted to be with us, a more diverse group (an Australian man, a Nigerian woman, a British woman, a South African man, and myself, an Asian American), than in an all-Latino group. However, though his English was decent, he still struggled to keep up with the conversation, so there was a trade-off.

[38]For a transcript of all the plenary addresses at Cape Town 2010, see Cameron, *Christ Our Reconciler*. A good companion volume to this is Lars Dahle, Margunn Serigstad Dahle and Knud Jørgensen, eds., *The Lausanne Movement: A Range of Perspectives* (Oxford: Regnum, 2014).

hallmark of evangelicals, namely Christocentrism. These sessions were primarily dedicated to evangelization of other worldviews.

The evening plenaries were focused on contemporary missiological issues, showing why a third Lausanne Congress was needed in a world post-Lausanne II. The topics addressed were

- China (Suffering Church, Religious Freedom)

- Broken World (Environment, Human Trafficking)

- Megacities and Diaspora

- Children and Young People, and Next Generations

- Responding to God in Worship and Prayer

Each evening also had a geographical focus: Asia, Middle East, Latin America, Africa and the Western world.

Though the plenary speakers were an indication that Cape Town 2010 had excellent non-Western representation, looking at the origin of the plenary speakers told another story: the congress was heavily Anglophone on stage. Almost all the Asian speakers were from former British colonies in South and Southeast Asia rather than East Asia, which is largely non-English-speaking (despite the prevalence of Koreans in world Christianity, they were largely missing from the platform), and the same was true of the African speakers, who were drawn from Anglophone Africa rather than Francophone.[39] Padilla DeBorst was educated in the United States and was born of an American mother. Even the management team of Cape Town 2010 included executive chairman Doug Birdsall and congress director Blair Carlson, both Americans; LCWE international director Lindsay Brown from Wales; and chair of the program committee Ramez Atallah of Egypt, program director Grace Mathews of India and chair of the participant selection committee Hwa Yung of Malaysia, all of whom were educated in the West. In addition, the closing ceremony, described below, was a Church of England liturgy. Perhaps this is just a matter of having patience

---

[39]One of the few exceptions was Daniel Bourdanné, general secretary of the International Fellowship of Evangelical Students (parent organization of InterVarsity Christian Fellowship, which runs the Urbana missions conference) and a Francophone African.

as the Lausanne movement slowly matures, as it grows into the realities of the global church.

In some ways, the Anglophone nature of missionary movements is not surprising, given how powerful American-British collaboration has been throughout history and politics. John Mott and J. H. Oldham were a combined force to be reckoned with at Edinburgh 1910, as were Billy Graham and John Stott at Lausanne I. (We see this geographical partnership yet again, going back two centuries to the origins of the modern missionary movement with the Baptist pioneers Adoniram Judson and William Carey.)[40] The American-Anglo face of Lausanne III was American Doug Birdsall and Irishman Christopher J. H. Wright, who was chair of the Theology Working Group. Christians can sometimes be cutting-edge in terms of diversity leadership (e.g., Martin Luther King Jr.) and sometimes severely lagging behind the world (the Southern Baptist Convention only elected its first black president in 2012, Fred Luter, whereas the US did it in 2008). Doug Birdsall's successor as Lausanne's CEO[41] in 2013 was Michael Oh,[42] president and founder of Christ Bible Institute, a seminary in Nagoya, Japan. Though he does represent the Two-Thirds World with his home base in Japan, and he is ethnically Korean and a younger leader (having been elected at age forty-one), he is actually American by birth, nationality and education.[43] Will there come a day when the Two-Thirds World is represented by someone who is not of European ethnic background, who is not educated in the West,[44]

---

[40]See Allen Yeh and Chris Chun, eds., *Expect Great Things, Attempt Great Things: William Carey and Adoniram Judson, Missionary Pioneers* (Eugene, OR: Wipf & Stock, 2013).

[41]They changed the title from executive chair to chief executive officer during Birdsall's tenure.

[42]I first met Michael at the Lausanne 2004 Forum in Pattaya, Thailand, the first Lausanne event for both of us and where Doug Birdsall was installed as executive chair of Lausanne. We got to know each other further through subsequent Lausanne gatherings, most notably the Younger Leaders' Gathering at Port Dickson, Malaysia, in 2006.

[43]Still, it is worth noting that Michael Oh was only the first of several younger Asian Americans to helm a major missions organization. In 2016, Sharon Koh became the executive director of American Baptist International Ministries (the oldest denominational missions board in the United States), and Tom Lin, former director of the Urbana missions conference, became the president of InterVarsity Christian Fellowship USA. This is quite a remarkable trend of this demographic occupying positions that had never been held by a non-white person before.

[44]This was John Stott's strategy with his Langham scholarships: they are offered to bright Two-Thirds World Christian leaders to receive an all-expenses-paid PhD at the top research universities in the West. The only stipulation is that they *must* return to their home country upon completion of their doctorate in order to serve the church and academy in their nation of origin and to prevent "brain

who is not born and raised in the West?[45] That would be fully ground-breaking in terms of true Global South leadership in the church. The secular world has already seen people such as Nelson Mandela be able to succeed without affiliation with the West.

Perhaps another way to view Birdsall and Wright (or Graham and Stott) is not in terms of their national origins but in terms of their roles: a partnership between an evangelist and a theologian. This has biblical precedent, as Paul and Apollos formed this kind of team: the missionary/evangelist plants the seed, and the pastor/theologian waters the flock—but ultimately God makes it grow (1 Cor 3:5-9). Birdsall and Wright made this very point at a scholars' reception for professors and academics at Cape Town 2010. Birdsall, a career missionary of twenty years in Japan, said that a missionary/evangelist brings the gospel *to* a people, while a theologian brings the gospel *through* a people, and both are needed because theology is ultimately missional. Carey also had his theologian friend Andrew Fuller support him, even if it was Fuller himself who dismissed Carey's "pleasing dream" of Cape Town 1810. Diversity in roles (1 Cor 12) is just as important as diversity in nationality or race.

Was there a hero at Lausanne III? Unfortunately neither Graham nor Stott, the heroes of Lausanne I, could attend due to health reasons,[46] so the torch was passed on to a new generation of heroes—however, none that were as easily identifiable, as nobody on the Cape Town 2010 management team is a household name. The most recognizable names actually came from a few of the plenary speakers (such as John Piper) from Graham's and Stott's generation, most notably from Latin America (René Padilla and Samuel Escobar).[47] But the hero is not simply the person who organizes the conference; it could be someone who made a notable address or history-changing speech, like Azariah at Edinburgh 1910, or Winter at Lausanne 1974. Interestingly, probably the most memorable

---

drain." Essentially, Stott was attempting to help the Two-Thirds World churches with the fourth self: self-theologizing.

[45]As mentioned above, even Pope Francis fails two of these three criteria, being ethnically Italian as well as educated in Europe. But so do people like Aung San Suu Kyi and Mahatma Gandhi, who were both educated in England.

[46]Stott died a year later, on July 27, 2011.

[47]See chapter seven for a review of the Latin American evangelical heroes.

speech of the entire Congress was not given by a celebrity speaker like Joni Eareckson Tada or Rick Warren,[48] but rather was made by a young girl from North Korea named Gyeong Ju Son.[49] Her testimony[50] about her escape from that country and her continuing love for her land garnered a rousing standing ovation from the entire congress. Two other moving presentations were about Islam: a heart-wrenching but hopeful talk on the third day by American Elizabeth "Libby" Little, who spoke on the recent martyrdom of her husband, Tom, in Afghanistan,[51] and a radical, eye-opening address on the penultimate day by Turk Ziya Meral[52] on an appropriate way for Christians to interact with Muslims.[53] Perhaps this is a good sign that youth and women and the Two-Thirds World are not overlooked in the future of the missional world. Also, it is significant that, though much has changed since Lausanne I and II, not much has changed: communism and Islam are still two of the biggest challenges to Christianity today.

The afternoons were dedicated to twenty-four multiplexes—small breakout sessions of various topics such as how to evangelize oral learners, how to use technology to evangelize, how to have gender partnership for mission, how to minister to the poor, how to minister to children, and how to raise up the next generation of leaders. The multiplexes, combined with the plenary sessions, identified over thirty critical missiological issues that Lausanne wanted to address in the next decade.

There were clear nods to Urbana, the triennial student missions conference in North America sponsored by InterVarsity Christian Fellowship,

---

[48]The former led the penultimate evening plenary, while the latter was scheduled to speak on the later morning plenary of the second day but due to his schedule was unable to make it.

[49]She also goes by her Anglicized name, Sarah. At Cape Town 2010, she was at the end of high school, and she eventually ended up going to Biola University, which is the university where I teach.

[50]"Testimony: 'I Know the Gospel Is True,'" in Cameron *Christ Our Reconciler*, 17-19.

[51]It is interesting, or ironic, that Libby Little—whose husband experienced present physical suffering—spoke right after John Piper, who emphasized eternal soul suffering.

[52]Meral pointed out three failures of evangelicals in mission: (1) understanding the future of the church in the Islamic world; for example, there is a myth that the church always grows under persecution—but in reality, many churches in the Islamic world are being wiped out completely; (2) perpetuating twentieth-century modernist missions such as tracts, Bible smuggling and faith support-raising, which are no longer effective today; (3) understanding the Islamic world correctly—for example, the Western world gets carried away by security and diplomatic issues.

[53]Neither of these presentations was recorded or published in the *Christ Our Reconciler* book for security reasons.

which draws eighteen thousand university students each time. The drama team was from Urbana, and several of the speakers have also made appearances on the Urbana platform, such as Brenda Salter McNeill, Ruth Padilla DeBorst, Calisto Odede and Ramez Attalah.

Though there was hardly any explicit reference to the other 2010 conferences and only a few mentions of Edinburgh 1910,[54] the fact that the general secretary of the World Council of Churches, Olav Fykse Tveit, came to bring greetings during the opening ceremony was a sign of ecumenical friendship in both directions. This was followed by a parade of flags and a "Welcome to Africa" song, to remind the congress of the land and people who are serving as the host. Two presentations about Lausanne I and Lausanne II were next to serve as a reminder of the movement's history, the latter presented by Bishop Efraim Tendero, a Filipino who proudly described the 1989 congress that occurred in his native land and who would later succeed Geoff Tunnicliffe as the general secretary of the World Evangelical Alliance in 2015. It is heartening to see both Lausanne's and the WEA's leadership shift to the Two-Thirds World with the election of Michael Oh and Bishop Ef (as he is affectionately known), respectively.

EVANGELICAL PARTNERSHIP

Cape Town 2010 was so large and had such a sweeping scope that it was difficult to narrow down any particular foci of the congress. Yet, if there was one clearly identifiable marker, it was evangelical partnership, which also happened to be the theme of the final plenary session. The most important of the four stated goals of Cape Town 2010 (the other three being truth about the uniqueness of Christ, identification of key missiological issues and the emergence of new initiatives in mission) was the network of friendships and alliances that emerged. This makes sense, because Lausanne is not a missions organization; it is a missionary *movement* and thus functions as an umbrella that links evangelical missions organizations. At Cape Town, the world's evangelical missional leaders connected as never before. If missions is the mother of ecumenism, it was surely shown by evangelical mission leading to evangelical unity.

---

[54]Actually, what is most surprising is that Cape Town 2010 never mentioned William Carey's suggestion for a Cape Town *1810* conference.

In this unity there was a solidarity to really get things done. Strong identity lends itself to concerted action. Simon Sinek, in one of the most-watched TED Talks, called "How Great Leaders Inspire Action,"[55] posited that effectiveness has much more to do with *why* a person or organization does something than simply *what* they do. Those whose foundation is the *why* become global leaders, whereas those who start with the *what* do not get as far. Cape Town 2010 really knew *who* they were as a global body of evangelicals, which meant they also knew the *why*—evangelicals care about the *euangellion* (the gospel). Yes, there were sessions dedicated to evangelism and the poor and human trafficking, but reconciliation was the emphasis that resonated the most. Though the Bible studies each morning were focused on the book of Ephesians, the theme of the conference came from 2 Corinthians 5:19, "God in Christ, reconciling the world to himself." This is perhaps *the* best definition of mission in the Bible, with the acknowledgment of the *missio Dei* (God as prime mover) and taking the broken and restoring it to wholeness, whether that be the physical body or the spirit or institutional structures or relationships. This makes for an interesting contrast with Edinburgh 1910 and Tokyo 2010: the former had evangelization as its theme, the latter had discipleship, and Cape Town 2010 had reconciliation.

Two profound examples of reconciliation happened, one on stage and one off stage, neither of which were upstaged by the Westerners as at Tokyo 2010.[56] First there were Palestinian Shadia Qubti and Israeli Dan Sered, who gave a powerful testimony about reconciliation in a plenary session.[57] Second, Brazilian-African reconciliation happened behind the scenes when the Brazilian delegation presented the following statement to the African delegation on October 24, 2010:

> After the discovery and for almost 400 years the Brazil colony and the independent Brazil relied on slave labor for the formation of plantations, for

---

[55]See www.ted.com/talks/simon_sinek_how_great_leaders_inspire_action.

[56]As described in chapter three, the racial reconciliation should have been between the Japanese and the Koreans, but instead it turned into an American-Japanese display. Not that the latter was wrong or unnecessary, but sometimes Westerners do not need to be the saviors of the world, and part of Two-Thirds World churches coming into their own is that they should be allowed to work things out without Western assistance.

[57]Shadia Qubti and Dan Sered, "Testimony: Palestinian-Jewish Reconciliation," in Cameron, *Christ Our Reconciler*, 53-54.

digging our mines, for building our houses, our cities and our nation. So we have committed the sin of kidnapping people, destroying families and villages; we have left behind plenty of orphans, destroyed homes, villages and harmed deeply your nations.

We have committed the sin of assassination, of treating human beings made in the image of God as beasts, imposing on your people moral, psychological and physical violence, abuse and suppression—and sub-human conditions of life. We have committed the sin of destroying whenever possible their national, ethnic and familiar identity.[58]

The result was repentance by the Brazilians, forgiveness by the Africans, reconciliation between the two groups and the ability to move forward in the power of the Holy Spirit. If this had been seen by all congress participants, I am sure it would have elicited the same type of response as to North Korean Gyeong Ju Son's testimony and have been stamped indelibly in the minds of the people as one of the highlights of Cape Town 2010.

The congress had good representation of different cross-sections of people, despite all being from the evangelical stream of Christianity (Pentecostals were considered evangelicals at Cape Town 2010). Of the delegates, 47 percent were under age fifty,[59] and fully one-third were women. However, the issue of women—not their presence but their roles—was one that caused some consternation. One of the difficulties of gathering a worldwide body of Christians, even ones who are as unified as evangelicals, is the diversity within them. Some debatable issues do not need to be addressed because they are the purview of the local church, such as whether to do paedobaptism or credobaptism, or one's view on eschatology. Some, however, cannot be avoided: namely complementarianism and egalitarianism. Strictly on the level of whether or not women can preach and/or exposit the Bible, the fact that a woman (Ruth Padilla DeBorst) and a well-known complementarian (John Piper) shared the stage proved to be a logistical and theological difficulty. The Lausanne Movement, in wanting to honor points of view of evangelicals from

---

[58]Valdir Steuernagel, "A Latin-American Evangelical Perspective on the Cape Town Congress," in Dahle, Dahle and Jørgensen, *Lausanne Movement*, 317.

[59]This may not seem like a lot, but missiological circles tend to run older, as usually over twenty years on the mission field is required, plus a doctoral degree, in order to ascend to leadership.

around the world, also had to make a decision on this, because either women were allowed to preach on stage or they were not. There was no way to *not* decide on this issue. Lausanne sided with egalitarianism, mostly by showing it, but at one point even verbally acknowledging it from the platform with Chad and Leslie Segraves's presentation "Partnership—Men and Women" during the second plenary session on the last day, as well as in one of the multiplex sessions, "Men and Women: A Powerful Team for the Completion of the Great Commission." This issue is further complicated by the fact that the terms *complementarian* and *egalitarian* are not familiar in a variety of global contexts because of how they reflect certain Western theological perspectives, and also because many non-Western contexts are heavily patriarchal and traditional in gender roles. Culturally these would fall more in line with complementarianism,[60] yet at the same time many are more accepting of female preachers than some Westerners are, especially in places with more Pentecostal presence, which is the fastest-growing form of Christianity around the world today.[61] So, despite the vast amount of evangelical agreement on core issues, diverse issues still remain—but thus is the nature of the church: unity in diversity (cf. Rev 7:9).

John Piper was also at the center of another, more public form of controversy at the congress, this time on the subject of holistic mission. Paul Eshleman, on day four of the congress, issued the same call to frontier missions that he did at Tokyo 2010, calling for everyone to adopt an unreached people group. This had its own share of controversy, as mentioned in chapter

[60]My friend Kevin Johnson, a missionary teammate with me in Mexico a few years ago and now teaching at the Biblical Seminary of Colombia, wrote in his blog (www.kevinuwm.blogspot.com, "Gender Equality Conference," July 13, 2014): "One of the primary reasons for the significant presence of female seminarians, however, has to do with the prevalence of Pentecostalism in Colombia. Some significant Pentecostal denominations, like the Foursquare Church, were started by women (i.e. Aimee Semple McPherson), and most Pentecostals have recognized female preachers since their beginnings. For example, I know one male seminarian here whose mother was a pastor who founded a church in the rural outskirts of Medellín and a man who works in the extension office whose grandmother was a pastor. For most egalitarians here, their viewpoint has nothing to do with theologically 'liberal' or 'feminist' ideology and everything to do with churches that are committed to the Great Commission and have been open to providing opportunities for women to be part of that at every level. Whether one agrees with their exegesis or not, I think that's worthy of respect."
[61]For the biblical injunction about how to handle theological differences between evangelicals on essential vs. nonessential issues, see Allen Yeh, "The Road Ahead: Essentials vs. Nonessentials," in Yeh et al., *Routes and Radishes*, 40-41.

three, but Piper's comments stirred an even greater reaction. In his plenary address on the morning of day three, he said:

> I draw out this implication of the cross [everlasting suffering in hell] to hold together two truths that are often felt to be at odds with each other, but which belong together: (i) that when the gospel takes root in our souls, it impels us out, towards the alleviation of all unjust suffering in this age. That's what love does! (ii) that when the gospel takes root in our souls, it awakens us to the horrible reality of eternal suffering in hell, under the wrath of a just and omnipotent God. And it impels us to rescue the perishing, and to warn people to flee from the wrath to come (1 Thessalonians 1:10). I plead with you. Don't choose between these two truths. Embrace them both. It doesn't mean that we will all spend our time in the same way. God forbid. But it means we will let the Bible define reality and define love. Could Lausanne say—could the evangelical church say—*we Christians care about all suffering, especially eternal suffering*? I hope we can say that. But if we feel resistant to saying, "especially eternal suffering," or resistant to saying, "We care about all suffering in this age," then either we have a defective view of hell or a defective heart. I pray that Lausanne would have neither.[62]

Was Piper drawing evangelicals back to the "Great Reversal"? Was he going against the spirit of *The Lausanne Covenant*, which advocated holistic mission? John Stott, almost a decade after Lausanne I, made a famous analogy in the Lausanne Occasional Paper 21, drafted in 1982 at the International Consultation on the Relationship Between Evangelism and Social Responsibility in Grand Rapids, Michigan. He wrote:

> Social activity not only follows evangelism as its consequence and aim, and precedes it as its bridge, but also accompanies it as its *partner*. They are like the two blades of a pair of scissors or the two wings of a bird. This partnership is clearly seen in the public ministry of Jesus, who not only preached the gospel but fed the hungry and healed the sick.[63]

---

[62]John Piper, "Ephesians 3:1-21," in Cameron, *Christ Our Reconciler*, 83-84.

[63]"Evangelism and Social Justice: An Evangelical Commitment," Lausanne Occasional Paper 21 (1982), www.lausanne.org/grand-rapids-1982/lop-21.html. C. S. Lewis makes a similar statement in *Mere Christianity* (New York: HarperCollins, 1952), 148: "Christians have often disputed as to whether what leads the Christian home is good actions, or Faith in Christ. I have no right to speak on such a difficult question, but it does seem to me like asking which blade in a pair of scissors is most necessary."

Can one wing be higher than another or one blade stronger than another? It must be said that some Two-Thirds World theologians still feel that Stott's analogy is too dichotomistic and that Jesus' mission was not as black and white as that (cf. Lk 4:18-19, where proclamation clearly is not just verbal). And some Western evangelicals still take Piper's side[64] and elevate the spiritual over the physical.

Regardless of the controversies, Cape Town 2010 still had much more strength in its bonds than weak links. The identity of evangelicalism served the Congress well for its purposes of global mission.

TECHNOLOGY

As mentioned above, global cutting-edge technologies were one of the main hallmarks of Cape Town 2010. Following the 2010 World Cup was a brilliant stroke, and this congress attempted technological leaps that have never been tried at a major missions gathering. Much of it was due to the simple reality that the Internet was not something that existed at Lausanne II.[65] However, technology is always a double-edged sword: it can create massive advantages if it works right, but the set-up is incredibly time consuming, and if something goes wrong and too much is reliant on it, the enterprise could be severely handicapped.

GlobaLink was an attempt by the congress organizers to have people worldwide be able to join in live if they were unable to afford the time or money to come, or if they applied and were not accepted due to the 4,200-person limit. Six hundred fifty physical GlobaLink sites were set up in ninety-one countries and drew 100,000 unique visits to the website from

---

[64]E.g., Ligon Duncan, "An Unpopular Doctrine," *Ministry and Leadership*, Spring–Summer 2011, 6-7: "Social justice is rightly concerned with people who are suffering. Our Lord suffered for us. You want other people to receive the mercy that you received. You want to show the mercy that you have been shown. So you become concerned for all suffering, especially *eternal*. . . . Is the Great Commission to make disciples or to love our neighbor? Is there a priority on sharing the gospel or on ministering to the urgent and manifold needs of millions worldwide? Should we care about their destiny or present predicament? . . . We whose hearts have been changed by grace and who embrace Jesus' teaching on hell want to do all in our power to relieve human suffering now and to proclaim the gospel with all of our might, so that as many as possible will hear, and turn and flee the wrath to come. . . . Hell, rightfully understood, does not make us hard; it makes us tender, . . . moves us to action and gives us a perspective that refuses to merely work for the good of people now but always and especially for their everlasting good."

[65]Technically, the Internet was in its nascent stages in the 1980s, but it was not widely available (or strong enough) for global usage.

185 countries during the week of the congress. This way anybody could join in using a live-stream or time-delayed viewing of the sessions, making Lausanne more of a household name, which was one of its public relations problems in the past; more importantly, however, it did not completely sideline the average layperson in the cause of mission. The professionalization of missionary work has caused some harm in that it disconnects the local church from the work in the field.

GlobaLink had some glitches but mostly seemed to work fine until the middle of the congress when a malicious virus made it crash. The source was likely China, which has been accused of a number of cyber attacks on various countries in recent years.[66] Imagine the joy when two stewards from India—Unisys Global Services employee Vijay Kumar and Pastor Daniel Singh, who just happen to be cousins—solved the problem in a matter of two short hours! It is amazing that a possible Chinese cyber attack was countered by an Indian solution. Not only does this reflect what Vinoth Ramachandra said at Edinburgh 2010 that India is not just about mystical religions but also about modern tech,[67] but it shows that world problems and solutions do not always involve the West. The Two-Thirds World can hold its own, suggestive of the "three selfs."

Speaking of the Chinese (the Christian ones, not the ones responsible for cyber attacks), they were nearly completely missing from Lausanne III[68] as well as from Tokyo 2010—an unfortunate link between the

---

[66]When the Chinese president, Xi Jinping, visited Seattle in September 2015, in his first address he pledged to fight cyber attacks against the United States and other countries, even stressing that the Chinese government itself has been victimized. This indicates some of our tendencies to implicate the government or the entire country/culture in crimes when only some rogue segments of the nation are at fault. A similar example is the common reaction of Westerners in equating radical terrorist Muslims with all Muslims. See Todd C. Frankel, "China's President Pledges to Fight Cyberattacks," *The Washington Post*, September 23, 2015, www.washingtonpost.com/business/economy /chinas-president-pledges-to-fight-cyber-attacks-stresses-reforms/2015/09/22/2f019aa6-6c35-4 c7f-9e15-6df3278c12ed_story.html.

[67]See chapter four, note 36.

[68]Brent Fulton, "From Cape Town to Seoul," *China Source*, July 23, 2013, www.chinasource.org /resource-library/from-the-west-courtyard/from-cape-town-to-seoul. However, the Chinese Christians eventually had a historic breakthrough: "Nearly three years later, about 100 of these leaders were able to join their counterparts from around the world in Seoul, Korea, for the Asian Church Leaders Forum. This meeting was historic in that it represented perhaps the first time that such a broad spectrum of Chinese church leaders from multiple regions of China and multiple streams within the unregistered church was able to meet with an equally broad spectrum of international evangelical leaders." Speakers included Patrick Fung of OMF International, Daniel Bourdanné of IFES, Joshua Ting of Chinese Coordination Centre of World Evangelism (CCCOWE),

evangelical 2010 conferences! Some two hundred Chinese Christians had applied for and gone through all the appropriate channels and had been cleared for departure. Then at the last minute they were detained at their respective departure airports in China, their passports were confiscated, and they were not allowed to continue on to South Africa. Ironically, this was like history repeating itself: Chinese couldn't come to Lausanne II either because the Tiananmen Square uprising a month prior made the Chinese government disallow international travel.[69] However, the reasoning was different for this exclusion: Chinese governmental leaders said that they were offended that the official government-sponsored Three Self Patriotic Movement (TSPM) Church was not invited but house church leaders were. This was not due to political reasons, but rather theological reasons, namely, ability to affirm *The Lausanne Covenant*. The TSPM leaders were invited to be observers, alongside Catholic and Orthodox observers, but they declined. Chinese today are the second-largest Christian population in the world after sub-Saharan Africa,[70] and missing them meant that Cape Town 2010 was not truly representative of what it should have and could have been. Archbishop Henry Orombi of Uganda noted that "not having China at the world mission conference is like not having Brazil at the World Cup."[71] Or, to go back to history, the omission of China at Tokyo and Cape Town 2010 is reminiscent of Latin America being left out of Edinburgh 1910. At least the Cuban delegation, despite also having a communist government, made it safely through to the Cape Town congress.

Other aspects that showed the advantages of technology included the following: there was much media attention on the congress from news outlets working with the Cape Town 2010 communications team, and they

---

Thomas Wang of Great Commission Center, JaeHoon Lee of Onnuri Church and James Hudson Taylor IV, great-great-grandson of the British missionary pioneer to inland China.

[69]Kåre Melhus, "To Tell the Whole World: Three Lausanne Congresses Seen from the Press Centre," in Dahle, Dahle and Jørgensen, *Lausanne Movement*, 90.

[70]Asia has interesting polarities when it comes to Christianity. Though it is only 3.8 percent evangelical, it has the highest number of evangelicals of any continent; yet it is the only continent in the world where Christianity is not the majority religion.

[71]Michelle A. Vu, "Chinese Delegates Barred from Travel Send Greetings to the Lausanne Congress," *The Gospel Herald*, October 19, 2010, www.gospelherald.com/articles/46737/20101019/chinese -delegates-barred-from-travel-send-greetings-to-lausanne-congress.htm.

produced a high-quality color newsletter each day to keep all congress delegates highly informed. However, the negative effects of technology could also be seen: some sensitive sessions, despite prohibitions from the platform, were posted by people immediately onto social media such as YouTube or Twitter, showing how difficult it is to control people and information, even when lives are potentially at risk, and even from well-intentioned people who simply were excited about what they heard.

Two final pieces of technology are worth mentioning, because they revealed the Western-leaning nature of the congress, whether by necessity or not. The first was a video shown at the opening ceremony called "From Pentecost to Edinburgh,"[72] tracing the missionary movement throughout its first 1900 years of history. It was an excellently produced film in terms of quality and budget, providing a sweeping glance at missions history from the first century to Edinburgh 1910 (one of the few nods that Cape Town 2010 gave to its link to the Edinburgh centenary). However, one of the major criticisms of this video—as refreshing as it was to have history included— was that it did not really tell the story of the expansion of the church in Asia and Africa; it was mainly a recounting of Western missionary endeavors and their impact *on* the Two-Thirds World. Philip Jenkins's helpful 2008 book *The Lost History of Christianity: The Thousand-Year Golden Age of the Church in the Middle East, Africa, and Asia—and How It Died* fills in much of the missing pieces, but more scholarship on this area needs to be written.[73]

The second issue concerned the translation headsets, but the Anglophone bias cannot be faulted here,[74] because it was not a cultural preference but a functional necessity. Tokyo 2010 also had to make translation accommodations, but because Cape Town 2010 was so massive, the accomplishment was all the more impressive. Other than English they had seven official congress languages: Arabic, German, Portuguese, Spanish, French, Mandarin and

---

[72]Part one: www.youtube.com/watch?v=oO8VNvNDOrk; and part two: www.youtube.com/watch?v=RY_vertBFdI.

[73]Philip Jenkins, *The Lost History of Christianity: The Thousand-Year Golden Age of the Church in the Middle East, Africa, and Asia—and How It Died* (New York: HarperOne, 2008).

[74]American theologian Robert McAfee Brown spoke Spanish in his address at the World Council of Churches General Assembly in Nairobi in 1975 and famously (or infamously) explained that English is "the language of imperialism." Unfortunately, Brown forgot that Spanish was also an imperialistic language from Europe that took over the Americas and symbolized genocide. If he could have given his address as Nahuatl or Quechua, that would have better proved his point!

Russian (surprisingly, not Korean). Still, English was the official language of business from the platform for practically all the sessions. Headsets were only for those who didn't understand English, so they had translators working around the clock to facilitate understanding for much of the linguistic diversity around the world. Logistically, English made the most sense, because it is the lingua franca of the world today, and also because of the permutations that would be needed to translate seven ways from every language; that is, it is one thing to translate from English to Arabic and to Chinese and to French, but the scope is another thing entirely to translate from Chinese to Arabic as well as English to Portuguese as well as Spanish to Russian, and every other possible combination. The number of translators required would be enormous.

PRAYER AND WORSHIP

Evangelicals are known not only for preaching the Word and for strong Christology but also for acknowledging the primacy of prayer as an essential component of a personal relationship with God. Even William Carey, in his *An Enquiry*, implored missionally minded people toward "fervent and united prayer." There were 24/7 prayer rooms open nonstop throughout the congress, and the evening plenary sessions had geographical foci, which included focused corporate prayer for one continent each night.

The plenary on the penultimate evening was dedicated to prayer, as the table groups spent time praying over *The Cape Town Commitment*. In addition, Patrick Fung, director of OMF, gave an impassioned plea for humility the final day in the later morning plenary session, calling the evangelical world not to a global equilibrium but to a kingdom equilibrium where the focus is not on us but on discipling the world. He cautioned against unidirectional financial giving, reemphasized reconciliation as the heart of the gospel and the foundation of partnership, and ended with an eye-opening quote:

> I hear many comments about twenty-first-century mission belonging to Asia, or belonging to the Chinese. But I'm concerned that many of us Asians may be repeating the same mistake that Western Christians made in the past: that is, equating economic and political power with advances in spreading the gospel. We continue to reinforce the notion that the spreading of the gospel

is always from the powerful to the powerless, the haves to the have-nots, and there is a sense of Asian triumphalism which makes me very nervous. I stand before you today and confess that I pray daily for myself, my people and the Chinese church, that Christ will keep us humble, and grant us mercy and grace.[75]

This is why this book is subtitled *Twenty-First-Century Mission from Everyone to Everywhere*, not *The Great Century of China*, as tempting as it is to dub it that. And being grounded in prayer helps to keep delusions of grandeur in check, a mistake of missionaries in past years. Even Kenneth Scott Latourette's dubbing the nineteenth century the Great Century of Missions may have been premature, as missionaries are as active today as ever before, except in the Two-Thirds World.

The closing ceremony was one of the grandest worship spectacles and experiences I have ever witnessed. It conjured up what heaven might feel like.[76] Archbishop Henry Orombi of Uganda, the honorary chair of the Africa host committee, presided, but he lost his voice so Doug Birdsall had to serve as a last-minute substitute. The liturgy was based on the Kenyan Service of Holy Communion—appropriately, it celebrated the host continent as well as Kenya, which is the country in the world with the highest percentage of evangelicals: 48.92 percent![77] However, the Western flavor still predominated: the Kenyan Service is still an Anglican liturgy, so it is based on a Western order of service rather than being indigenously created. The service also included the reading of the Nicene Creed.[78] An American— the gifted Ed Willmington, director of the Fred Bock Institute of Music at Fuller Seminary—composed the beautiful music and wonderfully conducted the opening and closing ceremonies, and though the orchestra was composed entirely of Cape Town people, all the music was Western too.[79]

---

[75]Patrick Fung, "Working Toward a New Global Equilibrium," in Cameron, *Christ Our Reconciler*, 176-81.

[76]Specifically Revelation 7:9-10: "After this I looked, and behold, a great multitude that no one could number, from every nation, from all tribes and peoples and languages, standing before the throne and before the Lamb, clothed in white robes, with palm branches in their hands, and crying out with a loud voice, 'Salvation belongs to our God who sits on the throne, and to the Lamb!'"

[77]In contrast, Turkey has the lowest at .01 percent.

[78]See the introduction and chapter two for an explanation of how Western this was.

[79]The music included songs by Chris Tomlin and Darlene Zschech of Hillsong and hymns such as "All Hail the Power of Jesus' Name" and "Crown Him with Many Crowns."

During the music, however, there were incredible accompanying visuals. First, there were images of Christ from cultures around the world displayed as everyone was singing. This was one area where there seemed to be no Western bias whatsoever; rather, it was a great example of contextualization and a demonstration that the Word must be incarnated among us. Second, an artist had spent the entire congress painting various delegates, and these pictures were shown in conjunction with the Jesus paintings.[80] This is appropriate, because God and his people together accomplish mission.

Lindsay Brown was the closing speaker and mentioned four hopes: (1) reaffirmation of the uniqueness of Christ; (2) identification of key issues the church needs to address in the next decade; (3) formation of partnerships and friendships; and (4) creation of new initiatives emerging out of this congress.[81] I discussed Christology and partnerships earlier in this chapter, but what are the key future issues as well as the new initiatives that need to be created?

Some of the things Lausanne III did well were to focus on areas the other four conferences did not touch upon, like the arts (beyond music, to areas such as drama and painting), the HIV/AIDS pandemic, and disability ministries. Some of the things that were missing (to be fair, not even the other 2010 conferences really engaged with them much either) were creation care and homosexuality, though they were addressed in *The Cape Town Commitment*. Surprisingly, Cape Town 2010 did not really touch on reevangelizing the West (the last geographical focus in the evening plenaries, intended to be dedicated to the Western world and Eurasia, did not even showcase this region). Tim Keller discussed the treatment of urbanization[82]—a key issue—but New York City is not a prototypical Two-Thirds World city and cannot be the yardstick by which all other cities are measured.[83] René Padilla, on the third night of the

---

[80]These paintings together were reminiscent of the tapestries in the Catholic Cathedral of Our Lady of the Angels (by artist John Nava) in Los Angeles, which portrays modern people intermingled with the saints. See www.olacathedral.org/cathedral/art/tapestries.html.

[81]Lindsay Brown, "We Have a Gospel to Proclaim," in Cameron, *Christ Our Reconciler*, 191-202.

[82]In 2008, the world experienced an urban tipping point: more than 50 percent of the global population now lived in cities rather than rural areas.

[83]See Timothy Keller, "God's Global Urban Mission," in Cameron, *Christ Our Reconciler*, 119-25. He gave some broad brush strokes of characteristics of cities: (1) multicultural, (2) work as a huge part of life, (3) disorder and change, (4) evangelism and social justice, (5) the arts, and (6) interdenominational.

congress (October 20), which focused the geographical spotlight on Latin America, offered one of the few prophetic criticisms[84] of the way evangelicals do mission, saying that (1) we need to focus on making disciples rather than making converts; (2) globalization is creating a great harm because it creates unjust economic systems, which are destroying humankind; and (3) destruction of the ecosystem ought to be of concern to Christians.[85]

Perhaps the most critical off-platform protest was called the "Statement of Lament for Evangelicals and the Legacy of Apartheid"[86] written by American Chris Rice, well known for his books on racial reconciliation from a Christian perspective.[87] This was appropriate because Lausanne III was practically in the shadow of Robben Island, where Nelson Mandela was imprisoned for twenty-seven years, from 1964 to 1982, and many of the participants visited the prison during or after the congress. Part of Rice's statement reads:

> This Lausanne Congress 2010 in Cape Town gathered in a land which 16 years ago stood in the grip of one of the greatest evils of our time—apartheid. We regret that this was not named or confessed at the opening of the Congress. . . . This leads us, with others, to lament our failure in much of the evangelical church both in South Africa and throughout the world who remained silent about or complicit in apartheid. . . . We call upon this Congress to join in this spirit of lament and confession.

These may all be true of New York City where Keller lives, but, for example, the two biggest cities in the world—Tokyo and Mexico City—are fairly monocultural by Western city standards. Also, though the arts are certainly represented among the poor, it tends to be a luxury of the elite, so many of the poorer world cities do not have a large focus on the arts.

[84]Along with Ziya Meral and Patrick Fung.

[85]These three points can be found fully explicated in René Padilla, "From Lausanne I to Lausanne III," *Journal of Latin American Theology* 5, no. 2 (2010): 43-50. Though creation care was addressed in a multiplex, Lindsay Brown finally mentioned it in passing at the closing ceremony. Considering that Andrew Walls highlights creation care as one of the five main components of twenty-first-century missiology, it is surprising that it was not mentioned more at Cape Town 2010.

[86]For the full text, see "Apartheid Legacy Lament," *Reconcilers with Chris Rice* (blog), October 22, 2010, https://reconcilers.wordpress.com/2010/10/22/apartheid-legacy-lament.

[87]One notable one, coauthored with Spencer Perkins, is *More Than Equals: Racial Healing for the Sake of the Gospel* (Downers Grove, IL: InterVarsity Press, 2000).

He and his associates distributed this printed document to everyone at Cape Town 2010 and collected signatures in support of it.[88] Often, to avoid triumphalism in the West (or in China, as Patrick Fung described), a theology of lament[89] ought to be employed, which is something quite unfamiliar in non-white or non-Western cultures but is much more common in Two-Thirds World theologizing.

IMPACT OF CAPE TOWN 2010

If the continuation committee was Edinburgh 1910's strength, Cape Town 2010 has this area well covered—remember that Doug Birdsall says that Lausanne can be thought of as the three C's: city, congress and a *continuing* movement. Unlike Tokyo 2010, which had to create a new structure of continuation (the Global Great Commission Network), or Edinburgh 2010, which has no plans beyond the limited-run Regnum Centenary book series, Lausanne already had structures in place and is now once more a thriving movement because Cape Town 2010 breathed new life into it.

One of Lausanne's weaknesses is also its strength. It is an umbrella movement, not an organization that exists unto itself, which is why people may have heard of, for example, OMF or InterVarsity but not Lausanne. But it is this flexible nature that enables it to be such a unifying force among evangelicals. Cape Town 2010 made Lausanne a much more recognizable, household name, but its end goal is not to perpetuate the Lausanne name; rather, it's to create a global network to enable worldwide missions organizations to do their job. Lausanne can also do this regionally under different names; for example, in the United States it is called the Mission America Coalition,[90] and in Africa it is called Mission

---

[88]This is reminiscent of when René Padilla, at the Lausanne 2004 Forum in Pattaya, Thailand, circulated a petition calling for protest of the invasion of Iraq by George W. Bush's administration at the time. This was not looked upon favorably by Lausanne executives because it was not officially sanctioned.

[89]See Soong-Chan Rah, *Prophetic Lament: A Call for Justice in Troubled Times* (Downers Grove, IL: InterVarsity Press, 2015), which came out of the Hispanic and Asian North American (HANA) theology and ministry consultation at Trinity Evangelical Divinity School, Deerfield, Illinois, on May 14–17, 2013, which I was also a part of.

[90]The Mission America Coalition had their US Leadership Consultation on World Evangelization April 4–7, 2011, in Orlando, Florida, which was a direct follow-up for the American delegates who attended Cape Town 2010. Their theme was "From Cape Town 2010 to Orlando 2011 . . . and the Future: Accelerating the Church Toward the Great Commission."

Africa. Even within Mission America, there are demographically specific conferences, such as the Lausanne Consultation for North American Younger Leaders.[91]

Lausanne also has produced, since 2012, a newsletter called *Lausanne Global Analysis*, endeavoring to "deliver strategic and credible information and insight from an international network of evangelical analysts to equip influencers of global mission."[92] The initial impetus came out of a meeting at Cape Town 2010,[93] and the *LGA* now publishes five to six issues per year, engaging with a wide variety of world issues from an evangelical perspective.

Even if Cape Town 2010 seemed to be *the* landmark 2010 conference, being the biggest and most prominent of them all that year, it definitely gave nods to the others. To have Paul Eshleman give the call to frontier missions paralleled Tokyo 2010, even if he was not the keynote speaker or the main focus.[94] To have the WCC general secretary bring opening greetings invoked Edinburgh 2010. To have the organizers of Cape Town 2010 (Doug Birdsall at Gordon-Conwell Seminary) and 2010Boston (Rodney Petersen at Andover Newton Theological School, Dana Robert at Boston College and Todd Johnson at Gordon-Conwell Seminary) all be based in the same city meant that there was conference-planning synergy in Boston.[95] Having Ruth Padilla DeBorst as one of the main plenary speakers, as well as having René Padilla and Samuel Escobar on stage representing the history of the Latin American Theological Fellowship, linked it with CLADE V (which, in turn, distributed *The Cape Town Commitment* in Spanish to all its constituents).

With this world changing so quickly, the question is, can Lausanne keep pace? Some huge global changes have taken place since 2010, including the Arab Spring[96] and the rise of ISIS, the world population hitting seven billion,[97]

---

[91]Held in Madison, Wisconsin, July 24–26, 2012.

[92]This is modeled on David R. Young's organization in England, Oxford Analytica. Originally it was going to be called Lausanne Analytica. Quote from www.lausanne.org/lga.

[93]I was invited to be part of this initial meeting, which was composed of a twenty-person think tank.

[94]Ralph Winter, founder of Tokyo 2010, gave the initial clarion call to minister to the unreached people groups at Lausanne '74, so there is a historical connection there too.

[95]Doug Birdsall and Todd Johnson were even based at the same institution, as the former was the director of the J. Christy Wilson Center for World Mission at Gordon-Conwell Seminary and the latter was the director of the Center for the Study of Global Christianity, also at Gordon-Conwell.

[96]Beginning December 18, 2010, in Tunisia, and fading in mid-2012.

[97]October 31, 2011, almost exactly a year after Cape Town 2010.

the election of the first Latin American pope,[98] the US Supreme Court decision on gay marriage,[99] and the growth of world megacities showing no signs of abating.[100] It seems like a Lausanne IV Congress can't come soon enough and certainly cannot be put off another fifteen years (the time between Lausanne I and II), and especially not twenty-one years (the time between Lausanne II and III)! Lausanne has now had congresses on three continents: Europe (Lausanne, Switzerland), Asia (Manila, The Philippines) and Africa (Cape Town, South Africa). It seems that Latin America should be the next location—we shall see if that is where Lausanne IV will be held! One idea is that it should be in Rio de Janeiro due to the infrastructure upgrades of the 2016 Olympics and 2018 World Cup, mimicking the precedent of Lausanne III, which was held in Cape Town following the hosting of the World Cup by South Africa.

In the meantime, Lausanne CEO Michael Oh has identified the vision for the future of the movement as "Connecting influencers and ideas for global mission," disaggregated into four priorities: (1) the gospel for every person, (2) an evangelical church for every people, (3) Christ-like leaders for every church and (4) kingdom impact in every sphere of society.[101] In addition, Lausanne's commitment to younger leaders (hearkening back to the focus on students at Edinburgh 1910) continues to be unwavering, as every generation there is a new Younger Leaders Gathering.

CAPE TOWN COMMITMENT

One of the things that made the *Lausanne Covenant* so amazing is not only its enduring influence but the amazing breadth and scope of the document, even while maintaining its brevity. René Padilla made his observation on what made the *Lausanne Covenant* so influential: "That a 2,700-word

---

[98]Pope Francis, on April 8, 2013.

[99]On June 26, 2015. Even earlier, on May 9, 2012, Barack Obama became the first sitting US president to support gay marriage.

[100]In a way, this echoes the direction of the biblical narrative. Andy Crouch, in *Culture Making* (Downers Grove, IL: InterVarsity Press, 2013), points out that we are moving from nature to culture, that is, from a garden (the Garden of Eden) to a city (the New Jerusalem). Crouch offers a modern supplement to H. Richard Niebuhr's seminal 1951 book, *Christ and Culture*, which examines the importance of culture in Christianity.

[101]Michael Oh and Justin Schell, "Lausanne's Renewed Engagement in Global Mission," *Lausanne Global Analysis* 4, no. 6 (November 2015), www.lausanne.org/content/lga/2015-11/lausannes-renewed-engagement-in-global-mission.

statement on evangelism should deal with such a wide range of subjects [fifteen in all] is in itself a proof that Evangelicalism on the whole is no longer willing to be identified as a movement characterized by a tendency to isolate evangelism, in both theory and practice, from the wider context represented by the nature of the Gospel and the life and mission of the Church."[102] If William Carey's *An Enquiry* put mission on the agenda for Protestants, the *Lausanne Covenant* put social justice back on the agenda for evangelicals.

Then came *The Manila Manifesto* at Lausanne II, which used the theme "The Whole Church Taking the Whole Gospel to the Whole World" to sum up the meaning of evangelism[103] (this phrase was also echoed from the stage many times at Lausanne III). Though this phrase may seem triumphalistic or naive, Dana Robert nuanced it at Edinburgh 2010:

> Lest it seem that the idea of "whole church" to the "whole world" represented shallow optimism, it is important to recognise it was also a cry of lamentation and call for repentance. Talk of the need for the "whole church" to reach the "whole world" recognized that previous mission efforts had been dominated by what Sri Lankan theologian D. T. Niles called "the westerity of the base." It also underscored that mission should pay greater attention to the "other" global forces of politics and economics.[104]

Nonetheless, despite this great watchword, the *Manila Manifesto* fell rather flat and did not have the impact of the *Lausanne Covenant*.

How does *The Cape Town Commitment* (*CTC*)[105] compare? *CTC* was different from its predecessors in that it was written both before *and* after the congress. Part one, "For the Lord We Love" (the confession of faith), was started five years prior to Cape Town 2010 and was presented in its final

---

[102]C. René Padilla, ed., *The New Face of Evangelicalism: An International Symposium on the Lausanne Covenant* (Downers Grove, IL: InterVarsity Press, 1974), 10-11.

[103]Chris Wright, "Editorial: 'The Whole Gospel': Lausanne Reflects on Its Own Vision," *Evangelical Review of Theology* 33, no. 1 (January 2009): 3.

[104]Dana Robert, "Plenary 1: Mission in Long Perspective," in *Mission Today and Tomorrow*, ed. Kirsteen Kim and Andrew Anderson (Oxford: Regnum, 2011), 63.

[105]Two years before *The Cape Town Commitment*, some prominent evangelical leaders (such as Timothy George, Os Guinness and Rich Mouw) drafted *An Evangelical Manifesto* in 2008. Though the attempt was commendable in trying to be a radical prophetic voice among evangelicals, it likewise gained little traction amongst most laypeople, partially due to lack of total agreement by evangelical leaders in being able to affirm it. The full text can be read at www .evangelicalmanifesto.com.

version there. Part two, "For the World We Serve" (the call to action), was the result of a listening process begun three years before Lausanne III, continued throughout the congress and finished four months later.[106] *Love* was the framing word for part one, as it was developed in ten subpoints:

1. We love because God first loved us.

2. We love the living God.

3. We love God the Father.

4. We love God the Son.

5. We love God the Holy Spirit.

6. We love God's Word.

7. We love God's world.

8. We love the gospel of God.

9. We love the people of God.

10. We love the mission of God.

Part two was composed of six key issues that became the structure of the Congress:

A. Bearing witness to the truth of Christ in a pluralistic, globalized world

B. Building the peace of Christ in our divided and broken world

C. Living the love of Christ among people of other faiths

D. Discerning the will of Christ for world evangelization

E. Calling the church of Christ back to humility, integrity and simplicity

F. Partnering in the body of Christ for unity in mission

The link between parts one and two can be seen as either belief and praxis or primary truths and secondary issues. The World Evangelical Alliance assisted in the production of this document, showing a further cooperative spirit.

Though it was a groundbreaking way to produce a document, it had logistical challenges. For example, the length was enormous. The *Lausanne Covenant* had a beautiful conciseness to it; the *Manila Manifesto* started to

---

[106]Part two of the *CTC* was released on February 11, 2011.

become unwieldy; and the *CTC* seems like a chore for anyone to read because it had to be produced in booklet form rather than being easily printable on a couple of sheets of paper. Unfortunately, the length alone seems to ensure that the *CTC* will never have the impact and effectiveness of the *Lausanne Covenant*. Another problem lay in the fact that, though everyone at the congress had access to part one, part two came out so much later, after everyone had scattered, thus inhibiting corporate discussion. And though the drafting committee kept working on part two during the congress, there did not seem to be much input from the general audience into the *CTC* during the course of Cape Town 2010, despite the fact that it was advertised as a congress.[107] The *CTC*, however, did reflect the congress not only in terms of what was discussed on the platform but also what was not. Some of the new or missing issues that *CTC* addressed that were not written in the documents produced from Lausanne I or II included oral cultures, seminaries, cities, children, prayer, HIV/AIDS, homosexuality, creation care and egalitarianism. What made the *CTC* overwhelming was its attempt to be thoroughly comprehensive, but this is also what made it magisterial. Striking a balance between the two is difficult, and in many ways, Lausanne cannot be faulted for trying. To leave something out for the sake of brevity when one knows that it is a crucial issue seems irresponsible—and yet, limiting the information for the sake of effectively communicating a particular message is something the apostle John knew about: "Now Jesus did many other signs in the presence of the disciples, which are not written in this book; but these are written so that you may believe that Jesus is the Christ, the Son of God, and that by believing you may have life in his name" (Jn 20:30-31).

Shortly after the *CTC* was written, the WCC came out with their own ecumenical missions document titled *Together Towards Life: Mission and Evangelism in Changing Landscapes*.[108] The process for writing it began at the ninth WCC General Assembly at Porto Alegre, Brazil, in 2006,[109] and was released seven years later at the tenth WCC General Assembly at Busan,

---

[107]Valdir Steuernagel, "A Latin American Evangelical Perspective on the Cape Town Congress," *Journal of Latin American Theology* 9, no. 2 (2014): 121.

[108]The full text of *Together Towards Life* can be downloaded at www.oikoumene.org/en/resources/documents/commissions/mission-and-evangelism/together-towards-life-mission-and-evangelism-in-changing-landscapes.

[109]I was in attendance there, the first WCC General Assembly ever held in Latin America.

South Korea, in 2013. Similar to the *CTC* being the third in a series, *Together Towards Life* (*TTL*) was not the first of its kind. This document was preceded by the 1982 WCC text *Mission and Evangelism—an Ecumenical Affirmation* (*MEEA*),[110] which was prepared by the WCC's Commission on World Mission and Evangelism. Similar to *CTC* and the earlier documents in its series, *TTL* differed from its predecessor in length (forty pages instead of fifteen) and in topics. *MEEA*'s seven points[111] are similar to the *Lausanne Covenant* in that they cover evangelism, social justice, holistic mission and so on.[112]

TTL, however, was a necessary update to *MEEA*. The introduction to *TTL* states:

> The Commission on World Mission and Evangelism (CWME) has, since the WCC Porto Alegre Assembly in 2006, been working toward and contributing to the construction of a new ecumenical mission affirmation. The new statement will be presented to the WCC 10th Assembly at Busan, Republic of Korea, in 2013. Since the integration of the International Missionary Council (IMC) and the World Council of Churches (WCC) in New Delhi, in 1961, there has been only one official WCC position statement on mission and evangelism which was approved by the central committee in 1982, *Mission and Evangelism: An Ecumenical Affirmation*. This new mission affirmation was unanimously approved by the WCC central committee on 5 September 2012 at its meeting in the island of Crete, Greece. It is the aim of this new ecumenical discernment to seek vision, concepts and directions for a renewed understanding and practice of mission and evangelism in changing landscapes. It seeks a broad appeal, even wider than WCC member churches and affiliated mission bodies, so that we can commit ourselves together to fullness of life for all, led by the God of Life![113]

TTL was a necessary update, as the time between *MEEA* and *TTL* (thirty years) was much longer than between the *Manila Manifesto* and the

---

[110]*International Review of Mission* 61, no. 284 (1982): 432-37.

[111]The seven topics are (1) conversion, (2) the gospel to all realms of life, (3) the church and its unity in God's mission, (4) mission in Christ's way, (5) good news to the poor, (6) mission in and to six continents, (7) witness among people of living faiths.

[112]Allen Yeh, "*Together Towards Life* and *The Cape Town Commitment*," in *Ecumenical Missiology 1910–2012*, ed. Kenneth R. Ross, Jooseop Keum, Kyriaki Avtzi and Roderick Hewitt (Oxford: Regnum, 2015).

[113]See www.oikoumene.org/en/resources/documents/commissions/mission-and-evangelism/together-towards-life-mission-and-evangelism-in-changing-landscapes.

CTC (21 years). *TTL* is structured with 112 paragraphs listed under four main sections,[114] each of which has four subsections,[115] all centered on the Spirit. It updates *Mission and Evangelism—an Ecumenical Affirmation* by not only highlighting contemporary issues but also creating a robust theological framework that was missing from *MEEA*.

Though *CTC* and *TTL* have much in common, their evangelical and ecumenical biases show. The former is more Christocentric and the latter more pneumacentric, for example. *CTC* would see diversity more as ethnic and cultural, *TTL* more as giving the marginalized an equal voice. *TTL* would affirm life as more justice-oriented while *CTC* as more spiritual. *CTC* would view unity as more interagency cooperation rather than denominational as *TTL* would.[116] (It seems that *TTL* is the document that perhaps Edinburgh 2010 should have produced rather than *The Common Call*[117]—showing that Edinburgh 2010 was more of a

---

[114](1) Spirit of Mission: Breath of Life; (2) Spirit of Liberation: Mission from the Margins; (3) Spirit of Community: Church on the Move; (4) Spirit of Pentecost: Good News for All.

[115]Subsections under 1: The Mission of the Spirit, Mission and the Flourishing of Creation, Spiritual Gifts and Discernment, Transformative Spirituality. Subsections under 2: Why Margins and Marginalization?, Mission as Struggle and Resistance, Mission Seeking Justice and Inclusivity, Mission as Healing and Wholeness. Subsections under 3: God's Mission and the Life of the Church, God's Mission and the Church's Unity, God Empowers the Church in Mission, Local Congregations: New Initiatives. Subsections under 4: The Call to Evangelize, Evangelism in Christ's Way, Evangelism, Interfaith Dialogue and Christian Presence, Evangelism and Cultures.

[116]See Michael Kinnamon and Brian E. Cope, eds., *The Ecumenical Movement: An Anthology of Key Texts and Voices* (Geneva: WCC Publications, 1997), 326-27. In comparing reports from Berlin 1966, Lausanne 1974 and Lausanne II (Manila) 1989 with reports from the Commission on World Mission and Evangelism (CWME of the WCC) meetings of Bangkok 1973, Melbourne 1980 and San Antonio 1989, the following analysis was given: "three significant differences are quickly apparent: 1. CWME documents typically stress that the 'spiritual and material gospels' are inseparable. . . . From the perspective of the Lausanne Covenant, this approach confuses categories since 'reconciliation with [people] is not reconciliation with God nor is social action evangelism nor is political liberation salvation.' This collapse of the spiritual and material means that insufficient attention is given to the invitational dimension of evangelism. . . . 2. Lausanne emphasizes the responsibility of all churches to be sending churches, just as early Christians understood themselves to be sent from Jerusalem to the ends of the earth. CWME texts look at the fact that churches are already present in nearly every culture, as well as at the history of western imperialism, and emphasize the need for indigenous churches to take responsibility for mission in their setting. The strategy is one of ecumenical partnership more than overseas evangelism. 3. The two groups differ on how Christians should relate to people of other faiths. . . . It is important to add that these differences are also found within and between churches that belong to the WCC. The most notable attempt to bridges these differences, both within the WCC and the wider Christian family, is the text 'Mission and Evangelism: An Ecumenical Affirmation.'"

[117]Even if *CTC* and *TTL* are overly long, perhaps *The Common Call* is overly brief, not being robust enough to cover sufficient territory. Striking the right balance of length is important, especially in

celebration and the WCC, like Lausanne, continues to be an ongoing working group.) However, both the *CTC* and *TTL* are thoroughly missional and, similar to how the two evangelical 2010 conferences (Tokyo and Cape Town) and the two ecumenical 2010 conferences (Edinburgh and Boston) balance each other out, a world with both *CTC* and *TTL* is, ultimately, a better one.

One more document needs to be mentioned: *The Seoul Commitment*. At the Asian Church Leaders' Forum (ACLF) in Seoul, South Korea, on August 21, 2013,

> Christian leaders from house church networks in mainland China overcame enormous hurdles to attend the recent Asian Church Leaders Forum in Seoul. . . . The participation of the Chinese leaders in the 300-strong ACLF marked the first time since 1949 that such a group of Chinese Christian leaders had taken part in a multi-national gathering. . . . The Chinese church was barely represented at The Third Lausanne Congress in Cape Town in October 2010 as Chinese participants were unable to leave China. In 2011 plans were laid quietly for a special event for these Chinese church leaders, to be held elsewhere in East Asia. More than 100 unregistered church leaders from mainland China arrived safely in Seoul, representing millions of Chinese believers.[118]

The inclusion of the Chinese house church voices made *The Seoul Commitment* different from any other worldwide missionary document in the past, and should be considered an addendum to the *CTC*.[119]

QUESTIONS

1. Do you agree with Kenneth Ross that Lausanne is more the spiritual heir of Edinburgh 1910 than is the World Council of Churches? How does one measure such a thing?

2. Is it practicable to have 4,500 people form a congress? Or should a gathering of that size simply be a conference?

---

this media-saturated age where attention spans have diminished but people continue to demand greater quality from products due to options.

[118]Lauren D'Avolio, "Chinese Christian Leaders Make History with Attendance at Church Leaders' Forum," *The Gospel Herald*, August 21, 2013, www.gospelherald.com/article/church/48661 /chinese-christian-leaders-make-history-with-attendance-at-church-leaders-forum.htm# .UhePqrzFYu7.

[119]The text of *The Seoul Commitment* is included in appendix C.

3. Which is the most biblical definition of mission: evangelization (the theme of Edinburgh 1910), discipleship (the theme of Tokyo 2010) or reconciliation (the theme of Cape Town 2010)?

4. Is non-Western leadership really "non-Western" if the people are from the Two-Thirds World but educated in the West?

5. If missions is the mother of ecumenism, does it make sense to have an international congress focused on, and composed of, just evangelicals? Does leaving out Catholics (the largest denominational body in the world) or Pentecostals (the fastest-growing form of Christianity around the world) give an inaccurate assessment of Christianity's global future, or does the definition of evangelicals as "enthusiastic Christians"[120] serve well enough as a vanguard and catalyst for mission?

6. Did Cape Town 2010 try to cover too many topics (and the same question can be asked of the *Cape Town Commitment*)? Is it a case of less is more? Should it have been more focused on one thing?

7. Were the post-Lausanne II topics the right ones to address in hindsight? Was there anything they missed?

8. How can you have ecumenical unity when people disagree on nonessentials? How do you decide when it is a topic you cannot avoid (like complementarianism vs. egalitarianism) as opposed to a topic that doesn't need to be brought up (like Calvinism vs. Arminianism)? Does Romans 14:1–15:7 speak to this at all?

9. Is John Stott's view of holistic mission more correct, or is John Piper's? Should we be more focused on eternal soul suffering, or are evangelism and social justice truly two wings of a bird or two blades of a pair of scissors? Another worthy exercise is to compare the *CTC* with *TTL*. Read both documents and see which gives a better definition of mission, or are both lacking and in need of the other to balance it out?

10. Were the Chinese Christians wrong in going through official channels and legal pathways to head to Cape Town 2010, even if it meant they made themselves easily identifiable and thus immediate targets? Would

---

[120]Brian C. Stiller, Todd M. Johnson, Karen Stiller and Mark Hutchinson, eds., *Evangelicals Around the World: A Global Handbook for the 21st Century* (Nashville: Thomas Nelson, 2015), 5.

availing themselves of "underground" channels be better—that is, does the freedom to act of their own accord outweigh the credibility they'd burn with the Chinese government as a result?

11. Was it okay that Cape Town 2010 did not address apartheid, even while being hosted by a country in which that was a devastating reality? How do you balance local versus global issues? Does it delegitimize your global ministry if you ignore the issues right in front of you, or is it sufficient that everyone has their own specific niche ministry—similar to the division of labor between apostles and deacons in Acts 6, or the division of the mission field into Jew (Peter, James and John) and Gentile (Paul and Barnabas) in Galatians 2? Yet, Galatians 2 also highlights ministry to the poor as a commonality among them, so there are some things that all Christians should be involved in. How do you distinguish?

12. Is it hubris for Lausanne to say they are the "whole church" taking the whole gospel to the whole world?

13. Is evangelicalism the future of world Christianity? Or is it Catholicism (the largest Christian denomination) or mainline Protestant denominations as represented by the World Council of Churches or Pentecostalism (the fastest-growing form of Christianity, especially in the Two-Thirds World)? Does evangelicalism have a strong future outside of the West?

2010BOSTON

THE CONCLUSION OF THE major 2010 conferences took place in Boston November 4–7.[1] It may have seemed anticlimactic because 2010Boston had to follow Cape Town 2010, which acted like *the* grand finale. But 2010Boston did not take it upon itself to be as comprehensive or as grandiose as Lausanne III. It decided to be the string that tied the others together rather than trying to be the center of attention—it was called "2010Boston" instead of "Boston 2010" in order to emphasize the year instead of the city. Its function was to be a summary of the 2010 conferences and an orientation toward the future. The conference program states: "This conference is not an event so much as a process. It is part of the centennial commemoration of the Edinburgh 1910 World Missionary Conference and comes as fourth in line after conferences in Tokyo, Edinburgh and Cape Town. It is part of a wider conversation with Christians around the world about the meaning of mission in the *twenty-first century*." Also, it is fitting that 2010 came full circle back to the city of Boston, because this is where it all began, when all the conference organizers met for a joint meeting on November 10, 2008,[2] thus serving as the impetus for this book. Sometimes the end does not have to

---

[1]Much of this was drawn from Allen Yeh, "2010Boston: The Changing Contours of World Mission and Christianity," *Missiology: An International Review* 39, no. 2 (April 2011, special electronic version).

[2]See figure 1.

have fireworks, or resign itself to petering out unspectacularly; ending with a deep sense of satisfaction is enough.

Boston is a place of new beginnings. The first Bible translation in the New World occurred there in 1661–1663 by John Eliot, who translated the Bible into Algonquin for the Native Americans. The city has a legacy of not only being the home of the Puritans,[3] conjuring up the spirit of the Protestant Reformation when people separated from the mother church for religious freedom, but also being the beginning of the American Revolution.[4] In both regards, it is countercultural: those calling themselves American Protestants are far from "conservative"—rather, they are the product of two major civilly disobedient nonconformist movements in history (just ask Catholics, or the Church of England, or the British)! New Englanders, like the Scots, were separatists from England, so there was a shared rebellious free spirit among them.

The same holds true of students. The university, originating as a place to train Christian clergy, was also the scene of many historical protest movements. There is something about the undergraduate age and the university campus that has become a cauldron for student activism, whether it was the Paris Uprising of 1832 (i.e., the June Rebellion) made famous in Victor Hugo's *Les Misérables*, the Tlaltelolco Massacre of 1968 right before the Mexico City Olympics, the Vietnam War protests at Kent State University in 1970, the Tiananmen Square protests of 1989 in Beijing or the University of Missouri racial protests of 2015. Perhaps it is the confluence of coming into adulthood (with all the intellectual powers and legal responsibilities that entails) combined with the freedom of living on one's own and not yet entering the life stage of marital responsibility. It is a time of change, of awareness, of heady optimism (or cynicism!), of unencumbered liberty and of naiveté/brashness, which causes university students to want to tackle life's greatest challenges. Whatever the case, students have been some of the greatest catalysts for change in the history of the world. It is no different with their involvement in world missionary movements.

---

[3]Technically, in 1629 they landed in Salem, a small town that today is a suburb just north of Boston.
[4]April 19, 1775, in the town of Lexington right outside of Boston, where the "shot heard 'round the world" was fired.

FROM EDINBURGH 1910 TO 2010BOSTON

If Tokyo was about frontier mission, and Edinburgh was about ecumenism, and Cape Town was about evangelicalism, then Boston was about students. 2010Boston never claimed to be *the* successor to Edinburgh 1910 and, in fact, consistently implicitly acknowledged that it did not have an identity outside of the other three 2010 conferences. Yet the emphasis on students was the very heartbeat of Edinburgh 1910, so it has more of a claim on being a modern-day 1910 than it may seem at first glance.

The Student Volunteer Movement for Foreign Missions was founded in July 1886 at a dramatic conference in Northfield, Massachusetts (made famous by Jonathan Edwards who pastored there), on the grounds of Dwight L. Moody's Mount Hermon School and sponsored by the YMCA. Two hundred fifty-one students from eighty-nine colleges and universities came to the Northfield conference. This became the catalyst to student missionary movements all across the country, the first chapter taking form at Princeton College in 1888 as the Princeton Foreign Missionary Society. Robert P. Wilder was the founder, and he led this group of students to sign a declaration of purpose: "We, the undersigned, declare ourselves willing and desirous, God permitting, to go to the unevangelized portions of the world."

Arthur T. Pierson later became the SVM's most well-known leader and elder statesman, emerging out of the Northfield conference. Professor Dana Robert of Boston University did her doctoral dissertation on A. T. Pierson,[5] so she has a deeply vested interest in student missionary movements as well; thus it was eminently fitting that she was one of the organizers of 2010Boston. And the organizer of CLADE V (Costa Rica 2012), Ruth Padilla DeBorst, did her PhD at Boston University, supervised by Dana Robert, so the organizers of these two conferences have direct relation with each other and to the city of Boston.

In 1891, the First International Convention of the Student Volunteer Movement convened in Cleveland. Its slogan was "The evangelization of the world in this generation." Sound familiar? This was the exact same slogan of Edinburgh 1910, and John R. Mott's famous clarion call was

---

[5]Later published as Dana L. Robert, *Occupy Until I Come: A. T. Pierson and the Evangelization of the World* (Grand Rapids: Eerdmans, 2003).

taken directly from SVM, which, along with the YMCA and the Student Christian Movement (SCM;[6] the SVM's British counterpart), was perhaps the greatest inspirations for the Edinburgh 1910 World Missionary Conference.[7]

As mentioned in chapter one, Edinburgh 1910 was the latter bookend of the Great Century of Missions, begun in 1792 with the publication of William Carey's *An Enquiry*. After the two World Wars, the SVM lost a lot of its earlier momentum, since the unbridled optimism of the Edinburgh 1910 watchword no longer seemed realistic or fitting after such global catastrophes, and disillusionment set in.

Biola University now has the last remaining vestige of the SVM in its Student Missionary Union (SMU), an entirely student-run missions organization founded in 1923.[8] This is fitting, considering that D. L. Moody, after founding Moody Bible Institute in 1886, inspired his cocrusader R. A. Torrey to help establish the Bible Institute of Los Angeles (BIOLA)[9] along with Lyman Stewart, Thomas C. Horton and Augustus B. Prichard. BIOLA was so committed to overseas missions that just a year after its founding it established an overseas sister institution, the Hunan Bible Institute in China.[10]

However, though the SVM is now largely defunct, new initiatives developed in the postwar years, like a phoenix rising out of its ashes. Edinburgh 1910 deserved its nickname as the birthplace of the modern ecumenical movement because it gave rise to the World Council of Churches in 1948. But when the SVM transitioned from missions to ecumenism, its membership actually declined.[11] The Student Foreign Missions Fellowship (SFMF), which was the missionary arm of InterVarsity Christian Fellowship, arose in its place. In 1946 the SFMF organized the first-ever

---

[6]From the SCM website: www.movement.org.uk/about-us/history.

[7]Brian Stanley, *The World Missionary Conference, Edinburgh 1910* (Grand Rapids: Eerdmans, 2009), 8.

[8]From Biola's SMU website: http://smu.biola.edu/about/history.

[9]In 1949, the Bible Institute of Los Angeles (BIOLA) formally achieved college status, dropping the acronym and rebranding itself as Biola College. In 1981, it underwent further reorganization and became Biola University.

[10]This property was confiscated by the Chinese government during the Communist Revolution of 1949.

[11]Norman E. Thomas, *Missions and Unity: Lessons from History, 1792–2010* (Eugene, OR: Cascade, 2010), 60.

Urbana missions convention in Toronto, Canada.[12] Samuel Zwemer invoked the Northfield conference of 1886 in his opening address, reminding them that they stood on the sixtieth anniversary of the crucial event that launched the SVM.[13]

Urbana has survived the test of time and is now a triennial convention drawing eighteen thousand university students from across North America. This book is, fittingly, published by InterVarsity Press, so it can be considered a tribute to university students worldwide, especially as I am also a college professor and this is my main sphere of influence.

2010Boston's theme was "The Changing Contours of World Mission and Christianity," which indicated a future orientation rather than one seeking to hold on to the past legacy of Edinburgh 1910. And yet it had some crucial commonalities with its progenitor.

THE HISTORY OF 2010BOSTON

Student involvement with missionary movements goes back much further than 1910. Some of the most esteemed universities in the world have produced some of the greatest missionaries. For example, David Brainerd was expelled from Yale in 1740 and so instead became a missionary to Native Americans and later inspired the greatest theologian in America's history, Jonathan Edwards, to do the same. Another Yale man, William Whiting Borden, also known as "Borden of Yale," died of cerebral meningitis at only age twenty-five while training for the mission field in Egypt in 1913. Though his life was tragically cut short, he inspired countless others after him to take up the missionary cause.

The American missionary movement was started by five undergraduate students at Williams College in western Massachusetts in what was known as the Haystack Prayer Meeting in August 1806. The reason for the odd name came from the fact that some students were praying for world missions and got caught in a thunderstorm, so they ended up taking shelter in a haystack while they made their commitment to missions. This

---

[12]From the Urbana website: https://urbana.org/history-urbana. The conference later moved to the University of Illinois at Urbana-Champaign (from which it derives its name) and then finally to St. Louis in 2006 after it outgrew the U of I facilities.

[13]Thomas, *Missions and Unity*, 60.

occurred just a decade and a half after publication of William Carey's *An Enquiry* and was directly inspired by that document, so there was yet again an Anglo-American link for the cause of world missions. The Haystack group was led by Samuel J. Mills, who formed the Society of Brethren[14] "to effect in the persons of its members a mission or missions to the heathens."[15]

Mills, in turn, influenced Adoniram Judson (who went to Brown University as an undergraduate) when the two of them attended Andover Theological Seminary[16] in Boston together. (Andover later ended up splitting into two, with one half—the liberal Unitarian faction—remaining as Harvard Divinity School, and the other half—the conservative Calvinist faction—joining Newton Theological Institution to become Andover Newton Theological School.) Mills and Judson went on to found the American Board of Commissioners for Foreign Missions (ABCFM) in 1810.[17] Adoniram Judson and his wife, Ann (née Hasseltine), then became the first intercontinental missionaries sent[18] from the United States when they set sail from Salem, Massachusetts, in 1812, to go to Burma.[19]

---

[14]The other four students were James Richards, Robert C. Robbins, Harvey Loomis and Byram Green. Mills also helped found the American Bible Society and the United Foreign Missionary Society.

[15]Thomas, *Missions and Unity*, 18.

[16]The oldest graduate school of theology in the United States, founded in the late eighteenth century as a continuation of education from Phillips Academy Andover.

[17]Today it is officially known as the American Baptist Foreign Missionary Society (ABFMS), but for marketing purposes it is branded as American Baptist Churches International Ministries (ABC IM). I was a member of the board of directors of ABC IM, from 2012 to 2015.

[18]As mentioned in chapter four, George Leile predated the Judsons as a missionary by thirty years. This is why the words *intercontinental* (Leile went to Jamaica, which was still in North America) and *sent* (Leile went of his own accord and did not have a sending body) are necessary to nuance the significance of the Judsons.

[19]The subject of my DPhil thesis from Oxford University was the Latino missiologist Orlando Costas. Every year the Boston Theological Institute (BTI) hosts the Orlando Costas Global Mission Consultation, named for him because Costas was the dean of Andover Newton Theological School (the first non-white dean of a mainline seminary in the US) and a huge shaper of the BTI. He was one who combined the best of evangelicalism, ecumenism and mission. In addition, Costas made history when he was commissioned to go overseas as a missionary at the very same church (Tabernacle Church) in Salem that Judson was commissioned before him. In fact, if you go to Tabernacle Church today, you can see the actual bench that these two men were commissioned on, and it has both Judson's and Costas's names engraved on it. For a BTI tribute to Costas, see Daniel Jeyaraj, Robert W. Pazmiño and Rodney L. Petersen, eds., *Antioch Agenda: Essays on the Restorative Church in Honor of Orlando E. Costas* (New Delhi: ISPCK, 2007).

The missionary movement caught fire not only on the American side of the Atlantic; university students rose up to the cause in both England and Scotland in the form of the Cambridge Seven[20] and the St. Andrews Seven,[21] respectively. These two ancient and venerable universities served as the seedbed of some of the most renowned student missionaries in history who inspired generations to come.[22] And the person who inspired them? None other than D. L. Moody, who also helped to fan the flame of student missionary activity in the United States.

Princeton, Yale, Williams, Brown, Andover, Cambridge, St. Andrews, Biola, Moody and more—clearly university students were major catalysts for the cause of world missions. Though Edinburgh is definitely a university city as well,[23] there is probably no city more synonymous with the university in 2010 than Boston, Massachusetts. Though the Philadelphia area has more colleges and universities than Boston, the ones in the Boston area have more renown: for example, Harvard, MIT, Wellesley, Boston University, Boston College and Tufts. One of the 2010 Boston speakers, Peter Phan of Georgetown University, in his plenary address called Boston the "intellectual capital of the world" and jokingly said that all scholars must pilgrimage here at some point in their lives to attain "academic salvation."

Some may object that New England is infamously the most secular region of the United States so perhaps Boston is not the ideal location for this conference. That certainly did not stop Tokyo or Edinburgh 2010 from holding their conferences there—Japan and Western Europe are two of the most

---

[20]John Pollock, *The Cambridge Seven: The True Story of Ordinary Men Used in No Ordinary Way* (Fearn, UK: Christian Focus, 2006). The seven were C. T. Studd, Montagu Harry Proctor Beauchamp, Stanley P. Smith, Arthur T. Polhill-Turner, Dixon Edward Hoste, Cecil H. Polhill-Turner and William Wharton Cassels.

[21]Stuart Piggin and John Foxborough, *The St. Andrews Seven* (Edinburgh: Banner of Truth, 1985). The seven were Professor Thomas Chalmers and six of his students: Alexander Duff, John Urquhart, John Adam, Robert Nesbit, William Sinclair Mackay and John Ewart.

[22]Cambridge is the second-oldest university in England, founded in AD 1209, while St. Andrews is the oldest university in Scotland, founded in 1413. This makes the United States' oldest university—Harvard—look young, as it was founded in 1636! But the Anglo-American Christian world cannot claim the university either in terms of the idea or in the antiquity of its founding. The oldest university in the Americas, San Marcos in Peru (1551), and the oldest university in Asia, the University of Santo Tomas in The Philippines (1611), predate Harvard as well. And the oldest university in the world is actually Al-Azhar University in Cairo, Egypt, founded in AD 970 by Muslims.

[23]The city of Edinburgh is home to several universities, such as the University of Edinburgh, Herriot-Watt University, Edinburgh Napier University and Edinburgh College of Art, among others.

secular places in the world today—but Soong-Chan Rah[24] points out that
Boston seems atheist, as evidenced by cavernous ancient churches that now
stand empty, if one only considers the white population of the city. Asian
American, Haitian, Hispanic, Brazilian and multiracial congregations are
bursting at the seams in the city, as well as in Christian fellowship groups on
the various university campuses throughout Boston.[25] To be fair, there still
stand some older churches that are alive and well, such as Park Street Church,
but the great Boston preacher Phillips Brooks (1835–1839)[26] would be cha-
grined that his Trinity Church today is a shadow of its former self. With the
environment in Boston as an example par excellence, Rah takes Philip Jenkins's world Christianity thesis in *The Next Christendom*—that the center of
gravity of Christianity has shifted to the Two-Thirds World—and applies it
to the domestic sphere. His thesis is that the center of gravity of Christianity
in the United States has shifted to ethnic minorities and immigrants. This is
the reason that the United States is one of the few nations in the West—
which includes Canada, Europe and Australia/New Zealand—to still be
majority Christian.

It is not only that large percentages of Christians are found among ethnic
minorities and immigrants, but Boston also benefits from the influx of students from all across the nation (and the world) who populate the campuses with Christian faith.[27] It is far from a secular city! And Boston also
has the distinct advantage of having one of the few theological consortiums
in the world, where a multidenominational collection of seminaries and
theological schools cooperate to cross-list classes, offer joint degrees and
share libraries. The Boston Theological Institute consists of ten schools,[28]

---

[24]When I was an MDiv student at Gordon-Conwell Theological Seminary, Soong-Chan Rah was my
  pastor at Cambridge Community Fellowship Church. My experience was of many thriving communities of Christianity among local ethnic minority congregations as well as on university campuses throughout Boston.

[25]Soong-Chan Rah, *The Next Evangelicalism: Freeing the Church from Western Cultural Captivity*
  (Downers Grove, IL: InterVarsity Press, 2009), 11-18.

[26]Author of the beloved Christmas carol "O Little Town of Bethlehem."

[27]J. D. Payne, *Strangers Next Door: Immigration, Migration and Mission* (Downers Grove, IL: Inter-
  Varsity Press, 2012).

[28]At the time of 2010Boston it was only nine schools, but Hebrew College (the only one from a non-
  Christian tradition) was added to the BTI in 2011, formally making it an interfaith theological
  consortium. Unfortunately, due to budget concerns Andover Newton had to formally close their
  Massachusetts campus in 2016 and found new life in merging with Yale Divinity School, bringing
  the BTI member schools back down to nine.

and its members are Andover Newton Theological School; Boston College School of Theology and Ministry, and Theology Department; Boston University School of Theology; Episcopal Divinity School; Gordon-Conwell Theological Seminary; Harvard Divinity School; Hebrew College; Holy Cross Greek Orthodox School of Theology; and Saint John's Seminary and Theological Institute. This represents a wide variety of Christian denominations and theological leanings. Two other major theological consortia in the United States are Berkeley's Graduate Theological Union (GTU)[29] and Association of Chicago Theological Schools (ACTS).[30]

2010BOSTON: CONFERENCE PROCEEDINGS

The consortium lent itself to a unique physical format: the BTI member schools took turns hosting, emphasizing the ecumenical nature of the proceedings. A multi-site conference takes good logistical planning, but given that 2010Boston was smaller in number, and Boston's public transportation system is easy to use, it actually ended up being quite doable. The three main organizers, similarly, were from different BTI institutions: Rodney Petersen, the BTI executive director, of Andover Newton Theological School; Todd Johnson of Gordon-Conwell Theological Seminary; and Dana Robert of Boston University, who was the one who came up with the idea for this conference in the first place.

The conference began at Boston's historic Park Street Church, representing evangelicalism. (Gordon-Conwell Seminary is forty-five minutes' drive north of downtown Boston and does not have readily accessible public transportation, so Park Street served as a surrogate, especially since the senior pastor, Gordon Hugenberger, is an adjunct professor at Gordon-Conwell.) The next day, the conference moved along the Green Line "T" (subway) to Boston University, representing mainline Methodism, and to Holy Cross, a Greek Orthodox school. The third day was hosted by Andover

---

[29]Eight member schools: American Baptist Seminary of the West, Church Divinity School of the Pacific, Dominican School of Philosophy and Theology, Jesuit School of Theology at Berkeley, Pacific Lutheran Theological Seminary, Pacific School of Religion, San Francisco Theological Seminary and Starr King School for the Ministry.

[30]Eleven member schools: Bexley Seabury Seminary Federation, Catholic Theological Union, Chicago Theological Seminary, Garrett-Evangelical Theological Seminary, Lutheran School of Theology, McCormick Theological Seminary, Meadville Lombard Theological School, Mundelein Seminary of University of St. Mary of the Lake, North Park Theological Seminary, Northern Baptist Theological Seminary and Trinity Evangelical Divinity School.

Newton Theological School, from the American Baptist and United Church of Christ traditions, and Boston College (Roman Catholic), including the historic Episcopal Church of the Redeemer. On Sunday, the final day, the conference concluded at Harvard University and its Memorial Church. Throughout the four days, the conference participants literally became pilgrims, which is a theologically appropriate way to think about the Christian life. Dana Robert pointed out that because this conference kept moving, it represented the fact that there is no one theological center of Christianity. Likewise, when people ask why there need to be *four* conferences in 2010 celebrating the centenary of Edinburgh 1910, a similar answer can also be given: there is no one geographical center of Christianity today. Robert also mentioned that this conference was intentionally modeled after the New York City 1900 missionary conference, which also moved from site to site. Though only five of the nine BTI schools served as host sites, the fact that the conference embraced a spectrum of Christian faith traditions and was hosted by both educational institutions and churches made it a wonderfully diverse smorgasbord of visual, theological and cultural riches over an extended weekend.

Was there a hero at 2010Boston? That seems like the wrong question to ask, given that the whole concept of 2010Boston was about diffusion of geography and denomination. Nobody was the star of the show, no BTI school was the main site, and no celebrity speaker was the main keynote. Conference organizers were very self-conscious about it being only one of four conferences, not making itself out to be *the* main 2010 conference or even the grand finale. It also was about students, making it the most grassroots of all the 2010 conferences. If there was any one conference that had no hero and was proud of that fact, it was 2010Boston. Rather, it paid homage to the past with reference to Edinburgh 1910 and student missionary efforts throughout history, to the present with the BTI and the 2010 conferences, and to the future.

The size of the conference was almost three hundred, about the same size as Edinburgh 2010, making it a nice mirror to the latter as they represented ecumenism among the major conferences of 2010. The constituency also fluctuated greatly, as many students from these respective BTI schools came, but often just for the session geographically closest to them. Yet there remained a core group of perhaps 150 who made the pilgrimage from site to site, and the unity and consistency from this core was very rewarding.

Nine keynote addresses from speakers of various denominational backgrounds, as diverse as the host BTI member schools, were spread out over four days. The first two addresses were historical pieces, and the other keynotes covered subjects like theological education, peacekeeping, interfaith dialogue and the *missio Dei*. There were also eight workshops ("breakout sessions") on the afternoons of the two full days of the conference (Friday and Saturday), an intentional tribute to the eight themes of Edinburgh 1910,[31] except updated for today's world:

1. Changing Contours of Christian Unity (what ecumenism looks like after a century)

2. Mission in Context (world Christianity)

3. Disciple and Mission (discipleship and spirituality)

4. Education for Mission (theological education)

5. Mission and Post-Colonialism (disentangling mission from its colonial legacy)

6. Mission Theology in a Pluralist World (how to interact with the diversity of faiths and the violence that sometimes accompanies it)

7. Mission and Post-Modernity (how to reach the secularists and the relativists)

8. Salvation Today (what soteriology looks like in all its forms; holistic mission)[32]

BTI director Rodney Petersen clarifies the parallels with Edinburgh 1910: "Boston themes 1 (Unity), 4 (Education for Mission) and 8 (Salvation Today) related to Edinburgh themes 8 (Cooperation and Unity), 5 and 3 (Preparation of Missionaries and Education in Relation to the Christianization of National Life) and 1 (Carrying the Gospel) respectively. Boston themes 2, 3,

---

[31]For a list of the eight Edinburgh 1910 themes, see chapter one.

[32]All the main sessions—nine keynote addresses, three 2010 conference reports and the best five student papers—are helpfully compiled in Todd M. Johnson, Rodney L. Petersen, Gina A. Bellofatto and Travis L. Myers, eds., *2010Boston: The Changing Contours of World Mission and Christianity* (Eugene, OR: Pickwick, 2012).

5, 6 and 7 were only loosely related to Edinburgh themes 2, 3, 7, 4 and 6 respectively. Differences between the two conferences' themes are the result of BTI faculty interests and reflect the contemporary issues of globalization, contextualization, and the evolution of mission studies."[33]

As important as the keynotes were, it seemed like the workshops were really the heart of 2010Boston: "As evidenced by the regions of the world and theological traditions represented, the issues in and for pastoral ministry raised, and the global concerns addressed, the students and their papers—more than any other component of the conference—represented the current shape of world Christianity and Christian mission."[34] Unlike Edinburgh 2010 or Cape Town 2010, which were working conferences with the delegates contributing to the formation of a document, the 2010Boston workshops were all papers given by students (thirty-six in total) with various faculty chairing the sessions. So it was not just student participation in a passive way as audience listeners; it invited them to be active participants and contributors in an empowering way. Unfortunately, due to the fact that there were only two afternoon sessions, attendees could not hear student papers on all eight themes (each session had two to three papers, so there was the possibility of hearing at least a couple of themes). However, audience

---

[33]Ibid., 275.

[34]Travis L. Myers, "The Student Paper Workshops of 2010Boston," in Johnson et al., *2010Boston*, 155-56. The papers covered topics such as "the many ambiguities, complex dynamics, and local implications of globalization; ecological crises, and Christian responsibilities toward creation; the contested meaning and value of short-term mission (or 'Christian service') trips; the liberation and restorative care of women and children in sex slavery; and the appropriate theological impetuses and practical modes for interreligious dialogue, evangelism, and disciple-making activities (including catechesis, sacramental theologies, and education for mission). More context-specific studies included topics like emergent/missional liturgical forms among Anglicans in 'post-Christian' England; post-conflict reconciliation initiatives in Colombia; and student movements for Christian mission in China. Students presented work from different academic disciplines (including history, biblical studies, theology, philosophy, sociology and demography) with most of the studies being interdisciplinary to some degree. Several students also exhibited the creative and ecumenical incorporation or synthesis of resources from theological traditions other than their own. In addition to BTI schools, students who either presented papers or participated in responsive dialogue during the workshops came from a variety of academic institutions, such as Yale Divinity School (New Haven, CT), Pittsburgh Theological Seminary, Palmer Theological Seminary (Philadelphia, PA), Westminster Theological Seminary (Philadelphia, PA), Asbury Theological Seminar (Wilmore, KY), Fuller Theological Seminary (Pasadena, CA), Luther Theological Seminary (St. Paul, MN), Trinity Evangelical Divinity School (Deerfield, IL) and Wake Forest University (Winston-Salem, NC). International students from these schools originated from nations such as Germany, Japan, Korea, China, Taiwan, Indonesia and India."

members had the opportunity to share their ideas, thoughts and reflections on what they heard in the closing session of the conference, adding yet another unique format of idea exchange.

ORIENTED TO THE PAST: TRADITION

It was not only the polycentric nature of the physical venues that was striking, but the denominational scope from varying traditions. Every day the conference attendees drank deeply of different worship styles, but especially notable were the styles that seemed more traditional and evoked the past, especially since this was a conference so much about the future.

One of the most striking examples of this was the session held at Holy Cross Greek Orthodox School of Theology, where everyone participated in an Orthodox vespers service, which was the most "different" worship all week. Throughout the spoken/sung liturgy, there was a refrain that recurred four times: "You took pains to put an end to the blasphemy of Arius. Suffering for the sake of the eternal and consubstantial trinity, you overcame the impious Macedonius, the adversary of the Spirit . . . and put to flight the heresy of Nestorius in your zeal for the Church of Christ." In order for the conference to discuss the "changing contours of world mission and Christianity," there needs to be a beginning, and the reference to the original ecumenical councils is a reminder of the early church in the Greek/Mediterranean world, even as world Christianity is upon us. It is interesting that diversity is now the norm, and the "traditional" is now the "different."

Dana Robert gave the opening plenary talk at Park Street Church on the first night, titled "Boston, Students, and Missions from 1810 to 2010," providing historical context for why 2010Boston is all about students, and discussing the many contributions that students have made in the past for the worldwide missionary movement.[35]

Perhaps the most prophetic—and, interestingly, the most liturgical—talk was Ruth Padilla DeBorst's (Latin American Theological Fellowship) talk at Boston College on the third day of the conference. It was maybe the most moving address of the whole conference, titled "Wooden Boxes and Latticed

---

[35]Dana L. Robert, "Boston, Students, and Missions from 1810 to 2010," in Johnson et al., *2010Boston*, 13-27.

Windows: Christian Witness and Post-colonizing Mission."[36] She proposed that public confession (via remembering, releasing and reconciling) needs to be a part of our Christian witness in order to extricate ourselves from colonization and power, which are always a bad combination for authentic Christianity. She had a constant refrain: "Forgive us, Father, for we know not what we do, or perhaps we know all too well, and find it too costly to change." This message would have fit in perfectly with the reconciliation theme at Cape Town 2010 had she not already been assigned to be an Ephesians Bible expositor! Especially notable was how she started with remembering the horrors of apartheid in South Africa—perhaps Chris Rice would not have had to circulate his petition if she had presented this talk at Lausanne III.

The daily worship music was led in a wonderful, folksy, intimate way by the young Tracy Wispelwey of the Restoration Project, who wrote many of the songs and, in fact, was one of the musicians at Edinburgh 2010. Despite this being an "academic" conference, worship was very much a major component of it (and all four conferences), to the delight of all present. The youth and newness present in this balanced out the tradition and ancientness of some of the other styles of worship.

ORIENTED TO THE FUTURE: A MORE ACCESSIBLE CHRISTIANITY

Unlike Tokyo, Edinburgh and Cape Town, which were all invitation-only, Boston was open to all. This made the number of attendees a mystery until the conference actually began. Though the quantity of people was initially unknown, the people intentionally sought after were academic in nature, particularly students and researchers. In the subject of world Christianity, a relatively new field of study, the number of published scholars is small, and the average age is not on the younger side.[37] The not-by-invitation nature of this conference meant that it was not only for the self-perpetuation of older established scholars, but to generate fresh interest in this field. This

---

[36]Ruth Padilla DeBorst, "Wooden Boxes and Latticed Windows: Christian Confession and Post-Colonizing Mission," in Johnson et al., *2010Boston*, 110-23.

[37]This is evident by the participants who regularly come to conferences such as the Yale-Edinburgh group, International Association of Mission Studies (IAMS) and Evangelical Missiological Society (EMS). In contrast, many younger scholars come to conferences like American Academy of Religion (AAR) and Evangelical Theological Society (ETS). However, it is perhaps not surprising that the demographics of missiologists is perpetually older, as the people most qualified to contribute are those who have spent considerable time on the mission field.

made 2010Boston the best representative of young people among the four 2010 conferences.

Technology, on a small scale, was also visible and well in effect. Cape Town 2010 may have had the big advances such as GlobaLink, but sometimes smaller technologies are more accessible to all. Todd Johnson and Kenneth Ross point out that at Edinburgh 1910, "technological advance was hailed as the handmaid to the spread of the gospel worldwide."[38] For 2010Boston, this meant students accessing the website, writing blog posts, making YouTube videos and availing themselves of a live Twitter feed throughout the whole conference.[39] Students are experts at these types of social media, and information technology allows people to be voices rather than voiceless. Throughout history, technology has aided the spread of the gospel, whether it be the Roman roads in the apostle Paul's time that linked the entire Mediterranean world and greatly expedited his three missionary journeys, or the Gutenberg printing press that helped Martin Luther put the Bible into the hands of laypeople and spurred on the Protestant Reformation, or the ships during the colonial era that aided missionaries to travel globally but turned out to be a double-edged sword in that missionaries got conflated with the imperial enterprise, or radio and television that helped Billy Graham to become the most prolific evangelist in the history of the world. Today, Facebook can connect people like never before, in ways that previous missionaries could not even have dreamed of, and tools like this are in the wheelhouse of students.

Brian Stanley, who wrote the book on the definitive history of Edinburgh 1910, was the second keynote speaker, thus giving 2010Boston legitimacy to be a centenary celebration, especially since he was not a speaker at any of the other conferences. Stanley gave his lecture, "Discerning the Future of World Christianity: Vision and Blindness at the World Missionary Conference, Edinburgh 1910," on the morning of the second day at Boston University. Despite the title, he mainly talked about the past, but he evoked the future by pointing out some blind spots that the Edinburgh 1910 organizers,

---

[38]Todd M. Johnson and Kenneth R. Ross, eds., *The Atlas of Global Christianity* (Edinburgh: Edinburgh University Press, 2009), xvi.

[39]Gina A. Bellofatto, "2010Boston from the Student Perspective," in Johnson et al., *2010Boston*, 245.

for all their brilliance, had, such as underestimating the tenacity of Islam and overestimating the influence of the West. These are good lessons for twenty-first-century Christians to learn, in order to avoid making similar mistakes in the future.[40]

The Emergent Church[41] was not evident at any of the four 2010 conferences except Boston. Though the label "Emergent" was never used,[42] its presence was felt by the inclusion of its most prominent spokesman, Brian McLaren, as one of the plenary speakers. His talk, titled "Christian Mission and Peace-Making: Discerning Our Secret Non-Weapon,"[43] focused on creating a metanarrative that promotes mission not as a specialized category but as part-and-parcel of what it means to be a Christian. This is in keeping with one of the main characteristics of Emergent, which is often described as "missional."[44] Thus it is surprising that Emergent, which takes so much of its core identity from mission, was not present (or at least not obvious) at any of the other three 2010 conferences. Part of what it means to be missional, according to McLaren, is to not create "us-them" categories, because as soon as you "other" someone, you alienate them. This is definitely a more invitational approach to missions that we would do well to think about for the future in order to make Christianity more accessible to all.

Archbishop of York John Sentamu gave the closing talk at Harvard University's Memorial Church, after which a panel discussion with all the 2010Boston speakers on stage fielded questions from the audience. In a

---

[40]Brian Stanley, "Discerning the Future of World Christianity: Vision and Blindness at the World Missionary Conference, Edinburgh 1910," in Johnson et al., *2010Boston*, 47-63.

[41]Not to be confused with the emerging church, which is more of an umbrella term under which Emergent can be included.

[42]Rodney L. Petersen, "Strategies for Holistic Mission: An 'Emergent' and Emerging Church," in *Tracing Contours: Reflections on World Mission and Christianity,* ed. Rodney L. Petersen and Marian Gh. Simeon (Newton Centre: Boston Theological Institute, 2010), 149: "The *'Emergent'* and *emerging church movement* is developing in relation to this missional conversation, a 21st [*sic*] Christian church whose participants seek to engage postmodern people, especially the unchurched with a missional approach to Christianity so as to reshape belief, standards and methods to fit contemporary realities. Scot McKnight identifies five themes within this trend: *prophetic, postmodern, praxis-oriented, post-evangelical and political* . . . a definition of the movement that defines 'emerging' in this way: as those who practice 'the way of Jesus' in the postmodern era."

[43]Renamed as "Finding the Seventh Story," in Johnson et al., *2010Boston*, 124-31.

[44]Its own website, www.emergentvillage.com (no longer active), used that word: "Emergent Village is a growing, generative friendship among missional Christians seeking to love our world in the Spirit of Jesus Christ."

Venn diagram sort of situation, 2010Boston was able to share Sentamu with Harvard's William Belden Noble Lecture Series, which has been ongoing since 1898. The archbishop gave three lectures for the Noble Series on the theme "Who Is Jesus and What Does He Mean to Those Who Put Their Trust in Him?," the first of which was the Sunday sermon and also the ninth and final keynote address for 2010Boston, titled "Part I—God's Mission Is Performative." The following two days (November 8–9), after the conference was over, he continued his series with "Part II—God's Mission Is Transformative" and "Part III—God's Mission Is Restorative Justice." He insisted that Christ must shape our theology, and culture itself must be converted. Even postcolonials who point fingers at others must think about their own culture. He brought it back to the goal of mission, insisting that the most crucial question always must be, do we ultimately look like Jesus?

A FITTING END TO 2010

2010Boston was deliberately placed at the end of 2010 to study the other conferences and sum up the year. Unlike the others, Boston styled itself as an academics', rather than missionaries', conference. This is not to say that the other three were not committed to academic reflection, but their main goal was scholarship as a springboard to action. The summary of the year was provided primarily by retired professor Norman Thomas of United Theological Seminary (Dayton, Ohio) who gave a 2010 overview on the first day in a pre-conference Edinburgh 1910–2010 debriefing (although he did not attend Tokyo 2010, Edinburgh 2010 or Cape Town 2010), as well as a panel discussion, which I participated in.

This panel happened on the second day of the conference, when I (from the American Baptist denomination) and two others (Kapya John Kaoma, an African who did his ThD at Boston University and who is from the Episcopal tradition; and LouAnn Stropoli, an American who works at Gordon-Conwell Seminary and is licensed with the Conservative Congregational Christian Conference) presented on the three previous conferences: Tokyo, Edinburgh and Cape Town, respectively.[45] However, a question about

---

[45] All three presentations can be found in Johnson et al., *2010Boston*, 254-72: Allen Yeh, "Tokyo 2010: Global Mission Consultation"; LouAnn Stropoli, "Lausanne III: A Success?"; and Kapya John Kaoma, "Witnessing for Christ Today: Christian Mission Beyond Edinburgh 1910."

evangelical versus conciliar ended up becoming the centerpiece of this panel discussion.

The panel was moderated by Episcopal bishop Ian Douglas. Douglas observed four commonalities among the 2010 conferences: (1) an embrace of the nature of Christianity as a world phenomenon, which presupposes a paradigm of plurality of missiological perspectives; (2) an attempt to heal or overcome divisions of the last half-century of mission, which was divided between evangelism and social justice; (3) that all four conferences were primarily Protestant; and (4) Faith and Order[46] did not seem to be primary. Douglas also categorized Tokyo and Cape Town as "evangelical," that is, emphasizing proclamation evangelism and having a constituency composed of practitioners, as opposed to Edinburgh and Boston as being "conciliar," or focused on ecumenical unity and having more of an academic bent. He asked the following questions: "How genuine is the healing of the social justice/evangelism rift?" "Have we overcome the division between evangelicals and conciliar Protestants?" and "What does the overwhelming dominance of Protestants, and the lack of focus on Faith and Order, say about the nature of ecumenism?"

To many of the Majority World participants (and to some of the Western participants as well), the evangelical-conciliar divide seemed like an artificial way to view these conferences. Speakers such as Dana Robert, Ruth Padilla DeBorst, Brian Stanley, Daniel Jeyaraj and John Sentamu could not be classified as solely one or the other. And the publisher of the Edinburgh 2010 Centenary Series is Regnum, an evangelical publisher. Perhaps speaking of evangelicals versus conciliars is a twentieth-century distinction (such as the fundamentalist-modernist controversy) that is no longer relevant today except as a historical curiosity. Also, to think of evangelicals as only practitioners belies the fact that the *Tokyo Declaration* and especially the *Cape Town Commitment* are documents with plenty of academic rigor to them. Certainly they were more robust than Edinburgh 2010's *Common Call*, which Norman Thomas called "theological pablum"—but it is worth noting that plenty of people also have benefited from, and reflected thoughtfully on, the *Common Call* since its publication. However, it is true that

---

[46]One of the two streams that came out of the International Missionary Council, along with Life and Work, that eventually led to the formation of the World Council of Churches.

Edinburgh and Boston were more ecumenical in the sense that they had Catholics and Orthodox in attendance as participants, not simply as observers. But perhaps Protestants are more drawn to these kinds of ecumenical missionary conferences because they well understand diversity, since they do not have one geographical or ecclesial center. It is inherent in the nature of Protestantism, especially evangelicalism, to have a multiplicity of expressions yet be united around the Bible, and that serves them well in being a resilient version of Christianity well suited to the twenty-first century.

The links with the other 2010 conferences were striking, intentional and manifold. Tracy Wispelwey was one of the worship leaders at Edinburgh 2010. The fact that 2010Boston deliberately echoed Edinburgh 2010 by having Dana Robert (professor at Boston University) as the opening speaker and John Sentamu (Anglican archbishop of York) as the closing speaker suggests that the emphasis on women (Robert) and the Global South (Sentamu is originally from Uganda) is another reality of the world today. Ruth Padilla DeBorst (a Latin American woman) was a speaker at Cape Town 2010 and 2010Boston, and she embodies *both* the female and Southern traits that are so characteristic of world Christianity today. Philip Jenkins wrote about the present and future contours of Christianity: "The average Christian today is a poor Nigerian or Brazilian woman. Soon, the phrase 'a White Christian' may sound like a curious oxymoron, as mildly surprising as 'a Swedish Buddhist.' Such people can exist, but a slight eccentricity is implied."[47] Henry Orombi, Anglican archbishop of Uganda and honorary chair of the Africa Welcome Committee for Cape Town 2010, is a fellow countryman with Sentamu—thus high-ranking Anglican clergy from Uganda closed Edinburgh 2010, Cape Town 2010 and 2010Boston.

There are links between the conference planners as well. Ruth Padilla DeBorst (a Latin American) was Dana Robert's (a North American) protégé just as Lamin Sanneh (an African) was Andrew Walls's (a European), but their students have come of age, similar to how Two-Thirds World churches have come of age and now are partners and equal contributors rather than learners. These are concrete examples of the Two-Thirds World churches

---

[47]Philip Jenkins, *The Next Christendom: The Coming of Global Christianity* (Oxford: Oxford University, 2002), 3. The first part of this quote is originally from Dana L. Robert, "Shifting Southward: Global Christianity Since 1945," *International Bulletin of Missionary Research* 24, no. 2 (April 2000): 50.

taking hold of not just the three selves but the fourth self: self-theologizing. Not only do these tandems represent the partnership of the Global South with the Global North, but Padilla DeBorst–Robert adds a female dimension to the Sanneh-Walls duo.

Another link is that Todd Johnson, one of the 2010Boston organizers, is Ralph Winter's son-in-law. Thus, the Robert–Padilla Deborst partnership in two of the conferences (Boston and Costa Rica) is similar to the Winter-Johnson partnership (Tokyo and Boston). And the ongoing partnership of Walls-Sanneh takes place every year with the Yale-Edinburgh Group.[48]

Speaking of Todd Johnson, he was the only person other than me to attend all four 2010 conferences, and one of the main reasons was that he was presenting on his monumental *Atlas of Global Christianity* (coedited with Kenneth Ross and published just in time for 2010). This magnificent work also helped to link all four 2010 centenary events.

IMPACT OF 2010BOSTON

It does not seem that 2010Boston had the same plans for continuation as the other 2010 conferences. There was no continuation committee, but the fact that the spirit of 2010Boston will live on in universities and students is sufficient. Not only have students been agents for mission, but the university itself is a mission field with the world coming to it in microcosm. Students do not have to go to a foreign country to preach to the nations: the world will come to the universities.

There was no document that came out of this conference, unlike at Tokyo 2010, Edinburgh 2010 and Cape Town 2010. However, there was a comprehensive book that was published on the conference proceedings called *2010Boston: The Changing Contours of World Mission and Christianity*, so at least the book serves as a published memorial to what happened and a resource for generations of mission scholars and practitioners to come. 2010Boston did not try to do too much, but wrapped up 2010 with a neat bow. It was more than just an academic exercise, it was a celebration: looking back toward history and remembering, looking at the present and celebrating, looking forward toward the future and wondering.

---

[48]See chapter two.

In considering theological education, there seems to be a glut of people with PhDs in theology and biblical studies in the West, and not enough jobs to sustain them all. There is a solution, but not one that many would choose to take: the need is so great in the Two-Thirds World. The problem is twofold: (1) people want a Western-level salary, and (2) they could end up importing Western theology to other nations. Hence the need for bidirectional education—Westerners need to be educated about other cultures so they know how to contextualize properly, and people from the Two-Thirds World need to be offered jobs in the West so that Westerners can learn from them.

In a way it is appropriate that these four conferences have toured in order through Asia, Europe and Africa, and finally to the Americas, because the gospel started in Asia (Israel and Turkey) two thousand years ago, made its way to Europe and Africa (Greece and Ethiopia in Acts 16 and 8, respectively), and finally the Americas, which were the last continents to receive missionaries. This exemplifies the Acts 1:8 formula of going from "Jerusalem" to "Judea and Samaria" and finally to the "end of the earth." It is perhaps instructive to realize, however, that the Americas (the US and Latin America) are now more Christian than any other continent on earth, while Asia is the only continent without a Christian majority today. This is one of the unique features of "reverse mission" that characterizes the world today.

In the final analysis, does 2010Boston represent "the Americas"? Is this the end of the story? If affirmative to the former question and negative to the latter, then the four conferences of 2010 once again—like a century ago—left Latin America off the map. It is to this next chapter that we will now turn.

QUESTIONS

1. What do you think about the eight workshop themes? Do they adequately serve as contemporary updates of Edinburgh 1910?

2. What do you think about 2010Boston's ecumenical diversity? Is it ecumenical in the same way as Edinburgh 2010?

3. Do you think that considering the four 2010 conferences as either evangelical or conciliar/ecumenical is an artificial division, or is it an appropriate way of thinking about certain divisions? Are these divisions only applicable to Western denominations, and/or to the twentieth century?

4. Should 2010Boston have had a document, like Tokyo 2010, Edinburgh 2010 and Cape Town 2010? If so, what kind of document should they have produced? How should it be distinctive from the others?

5. Should 2010Boston have had some continuation committee, or at least a book series come out of it like the Regnum Edinburgh 1910 Centenary Series, since it purports to be about students, universities and academics?

CLADE V (AKA COSTA RICA 2012)

IT IS PROMISING THAT many scholars are now seriously taking on world Christianity as a subject.[1] World Christianity is defined as the shift of the center of gravity of Christianity to the Majority World/Two-Thirds World, but sometimes the Majority World or Two-Thirds World remains a vaguely defined area—specifically, what geographical areas are we talking about? Usually it is defined as Asia, Africa and Latin America, sometimes with explicit mentions of the Caribbean and Oceania.

Unfortunately, Latin America is still seen as the excluded and forgotten continent by Westerners. For some reason, Latin America is not seen on par with Asia and Africa. There is a lot of historical precedent for this. For example, in 1893 Edward Millard and Lucy Guinness wrote a book about their missionary tour called *South America, The Neglected Continent*,[2] because it was hitherto unexplored by Protestants with regard to missionary work,

---

[1]The conference organizers never called it Costa Rica 2012, but I call it that just for parallelism with the other four, giving it a geographical location and a year. Then why not call it San José 2012, to have the name be a city like the others? Because "Costa Rica 2012" parallels the nomenclature of the landmark Panamá 1916 conference, which used the country name rather than the city. Nonetheless, this is a moot point as hereafter I will mostly only be referring to it as CLADE V out of respect for the conference's own way of referring to itself. See also Allen Yeh, "Lessons from 2010: Tokyo, Edinburgh, Cape Town, and Boston," *Journal of Latin American Theology* 6, no. 1 (2011): 14-27.

[2]Edward C. Millard and Lucy Evangeline Guinness, *South America, The Neglected Continent: Being an account of the mission tour of G. C. Grubb, and party, in 1893, with a historical sketch and summary of missionary enterprise in these vast regions* (New York: Fleming H. Revell, 1894).

unlike Africa and Asia. Hiram Bingham III (1875–1956), grandson of the famous Hiram Bingham I (1789–1869) who was part of the first missionary team to Hawaii, became even more famous than his grandfather for his "discovery" of Machu Picchu in Peru in 1911, as a result earning the first professorship of South American studies in the Western world, at Yale University. Bingham's uncovering of Machu Picchu was the impetus to validating Latin America as a viable field of study by Western academics, whereas Asian and African studies have had a long and storied history. This is confirmed by the well-known School of Oriental and African Studies (SOAS), which is part of the University of London—it does not include Latin America in its name. This trend continues today, as Mark Noll's second book on world Christianity only includes Africa and Asia.[3]

There are many possible reasons for this exclusion, especially with regard to Christianity and missions:

- Latin America is already deemed to be Christianized because of its cultural Catholicism.

- The 10/40 Window, a concept coined at Lausanne II, does not include Latin America within its geographical scope.

- Its close proximity to the US makes it not "exotic" or "distant" enough.

- Latin Americans themselves view North and South America as one single continent, not two, so there is no such thing as a separate field of *Latin American* studies.

- Because Latin Americans mostly speak Spanish or Portuguese and so many Latinos are of European ancestry, Latin America is viewed as an "extension" of Europe (completely forgetting all the indigenous genetics and cultural influences).

- While having poverty relative to the West, it does not seem to approach the destitution of places like Africa or India, so aid and compassion do not flow that direction as readily as to other places.

- The ancients of the "Old World" regarded the earth as consisting of three continents: Africa, Europe and Asia. In fact, ancient Christians equated

---

[3]Mark A. Noll and Carolyn Nystrom, *Clouds of Witnesses: Christian Voices from Africa and Asia* (Downers Grove, IL: InterVarsity Press, 2011).

this with the Trinity. When the New World was discovered, this disrupted the neat framework that people had constructed in their minds, and they did not know what to do with the information about this new land.

- At the famous Edinburgh 1910 World Missionary Conference, "the birthplace of the modern ecumenical movement," the Anglo-Catholics threatened to boycott (and thus disrupt the ecumenism of) the conference if the Protestants regarded Latin America as a mission field because they saw it as potential "sheep stealing."

- Modern books on Christian demography like *Operation World* and *The Atlas of Global Christianity* use self-identification to determine how many Christians are in each country or region of the world; therefore Latin America is always considered to be well over 90 percent Christian and never is considered to be a place that needs missions.

Yet, though Western history has been shortsighted with the omission of Latin America, we ought not be. Latin America deserves a chapter in the Edinburgh 1910 centenary conference series.

FROM EDINBURGH 1910 TO PANAMÁ 1916

William Carey did not only say that there should be an *1810* ecumenical conference in his "pleasing dream"; he gave a window between 1810 and 1812: "would it be possible to have a general association of all denominations of Christians, from the four corners of the world, kept there once in about ten years? I earnestly recommend this plan, let the first meeting be in the Year 1810, or 1812 at furthest." Therefore, anything between 2010 and 2012 would celebrate the bicentenary of his idea. Second, 1812 turned out to be the launch of the United States' missions movement with Adoniram Judson being sent overseas from the United States, so significant Carey-Judson missionary events were happening in this window.

Still, these were significant UK-US historical missionary events—what does all this matter to Latin Americans? Does CLADE V want to be considered along with the 2010 conferences? Is it trying to do its own thing, apart from the others? Does the fact that it was conducted entirely in Spanish—unlike any of the 2010 conferences—preclude participation from a worldwide audience? Does it even want to be linked with Edinburgh 1910?

The fact that Ruth Padilla DeBorst was at the planning meeting with the other 2010 conferences shows that it does deserve to be included in this volume, and the desire to not sideline Latin America once again also is a factor. Padilla DeBorst actually *intended* CLADE V to be in 2010,[4] but pushed it back two years because the 2010 calendar was already glutted with centenary conferences, and this would hamper the attendance in Costa Rica if Latin Americans were trying to attend any of the other 2010 conferences *plus* CLADE V in the same year. Also, having it two years later allowed a Spanish translation of *The Cape Town Commitment (CTC)—El Compromiso de Ciudad del Cabo (CCC)*—to be distributed among all CLADE V delegates for study, showing that there was theological and missiological agreement among Lausanne, the World Evangelical Alliance and the Latin American Theological Fellowship.[5] Marcos Amado, the Latin American director for the Lausanne movement, wrote in the *CCC's* introduction: "*Por eso, mi oración es que el CCC ofrezca una contribución significativa para que la Iglesia latinoamericana pueda entender los tiempos en que vivimos y logre cumplir los propósitos de Dios en esta generación.*" ("Therefore my prayer is that the *CTC* offers a significant contribution toward the Latin American church to be able to understand the times in which we live and meets the goal of fulfilling the purposes of God in this generation.")

Because Edinburgh 1910 left Latin America off the map, the Latin Americans organized their own conference a few years later in Panamá 1916.[6] In a repeat of history, the Latinos organized their conference later, or *mañana*, too—Costa Rica 2012! Some might question why the Latinos at Cape Town 2010, some four hundred in number, needed another conference if they were not excluded this time. The problem is, though they were present (unlike the Chinese) in South Africa, they felt marginalized—so they still wanted a congress to call their own.[7] Part of their dissatisfaction came from the video that was produced about their region. Every evening at Cape Town

---

[4]The original physical promotional materials that were distributed listed CLADE V as being planned for 2010, as seen in figure 2.

[5]In Ruth Padilla DeBorst's mind, CLADE V follows in the spirit of Lausanne as exemplified in her article "From Lausanne III to CLADE V," *Journal of Latin American Theology* 6, no. 1 (2011): 7-13.

[6]Brian Stanley, *The World Missionary Conference, Edinburgh 1910* (Grand Rapids: Eerdmans, 2009), 304.

[7]Valdir Steuernagel, "A Latin American Evangelical Perspective on the Cape Town Congress," *Journal of Latin American Theology* 9, no. 2 (2014): 122.

2010 there was a regional video describing the state of Christianity, and while the Middle Eastern video was very well received and the Asia video was seen as adequate, the Africa and Oceania videos were not shown due to lack of time in production, and the Latin America video was not received favorably by Latinos because it was seen as inaccurately describing the state of Christianity in their continent. The Latin Americans said there was a lack of vibrancy in Latin American Christianity in the video's portrayal, and it had a negative tone toward Catholics.[8] To be fair, Latinos felt marginalized by Edinburgh 2010 as well.[9]

Figure 2. Original promotional materials for CLADE V

In order to understand Costa Rica 2012, it is enlightening to show a parallel with Panamá 1916. The latter, officially the Congress on Christian Work in Latin America, was held February 10–20, 1916, at the Hotel Tivoli in Panama City. According to the official report, "What seemed at the outset . . . a matter of deep regret turned out fortunately. . . . Consequently, for the time being, the representatives of Latin-American missions agreed to their omission at the Edinburgh [1910] Conference, reserving at the same time the privilege of identifying

[8]Interview with Todd Johnson.

[9]Víctor Rey, "The FTL, Edinburgh, Lausanne III, and CLADE V: A Forty-Year Journey," *Journal of Latin American Theology* 6, no. 1 (2011): 32: "The only public space afforded to Latin America [at Edinburgh 2010] was given to a Baptist pastor from Brazil who highlighted the mission priorities of the Baptist World Alliance. Latin American delegates felt less than well represented by this exposition."

themselves at some future time with a movement for a Latin-American conference."[10] Even though, for the sake of ecumenical unity, Latin America was omitted from discussion as a mission field,[11] those representatives at Edinburgh 1910 who had a previous concern and stake in Latin America still met over lunch and planned a conference solely for discussion of missionary work in Latin America. This way, they could have their cake and eat it too—that is, enjoy ecumenical unity at Edinburgh 1910 while also continuing their Latin American missionary work. Perhaps, in this way, it was similar to Edinburgh 2010 and Cape Town 2010—the former was for evangelicals to meet with Catholics and Orthodox, and so on, and the latter was for evangelicals to do their own work. These Latin American mission board representatives from Edinburgh 1910— who, incidentally, were all North Americans without a Latino among them— drafted a statement to be presented to the North American churches:

> The undersigned delegates to the World Missionary Conference, rejoicing over the success of that great gathering and the impulse it must give to the evangelization of the non-Christian world, feel constrained to say a word for those missions in countries nominally Christian that were not embraced in the scope of the Edinburgh Conference.
>
> We do not stop to inquire whether the dominant Churches in these lands are or are not Christian Churches, or whether they are or are not faithful to their duty; we only affirm that millions and millions of people are practically without the Word of God and do not really know what the Gospel is. If Christ's followers are under obligation to give the Word of Life to those who are strangers to it; to tell those who have a form of godliness without the power thereof that they may have both; to show those who have never received the Holy Ghost that the privilege is theirs for the asking; to rouse those who have a name to live and are dead to seek the abundant life—if these are obligations pertaining to discipleship anywhere, they are obligations to the populations above described.
>
> The Church must not forget that missions in the Latin and Oriental Christian countries are and long have been a legitimate part of the foreign missionary enterprise of the leading foreign missionary Societies of the

---

[10]*Christian Work in Latin America: Survey and Occupation, Message and Method, Education: Being the reports of Commissions,* [sic] *I, II and III presented to the Congress on Christian Work in Latin America, Panama, February, 1916, with a general introduction and full records of the presentation and discussion of each report* (New York: The Missionary Education Movement, 1917), 6.
[11]See chapter one.

United States and Canada. As such they could claim the right to consideration in any World Missionary Conference. The American Societies in waiving the claim did not admit that these missions to peoples nominally Christian are not properly foreign missions and ought not to be carried on; but yielded their preference in view of the fact that foreign missions in Great Britain and in Continental Europe mean missions to non-Christian peoples, and that British and Continental societies are organized on this narrower basis. This and other facts made it clear to the American Executive Committee that if the Conference were to unite all Protestant Churches it must be on this basis; and the World Conference was restricted by the addition of the words "to consider missionary problems in relation to the non-Christian world." The Committee was justified in making the concession. The Conference was a glorious demonstration of the loyalty of Protestant Christianity to Christ, of its unity of spirit, and of its purpose of active cooperation in evangelizing the world.[12]

Though this was a Latin American congress, the US American influence was palpable. As is clear from the statement above, they were the ones organizing Panamá 1916 because the Europeans (Germans and Anglo-Catholics) omitted Latin America at Edinburgh 1910. Also, the location was determined by the fact that the Panama Canal, created and operated by the United States, was opened two years prior in 1914, making Panama literally the crossroads of the world, linking North and South America, and the Pacific and Atlantic oceans. The Panama Canal was a show of the United States' wealth, strength and ingenuity. It was also difficult for Europeans to be fully involved as World War I[13] occupied much of their attention, which was yet another reason the US Americans were more closely involved with Panama. Finally, John R. Mott chaired the advisory committee for Panamá 1916, linking it inextricably with Edinburgh 1910. It seems that any events in Latin America, whether political or social, almost inevitably involve the United States in some way. And perhaps it is no surprise that theological shifts in Latin America also reflect similar shifts in the United States.[14]

---

[12]*Christian Work in Latin America*, 7-8.

[13]July 28, 1914–November 11, 1918.

[14]José Míguez Bonino, "How Does United States Presence Help, Hinder, or Compromise Christian Mission in Latin America?," *Review and Expositor* 74, no. 2 (1977): 176: "Missions and missionaries came to Latin America as—conscious or unconscious—expressions and agents of a world view in which Protestant faith was integrated with a political philosophy (democracy in its American version), an economic system (free enterprise capitalism), a geopolitical/historical project (the United States as champion and center of a 'new world' of progress and freedom) and an ideology (the liberal creed of progress, education and science). Even a cursory

Originally the organizers had proposed having two conferences: one in the northern part of Latin America and one in the southern part. Instead, there was a pre-conference held in New York City on March 12–13, 1913, with the great missionary statesman Dr. Robert E. Speer as chair. A second pre-conference was held in June 1914 in Montevideo, Uruguay, thus being the first international missions conference in South America![15] The Montevideo conference was organized by the YMCA in Brazil, Uruguay, Argentina and Chile. Similar to Edinburgh 1910, it focused on students, it organized itself around commissions, and it had a continuation committee.[16] For the final location of the conference, the two largest cities in Latin America were considered: Buenos Aires and Rio de Janeiro. The former was struck off the list because it was considered too far for most delegates, and the latter was discounted because they spoke Portuguese rather than Spanish.[17] Panama was finally selected as the location for the conference. And the name was changed from its original title, "Latin-American Missionary Conference," to "Congress on Christian Work in Latin America," because Latin Americans did not like the term *missionary* due to the fact that it seemed to be derogatory to them as being the imperialistic object of conversion, and the word *congress* was preferred to *conference* because "the latter in Spanish and Portuguese implies a lecture, while the former denotes a deliberative body."[18] That linguistic difference may be why CLADE V was called a congress as well, and it is the same reason why Lausanne III called itself a congress instead of a conference.

The types of people recruited for Panamá 1916 were diverse in scope: leaders of national churches, missionaries, mission board executives and

historical research into documents of mission boards, missionary conferences and missionary appeals would substantiate this point in relation to the more liberal American denominations, where this connection is more conscious and explicit. But a deeper investigation would show that it is even stronger, though less obvious, in the more conservative denominations and missionary societies where the commitment to the 'American dream' in its expansionist features was uncritically assumed, often without the de-absolutizing elements implicit in its own philosophy."

[15]*Christian Work in Latin America*, 10-11.

[16]The commissions were (1) Survey and Occupation, (2) Message and Method, (3) Education, (4) Literature, (5) Women's Work, (6) The Church in the Field, (7) The Home Base, and (8) Cooperation and the Promotion of Unity.

[17]*Christian Work in Latin America*, 11-12.

[18]Ibid., 17.

laypeople from North America, Europe and Latin America. There were 149 representatives from Latin America in attendance and 155 from the rest of the world—namely, the United States, Canada, England, Spain and Italy. In this nearly equal representation, Panamá 1916 differed in a very important regard from the African and Asian representation at Edinburgh 1910: though Panamá 1916 was organized by US Americans, there were plenty of Latin Americans in attendance, almost half. This cooperative spirit was exemplified by the fact that the conference had three official working languages—English, Spanish and Portuguese—and by the fact that the leadership was also shared: Professor Eduardo Monteverde of the University of Uruguay was chosen as the president of the congress.[19]

Edinburgh 1910, on the other hand—though it had plenty of African representatives in attendance—did not have any black Africans (though there were some African Americans); they were all whites who were missionaries in Africa or white Africans. In other words, Panamá 1916, while not originally a Latin American idea, greatly involved Latinos. Edinburgh 1910 only saw Africans as a target of missions it did not employ them as full partners. Interestingly, however, it did do that with Asians, having Asian representatives in attendance (even if there only were seventeen) as well as even having some Asians speak on the platform, most notably V. S. Azariah. This speaks to the Western concept of civilization at the time—there was a clear hierarchy of non-Western races in the minds of the Americans and the Europeans.

Similar to Edinburgh 1910, while the work of the commissions was important, the continuation committee was even more so. As the report on the congress noted, "The Panama Congress was not an achievement; it was a process of discovery."[20] The continuation committee at Panamá 1916 was simply a reworking and expansion of the preexisting Committee on Cooperation in Latin America (CCLA) and was the real work of the congress.

The connection between Panamá 1916 and Costa Rica 2012 is open to question. Is there a genetic relationship, or is the parallel simply a coincidence?

---

[19]The other Congress leaders were Dr. Robert E. Speer, chair of the congress when in session as a working body; the Rev. S. G. Inman (of the Christian Woman's Board of Missions), executive secretary; and Dr. John R. Mott, chair of the business committee.
[20]*Christian Work in Latin America*, 33.

Two conferences were held in 2016 celebrating the centenary of Panamá 1916: one at Fuller Theological Seminary from February 9 to 10 and one at Wheaton College from June 30 to July 2. The difference between the two is that the former looks at Panama as its own independent entity, whereas the latter conference, organized by the Latin American Theological Fellowship, links it to CLADE V. It is to the second perspective that we now turn.

THE HISTORY OF CLADE V

CLADE V, held in Costa Rica in 2012, was the fifth in a series of evangelistic conferences sponsored by the Fraternidad Teológica Latinoamericana (FTL), or Latin American Theological Fellowship.[21] The timing of it had less to do with trying to align it with Edinburgh 1910 and more to do with the Congreso Latinoamericano de Evangelización (CLADE), or the Latin American Congress on Evangelization, offering a new conference in its series approximately once every ten years.

Panamá 1916 and the five CLADEs were not the only Latin American conferences of note. Just as Panamá 1916 followed Edinburgh 1910, there were two Brazilian conferences that followed Lausanne '74. The first was in the city of Curitiba in 1976, featuring Samuel Escobar and René Padilla, who had spoken so powerfully two years earlier at the congress in Switzerland. It was organized by the Aliança Biblica Universitária do Brasil with the theme *"Jesus Cristo, Senhorio, Propósito e Missão"* ("Jesus Christ: Lordship, Purpose and Mission"), out of which was produced O Pacto de Curitiba (The Curitiba Covenant).[22] After Curitiba '76 came the first Congreso Brasileiro de Evangelização (Brazilian Congress of Evangelization) in Belo Horizonte in 1983,[23] with official Lausanne endorsement though not financial or organizational support. The theme of Belo Horizonte '83 was *"Que o Brasil e o mundo ouçam a voz de Deus"* ("Let Brazil and the world hear God's voice"), a clear and deliberate mimicking of the theme of Lausanne '74.

---

[21]FTL was birthed out of CLADE I, not the other way around. However, the FTL gave rise to the other CLADEs. The English name was formerly translated as Latin American Theological Fraternity, but the name was changed to "Fellowship" in 2006 to make it gender-inclusive yet keep the English acronym (LATF) intact. It remains *Fraternidad* in Spanish because the masculine in Spanish implies gender inclusivity, whereas it does not in English.

[22]Valdir Steuernagel, Samuel Escobar and René Padilla, "Pacto de Curitiba," in *Jesus Cristo: Senhorio, Propósito e Missão. Compêndio do Congresso Missionário* (São Paulo: ABU Editora, 1978).

[23]A second Brazilian Congress of Evangelization, also held in Belo Horizonte, was convened in 2003.

However, the FTL and CLADE's roots actually predate not only the Brazilian congresses but the Lausanne movement itself. They arose from ecumenical tensions within Latin America. It might be simplified as follows: CLADE comprised the Latin American evangelicals, CELA the mainline Protestants, and CELAM the Catholics. Below are lists of their meetings:

CLADE (Congreso Latinoamericano de Evangelización)—a meeting of Latin American "evangelical" Protestants

1. Bogotá, Colombia, 1969
2. Huampaní, Peru, 1979
3. Quito, Ecuador, 1992
4. Quito, Ecuador, 2000[24]
5. San José, Costa Rica, 2012

CELA (Conferencia Evangélica Latinoamericana)—a meeting of Latin American "ecumenical" Protestants

1. Buenos Aires, Argentina, 1949
2. Lima, Peru, 1962
3. Buenos Aires, Argentina, 1969
4. Oaxtepec, Mexico, 1978

CELAM (Consejo Episcopal Latinoamericano)—a meeting of Latin American Roman Catholic bishops

1. Rio de Janeiro, Brazil, 1955
2. Medellín, Colombia, 1968
3. Puebla, Mexico, 1979
4. Santo Domingo, Dominican Republic, 1992
5. Aparecida, Brazil, 2007

However, ecumenical divisions within Latin America are not as clear cut as that. The word *evangélico* is unlike the English word *evangelical* in that it does not necessarily connote the characteristics of the Bebbington Quadrilateral.[25] Instead, it is somewhat more equivalent to *Protestant*, though

---

[24]CLADE IV was not supposed to repeat in Quito but rather to meet in Bogotá, Colombia, but the latter site was canceled because of violence, so the Colombian leaders advised that it be moved. Quito was an easy last-minute substitute because it was the same venue as before.

[25]See chapter five. Although it must be said, perhaps Latin American *evangélicos* have more of a claim to the Bebbington Quadrilateral than Western evangelicals did in the twentieth century in the sense that they have more of a social conscience, exemplifying the "activism" role in addition to "biblicism," which makes them more resemble nineteenth-century Western evangelicals.

even that is inaccurate as Latin America never had a Protestant Reformation since it was missionized by the Catholics at the same time that the Reformation was starting in Europe. Nor are "evangelical" and "mainline" Protestantism a clean distinction, as someone like José Míguez Bonino, a well-known liberation theologian and active participant in the World Council of Churches, was also a member of the FTL.[26]

Both CELA and CLADE had momentous conferences in the same year, 1969. The tumultuous 1960s and '70s in Latin America affected these conferences greatly. There was a great need to distinguish between "conservative" (those who accepted the status quo, whether that be military or political or social), and "progressive" (those who longed for radical change and upheaval). It was impossible to separate theology from politics in that context. The fact that Protestants (*evangélicos*) were such a minority compared to the overwhelmingly Catholic milieu of Latin America made it even more tragic for them to be further atomized. Yet, CELA and CLADE were the first evidence of such a split among *evangélicos*.

CELA was the ongoing result of the continuation committee of Panamá 1916. Though CELA was significantly older than CLADE as a movement, it did not really break ground until its third conference. CELA I was held in 1949 in Buenos Aires, Argentina, spawned out of Robert Speer's Committee on Cooperation in Latin America (CCLA).[27] CELA II was held in 1962 at Lima, Peru. In contrast to CELA I, this second conference did exhibit a liberal-conservative bifurcation among the *evangélicos*. The liberal/ecumenical *evangélicos* dominated CELA II, a fact that did not sit easily with the conservative/evangelical *evangélicos*. This led to the formation of two groups: ISAL (Iglesia y Sociedad en América Latina, or Church and Society in Latin America) and the FTL, representing the ecumenists and evangelicals, respectively. So, the genealogy is as follows: Edinburgh 1910 indirectly led to Panamá 1916 which partnered with CCLA which led to CELA, which indirectly led to CLADE, which birthed the FTL, which affected Lausanne.

---

[26]José Míguez Bonino, *Faces of Latin American Protestantism* (Grand Rapids: Eerdmans, 1995), vii-viii: "I have been variously tagged a conservative, a revolutionary, a Barthian, a liberal, a catholic, a 'moderate,' and a liberationist. Probably there is truth in all of these. It is not for me to decide."

[27]Daniel Salinas, "The Beginnings of the *Fraternidad Teológica Latinoamericana*: Courage to Grow," *Journal of Latin American Theology* 2, no. 1 (2007): 27.

Like the foundations of CELA, the FTL beginnings took root in the United States. Peter Wagner and Pedro Savage (the former an American missionary to Latin America, the latter born and raised in Latin America to American missionary parents) established the FTL as a way for the more "conservative" *evangélicos* to dialogue. Wagner especially was controversial—he published and distributed a book that elicited strong responses, mostly negative, from Latin Americans who read it.[28] The main thrust of the book was a critical reaction toward "liberals" (both Protestant and Catholics), who appeared to be taking over the Latin American churches. Fuller Seminary's church-growth movement was proposed as the answer to Latin America's woes.[29] Orlando Costas, along with Samuel Escobar, René Padilla, Plutarco Bonilla and Rubén Lores, felt "*ofendidos con el propósito, el contenido y la metodología del libro*" ("offended by the purpose, the content, and the methodology of the book").[30]

CELA III and CLADE I were held in the same year, just months apart. CELA III met in Buenos Aires, returning to the same location as CELA I, while CLADE I took place in Bogotá, Colombia. In addition to CELA and CLADE, there was CELAM, the third player in the game. CELAM (Consejo Episcopal Latinoamericano, or the Latin American Episcopal Council) was the Roman Catholic bishops' conference, and it actually had its second conference in 1968, the year before CELA III and CLADE I. CELAM II was significant for being the "birthplace" of Latin American liberation theology and is often simply called "Medellín" (Colombia) in reference to where it was held.

CLADE I was a negative reaction to CELA III, just as CELA III was a positive reaction to CELAM II. In other words, when the Catholics developed liberation theology, it inspired the ecumenical Protestants in that direction, which in turn led to the evangelical Protestants breaking away. Much of the reaction of US evangelicals against CELA being a "liberal" conference had to do with their discomfort toward a fully Latin American lead-

---

[28]C. Peter Wagner, *Teología Latinoamericana ¿Izquierdista o Evangélica?* (Miami: Vida, 1969). Its English translation is *Latin American Theology: Radical or Evangelical? The Struggle for the Faith in a Young Church* (Grand Rapids: Eerdmans, 1970).

[29]Salinas, "Beginnings," 44.

[30]Orlando Costas, "Teólogo en la encrucijada," in *Hacia una teología evangélica latinoamericana: Ensayos en honor de Pedro Savage,* ed. René Padilla (Miami: Editorial Caribe, 1984), 26.

ership and suspecting that indigenous leadership will ultimately lead to liberalism. As such, CLADE was a US creation that did not have Latin American interests at heart—they deliberately styled themselves as an anti-CELA. It had the theme "Action in Christ for a Continent in Crisis," referring to the Western powers' view of Latin America through the lens of the Cold War.[31] Though most people in attendance at CLADE I were Latinos, there was nothing about the Congress's final document[32] that was in any way Latin American.[33] In contrast, CELA III not only attempted to address the political, social, economic and theological concerns of Latin America, but it sought to include Pentecostals and Roman Catholics. Though the founding of the FTL and the convening of CLADE I were thoroughly impetuses of the United States, by CLADE II the movement was back in the hands of Latinos much to their relief. Orlando Costas, René Padilla, Samuel Escobar and José Míguez Bonino ended up being prime movers at CLADE II.[34]

How did CLADE I compare to Panamá 1916? The similarity is that both were organized by US Americans. The difference is that Panamá had a little less than 50 percent Latinos in attendance, whereas CLADE I had far more. But Panamá 1916 seemed to be more respectful of the Latino voice whereas CLADE I was a thoroughly US enterprise. As a result, the Fraternidad Teológica Latinoamericana[35] was founded in Cochabamba, Bolivia, December 12–18, 1970, with an initial twenty-five members.[36] The newly formed FTL had to overcome differences between Peter Wagner and René Padilla in order to move forward, but they

---

[31]Ruth Padilla DeBorst, "Who Sets the Table for Whom? Latin American Congresses on Evangelization (CLADE) 1969–2012: A Revision with Eyes Toward a New Celebration," *Journal of Latin American Theology* 5, no. 2 (2010): 109.

[32]An English translation can be found in ECLA, "The Evangelical Declaration of Bogotá (Official Translation)," *Pulse* 5, no. 1 (1970).

[33]Salinas, "Beginnings," 33, 36, 40.

[34]Samuel Escobar, "The Legacy of Orlando Costas," *International Bulletin of Missionary Research* 25, no. 2 (April 2001): 52.

[35]The original name was the *Fraternidad de Teológos Latinoamericanos* (Fraternity of Latin American Theologians).

[36]The original founding FTL members who signed the *Declaration of Cochabamba* were Ismael Amaya, Francisco Anabalón, Pedro Arana, Robinson Cavalcanti, Enrique Cepeda, Samuel Escobar, Héctor Espinosa, Gerardo de Ávila, David Jones, Andrew Kirk, Emilio Antonio Núñez, René Padilla, Washington Padilla, Ericson Paredes, Oscar Pereira, Pablo Pérez, Mauro Ramalho, Asdrúbal Ríos, Peter Savage, Richard Sturz, Douglas Smith, Ezequiel Torrez, Cesar Thome, Virgilio F. Vangioni and Peter Wagner.

eventually did.[37] The FTL aimed to be founded on four principles: (1) the authority of the Bible, (2) contextualization to Latin America, (3) relation to the evangelical church in Latin America and its mission, and (4) social transformation.[38] It was at Lausanne I in 1974 where the FTL made its first international appearance, and it immediately had a profound effect, influencing the direction of John Stott and the *Lausanne Covenant* toward *misión integral* (holistic mission) and thus the Western missionary movement into the twenty-first century.

The Segundo Congreso Latinoamericano de Evangelización, or CLADE II, was held in Huampaní, Perú, October 31 to November 7, 1979. It was a deliberate follow-up to Lausanne '74, but this time it was under the Latinos' own terms and completely organized and half-funded by them,[39] exemplifying two of the three selves: self-governing and self-sustaining—unlike how CLADE I followed Berlin '66 without the Latinos' consent and was perpetuating a United States agenda. CLADE II was based on the *Lausanne Covenant*, similar to how CLADE V later did the same, adhering to the *Cape Town Commitment*. Even the motto for CLADE II was reflective of the motto of Lausanne '74: "That Latin America May Hear God's Voice." CLADE II ended up being a tremendous success, with "266 people from 21 countries and 39 evangelical denominations" in attendance.[40]

The third CLADE conference was held from August 24 to September 4, 1992, in Quito, Ecuador, with the theme "All the Gospel for All Peoples from Latin America" on the five-hundredth anniversary of Columbus's arrival in the Americas, a sore spot for most Latin Americans. The congress produced the *Declaración de Quito* (Quito Declaration), but both the congress and the declaration barely registered on the radar for US Americans.[41] For the FTL, however, it was an attempt to become even more ecumenical in scope with their fellow Latin Americans, inviting younger leaders as well as CONELA (Confraternidad Evangélica Latinoamericana) and CLAI (Consejo Latino-americano de Iglesias).[42]

---

[37]Salinas, "Beginnings," 58-64.
[38]Ibid., 69-71.
[39]Ibid., 116.
[40]Ibid.
[41]Ibid., 142.
[42]Padilla DeBorst, "Who Sets the Table for Whom?," 118.

The same city (though different venue) was used for CLADE IV,[43] which was held September 2–9, 2000, and had some twelve hundred participants to discuss how Latin American mission might look in the twenty-first century,[44] with the theme "The Evangelical Testimony to the Third Millennium: Word, Spirit, and Mission."[45] This congress, however, had as much effect as CLADE III. Similar to the Lausanne movement, which waned in the 1990s and required the touch of Doug Birdsall in 2004 to revive it, CLADE required a strong leader to bring it back to prominence, and that was found in the person of Ruth Padilla DeBorst, the daughter of C. René Padilla. The FTL is led by the general secretary, and Padilla DeBorst was the fifth person to hold the office, elected in 2008, after Pedro Savage of Peru (1970–1984), René Padilla of Ecuador (1984–1992), Tito Paredes of Peru (1992–2004) and Omar Cortés Gaibur of Chile (2004–2008).

CLADE V: CONFERENCE PROCEEDINGS

Just as Lausanne II was anemic compared to Lausanne I, CLADE III and IV seemed to be pittances compared to CLADE I and II. And just as Lausanne III restored the glory of the Lausanne movement, CLADE V attempted to do that for the FTL's congresses. The fifth CLADE was held in San José, Costa Rica, July 10–13, 2012, at the Vida Abundante Church. The theme was "*Sigamos a Jesús en su Reino de Vida. ¡Guíanos, Santo Espíritu!*" ("Following Jesus in His Reign of Life: Guide Us, Holy Spirit!"), with the stated purpose of using the Trinity as a framework:

> 1. Following Jesus, because as Christ's church we need to learn to follow our Lord and to incarnate with commitment and integral discipleship. 2. God's kingdom of life, because the reign of God is a reign of life, even in our Latin American context so burdened by multiple expressions of death. 3. Guide us, Holy Spirit! In the midst of triumphal celebrations about evangelicals' growth in numbers and power, ours is a plea, a cry, a confession of our

---

[43]Instead of the Anderson School, it was held at the SEMISUD, or the Latin American Seminary of the Church of God.

[44]Salinas, "Beginnings," 135-36.

[45]Samuel Cueva, "Mission Distinctives of CLADE V," *Journal of Latin American Theology* 8, no. 1, 2013): 48.

weakness and unfaithfulness in living as incarnated expressions of God's reconciling love.[46]

The congress had these stated goals:

1. Generate a participatory movement that engages Christians, churches, agencies, institutions, and movements in Latin America and the Caribbean with each other around the central themes.

2. Promote reflection on the gospel and its significance for human beings, society, and the whole of creation.

3. Contribute to the life and mission of twenty-first century churches in Latin America and the Caribbean with a growing awareness of contextual realities.

4. Serve as a platform for dialogue among Christians and between churches, ministries, networks, and Christian movements in Latin America, the Caribbean, and the rest of the world.

5. Foster opportunities for the FTL to extend its service as a facilitator of evangelical reflection and a platform for Christian dialogue in Latin America and the Caribbean.[47]

There was a participant's guide that was distributed to people prior to the congress.[48] This way, even people who were unable to attend CLADE V could participate in the process (while GlobaLink at Lausanne III was amazing, technology does not necessarily have to be employed for others to benefit from the congress!). The participant's guide included nineteen discussion questions organized around the Trinitarian theme:

Following Jesus on the Path of Life

1. If we look closely at what is taught or preached in churches, following Jesus seems almost to be a forgotten topic. Why?

2. What hermeneutical techniques help us read Scripture? Which specifically help us understand the Gospel accounts about Jesus?

---

[46]Padilla DeBorst, "Who Sets the Table for Whom?," 121.
[47]Ibid., 121-22.
[48]This was also published in the *Journal of Latin American Theology* 7, no. 1 (2012).

3. What happens when "false Christs" displace the Jesus of the Gospels? How can this be avoided?

4. How do liturgical practices (songs, prayer, sermons, gestures, rhythms, services) influence how we follow Jesus? What criteria help us be discerning regarding these practices?

5. In what ways do we sense and follow Jesus with our bodies? What are some life-giving ways we can coexist with others? What does it mean to bear witness to Jesus with all of our senses?

The Kingdom of the God of Life

6. Religious practices are ambiguous and can be alienating or even toxic. The same can be said of theology. What can help us determine if our discussions and our ideas about "following" and the "kingdom of life" are healthy and life-affirming?

7. What does "life" mean in the actual conditions in which we live? And can the "abundant" life start now? How?

8. We cannot talk about "life" in general without talking about the concrete specifics of particular people (for example, gangs, those without land to work, the displaced). How does the kingdom of life manifest itself in specific situations involving death?

9. What are the ecological and cosmic dimensions of the kingdom of life?

10. What life? What for and for whom? What abuses occur "in the name of life"? What happens when the groups that are disciplined or punished "in the name of life" are the very same people that the majority of Latin American and Caribbean Protestants scorn?

11. How are the kingdom of the God of life and current political projects and social movements related?

12. Where do we see the problem of theodicy in our continent?

The Spirit of Life

13. How is Pentecostalness expressed in our contexts? How can we tell the difference between the work of the *Ruach* of life from the spirits of oppression and death?

14. "Holistic mission" has been a predominant theme in past CLADEs. What are the intrinsic limitations to describing mission in this way? In what ways does the self-image built around "holistic mission" hinder more holistic ways of living as Christians, and how does it foster them? To whom or what does the concept of "holistic mission" attempt to speak, and what distinctions does it try to make?

15. What specific examples of "mission" or "being sent" can inspire us for Latin America and the Caribbean?

16. What are the main obstacles to abundant life on our continent? How do our churches respond to them? What are some of the concrete steps our churches are already taking to resist death and offer life? How do we keep going down that path?

17. What does our hope consist of? Does it help or hinder us in following the God of life?

18. Why is there so much abuse of power and corruption in Protestant churches? What structural flaws are there in our churches? How do these issues relate to theological education at all levels?

19. How can we best incorporate the pneumatological (spiritual) agency of women, youth, indigenous people groups, and people of African descent into our way of living, being church, and doing theology?

During the course of the congress, each day consisted of focusing on a different person of the Trinity (the first full day was dedicated to "*Seguimiento de Jesús por el camino de la vida*," or "Following Jesus on the path of life"; day 2 was "*El Reino de la vida*," or "The kingdom of life"; day 3 was "*El Espíritu de la vida*," or "The Spirit of life"; and the final day was "*Comunidad Trinitaria*," or "Trinitarian community"). Each day also had a corresponding verb that described the theme of the day: *Recordar* (*buscar a Jesús*), *agradecer* (*descubrir a Jesús*), *escuchar* (*duda y misterio*), *responder* (*la paz*), *celebrar* (*desayuno de la resurrección*). [Remember (look for Jesus), give thanks (discover Jesus), listen (doubt and mystery), respond (peace), celebrate (to be amazed at the resurrection)]. The morning sessions were devoted to a Bible study of John 20–21, followed by a late morning plenary session focused on particular geographical regions: Brazil, the Andes, the Southern Cone.

Afternoon sessions were breakout sessions, and in the evenings were plenary sessions continuing the geographical regional foci: Mesoamerica and the Caribbean, and North America. The last evening was a focus on the world. The final session of each evening was dedicated to the arts, whether song or dance or the visual arts, and each Latin American region got to bring their own contributions to the stage, demonstrating a musical cornucopia of diverse cultures. Similar to Cape Town 2010, CLADE V also had table groups around which discussion, reflection, confession and celebration occurred.

Some of the notable plenary addresses included:

- Pedro Arana Quiroz on the first day talking about ministry to women. Latin Americans know the role of women well, as Mother's Day is all-important in Latin America, much more significant than Father's Day! Also, the "patron saint of the Americas" is the Virgin of Guadalupe, who represents women as well as the indigenous.

- Sidney Rooy highlighting the invisible disabled community of Latin America.

- Hernán Zapata Thomack, a pastor from the New York/New Jersey region, talking about how we need to forge more bridges between North America and Latin America, represented by people like Orlando Costas, Justo González, Juciano Jaramillo, Lindy Scott and Juan Martínez, who have all contributed to both hemispheres. He called these the "twin" theologies of the FTL: north and south.

- Ian Darke, representative of the publisher Letra Viva, talking about the forthcoming *Comentario Bíblico Contemporáneo* (*CBC*), the first-ever one-volume commentary on the entire Bible written wholly by Latin Americans.

- René Padilla who stressed that the task of holistic mission is not yet done, and that we need to always be open to new theologies because there are always new generations that need them.

CELEBRATING THE PAST AND THE FUTURE

One of the most memorable and moving parts of CLADE V was when they had all the pioneers of the FTL on stage. Notably absent was Orlando Costas, who died in 1987 of cancer at the young age of forty-five; otherwise he would be around the same age as Padilla and Escobar. They comprised the "big three" *evangélicos* of the 1960s–1980s. Costas was the most prolific of the three in his publishing, and one wonders what he might have accomplished today had he still been alive.[49] Also poignantly absent was José Míguez Bonino, who passed away on July 1, 2012, just nine days before the start of CLADE V. There was a moving video tribute played about him. Emilio Antonio Núñez, the patriarch, the oldest of the original founding members of the FTL, was also missing. Despite the absence of these three titans (and a few others), for the most part all the others were in attendance. In none of the other 2010 conferences was there such a sense of history, as Ralph Winter died prior to Tokyo 2010, and Billy Graham and John Stott were too frail to attend Cape Town 2010, and there was nobody who exemplified a historical "hero" for Edinburgh 2010 or 2010Boston. But CLADE V had not just one "hero" on stage; it had seven "old lions,"[50] living testaments to the work of the FTL: Valdir Steuernagel, Samuel Escobar, Sidney Rooy, René Padilla, Juan Stam, Pedro Arana and Mervin Breneman. Three of them were North Americans, three Spanish Americans and one Portuguese American. But the spirit of Costas, Míguez Bonino, Núñez and others who have passed were with them as well.

However, celebrating the past is not enough: the future must also be embraced. Latinos must be open to international diversity; otherwise CLADE V would not be able to be included in the ranks of the 2010 conferences. Because Ruth Padilla DeBorst was doing her doctorate under Professor Dana Robert at Boston University, she also invited Robert to be a plenary speaker, providing even more bridges between CLADE V and Edinburgh 2010 and 2010Boston. As a trained missionary historian, Robert advocated relationships as part of missions theology, even pointing to the theme of friendship (which conjures up the image of V. S. Azariah at Edinburgh 1910, "Give us friends!"). In addition to Dana Robert, Professor Al Tizon of Palmer Theological Seminary in Pennsylvania, who did his PhD dissertation on the

---

[49]In fact, he had only finished the first of the trilogy that was supposed to be his magnum opus, published posthumously: Orlando E. Costas, *Liberating News: A Theology of Contextual Evangelization* (Grand Rapids: Eerdmans, 1989).

[50]As dubbed by Samuel Cueva in "Mission Distinctives," 38.

Lausanne movement,[51] was invited to speak on stage. As a Filipino American, he noted that he is both an outsider and an insider. Obviously, having Asian ancestry, he is not Latino. But the Philippines were the only Spanish colony in Asia,[52] and therefore he has some common culture and ancestry with Latin Americans.[53] Also joining Robert and Tizon on a global panel were Corneliou Constantinou from Romania, representing Eastern Europe, and Las Newman from Jamaica, representing the Caribbean. This diversity is a hopeful sign for future CLADEs, especially since "Latino" is not a race; it is a geographic designation. Latin Americans can be black, white, brown or Asian and are often *mestizo*, or mixed-race. It only makes sense that Latin Americans can embrace the diversity of the world's colors and cultures. The original FTL members were all male but they were Europeans and North Americans in addition to Latinos. Having females, Asians, Europeans and Afro-Caribbeans represented on stage signals exciting future possibilities for expansion in the FTL.

The closing ceremony was also representative of the past and the future, as it started by honoring two of the "old lions," René Padilla and Samuel Escobar, as well as ending with a children's choir and a prayer for the youth. The theme song, written by Joel Sierra, was sung and a statement from Lausanne to CLADE was read. There was a changing of the guard from Ruth Padilla DeBorst to a new general secretary, Marcelo Vargas, and Pedro Arana was established as the head of the new executive committee of FTL.

HOLISTIC MISSION

It seems that question 14 above, regarding *misión integral* (holistic mission), is the crux of it all for Latin American evangelicalism and the FTL. Keeping evangelism and social justice together is what put Latin American theology "back on the map" and is the hallmark of the movement, of the FTL who brought it to Lausanne's attention in 1974, and of René Padilla, who even

---

[51]Published as Al Tizon, *Transformation After Lausanne: Radical Evangelical Mission in Global-Local Perspective* (Eugene, OR: Wipf & Stock, 2008).

[52]Just as Brazil was the only Latin American colony in the Americas. This was intentional, as Pope Alexander VI, in 1494, drew the line dividing the West (Spanish colonies) from the East (Portuguese colonies) with the Treaty of Tordesillas (in Spanish) or Tordesilhas (in Portuguese).

[53]Cueva, "Mission Distinctive," 60-62.

wrote a book on the topic.[54] Padilla actually received his *misión integral* impetus from IFES (the International Fellowship of Evangelical Students), so the injection of this idea into the *Lausanne Covenant* also came from student movements, similar to Edinburgh 1910 and 2010Boston, which drew their fuel from students. However, one of the biggest criticisms is whether or not *misión integral* actually reaches the people whom it was intended to serve. One of the most damning criticisms (though couched in a humorous way) of Latin American liberation theology is "Liberation theologians chose the poor, but the poor chose Pentecostalism!" In a similar way, *misión integral* theory without practice does no good. Valdir Steuernagel made this very point:

> The movement of integral mission has a strong "Latino flavor." Latino leaders helped to identify in the Gospel the message of God who called us to full obedience and to design models and projects of incarnational witness by which beautiful signs of God's Kingdom would emerge and become a testimony to Christ. This movement, however, does not come without challenges. It has never been able to enter in a substantial way into the tissue of the churches in this continent. It has remained micro, and while being lived out at that level, it hasn't succeeded in being lived out at the level of the mega-churches, or to become a factor to impact society even in places where evangelical churches have become a substantial percentage of the population. We need to recognize that it also has, in many cases, suffered the temptation to stay quite cerebral, even if put in action, not being able to develop a spirituality of prayer, joy and emotions. We need help to deepen and expand the holistic understanding of the mission of the church in order for it to become *integral*.[55]

Certainly *misión integral* is one of the greatest examples of the fourth self, self-theologizing, at work in the Two-Thirds World: at the founding of the FTL, "Peter Wagner saw in Church Growth the answer to the supposed poor Latin American theological production, for Padilla it was the culprit. It was precisely the insistence on the mission of the church as 'numerical growth' that gave the

---

[54]C. René Padilla, *Misión Integral: Ensayos sobre el Reino de Dios y la Iglesia* (Buenos Aires: Ediciones Kairos, 2012).

[55]Valdir Steuernagel, "A Latin-American Evangelical Perspective on the Cape Town Congress," in *The Lausanne Movement: A Range of Perspectives*, ed. Lars Dahle, Margunn Serigstad Dahle and Knud Jørgensen (Oxford: Regnum, 2014), 315-16.

impression that training theologians was not important."[56] However, was there a need for CLADE V if *misión integral* was going to be repeated again? British theologian Andrew Kirk, one of the FTL's original members, observed:

> In general terms, I have the impression that the evangelical message ("good news" for the lost) is overshadowed by the promotion of a particular *misión integral*, emphasizing social issues ("good news" for the politically and economically oppressed and marginalized). The pendulum is swinging from one side to the other. I am not sure if the FTL (maybe it does not matter anymore) has even done biblical justice to the idea of the mission of God as one that is integrated, not just a series of disconnected parts. Nevertheless, this is a very general commentary on a complex problem. The discussion continues and without a doubt will involve different voices from within the FTL.[57]

When the FTL theologians began to self-theologize, coming up with *misión integral* and then influencing Lausanne in this direction in 1974, it changed the world when these concepts made it into the *Lausanne Covenant*. So it might be that this small band of Latino theologians is responsible for Western evangelicalism's reversal of the "Great Reversal" in the twenty-first century! This is another convincing reason to hold worldwide missionary conferences.

One may think that this is an example of the Two-Thirds World church finally maturing, but it must be noted that CLADE I was held in 1969, as opposed to Lausanne I, which was held in 1974—so CLADE predates Lausanne. It is true that CLADE was founded by the Billy Graham Evangelistic Association as an outgrowth of Berlin '66,[58] but so was Lausanne I—thus making Lausanne and CLADE siblings, although CLADE is the older sibling.

LATIN AMERICAN ECUMENICAL CONTEXTUALIZATION

CLADE V was trying to hold in tension two goals: to be a part of the worldwide body of Christians and evangelicals and to be distinctively Latin American. This is actually an enactment of what Andrew Walls calls the

---

[56]Salinas, "Beginnings," 47.
[57]Cueva, "Mission Distinctive," 64.
[58]Padilla DeBorst, "Who Sets the Table for Whom?," 110: "These organizations [the Billy Graham Evangelistic Association, the Evangelical Fellowship of Mission Associates (EFMA), and the International Fellowship of Mission Associates (IMFA)] had already organized congresses on evangelism in Asia and Africa after the large one in Berlin (1966). Now it was Latin America's turn."

Pilgrim Principle and the Indigenizing Principle: we are part of the universal City of God, yet we are all inculturated in a specific time and place.[59] We are aliens and strangers in this world, yet we are firmly rooted in it and in a particular language and culture. This realization of the two parts of our identity is necessary for all Christians. Therefore, CLADE V was *ecumenical* as well as *contextually Latin American*.

Regarding *ecumenism*: one of the goals of CLADE V was to critically reflect on the *Cape Town Commitment* in a Latin American way:

> At the [Cape Town] congress, the participants received only the first part of the document. The second part . . . just recently began to circulate in 2011. Latin American churches have before them a sizable challenge to thoroughly interact with this document and its deep theological richness. . . . Unfortunately, during Lausanne III there was no time to analyze the fruits of their labor. Now the challenge remains to contextualize Lausanne III for the Latin American church. We hope that CLADE V will be an excellent opportunity to do so. . . . CLADE V provides an ideally timed opportunity for such reflection as inspired by the Lausanne Movement.[60]

While the Latinos did see some imperfections in the *CTC*, they affirmed that (1) discipleship is fundamental, (2) the reality of globalization must be addressed and (3) creation care is a major concern that should be a focus of missiology.

Regarding Latin American contextualization: Latinos reflect on theology in some different ways from Westerners. One such way is reflection with "doubt and mystery," as described by Mexican Methodist Alejandra Ortiz Chacón in her address on the third day. Westerners often have a need to find answers, and living with uncertainty and lack of clarity is part of the journey of faith. Another is in the method of celebration. Each day the arts were incorporated, as this is a large part of the Latin American spirit—painting, poetry, drama, song and dance.[61] Songwriting, liturgy creation, painting, dance and so on are other forms of the fourth self. Self-theologizing does

---

[59]Andrew Walls, *The Missionary Movement in Christian History: Studies in the Transmission of Faith* (Maryknoll, NY: Orbis, 1996), 7-9.

[60]Rey, "FTL, Edinburgh, Lausanne III, and CLADE V," 36-37.

[61]The art and liturgy were compiled in the "Special Post-CLADE V Issue on Art, Liturgy, and Mission," *Journal of Latin American Theology* 7, no. 2 (2012). Part of the pre-process of CLADE V involved bringing together thirty artists (musicians, poets, painters, photographers and other artists) to gather in Heredia, Costa Rica, in spring 2011, to create art together.

not have to be limited to book writing or academic research! The songs at CLADE V were written and led wonderfully by people like Leonardo Álvarez of Chile, Santiago Benavides of Colombia, Carlinhos Veiga of Brazil, and Tracy Wispelwey of the United States. Yet another theme is humility versus power and how authority is exercised in a continent where there have been so many abuses of power against the poor. The way Scripture is used also is notable, as Westerners often focus on more "Greek" parts of the Bible like the Pauline Epistles while Majority World Christians often use more "Hebraic" texts like the Old Testament Prophets or, in the case of CLADE V, John. Also, given that Latin America is home to the largest river and forest on earth in the Amazon, creation care is of paramount importance to Latin Americans. And finally, CLADE V aimed to bring in Latin American diversity, not just in terms of the many regional foci each day but also in bringing outside voices such as Erika Izquierdo, representing the younger generation, and Catholic Juan José Tamayo, representing liberation theology and an ecumenical spirit. CELAM and CLAI even sent representatives to bring greetings to CLADE.

IMPACT OF CLADE V

Similar to Lausanne with its LCWE, CLADE has a built-in continuation committee for decades: namely, the FTL. Both CLADE and Lausanne are movements,[62] so they have flexibility to grow and change and adapt to the world's changing circumstances.

With CLADE V, like Cape Town 2010, there was the before, the during and the after. The CLADE V "process" involved:

1. CLADE V Participatory Movement (August 2009 to July 2012)

2. CLADE V Gathering (July 2012 in Costa Rica)

3. CLADE V Transformational Movement (July 2012 forward)[63]

---

[62]Steuernagel, "Latin-American Evangelical Perspective," 314. At CLADE V, on the first day, they stressed that "CLADE is a process, not an event." For Latinos, the journey is often as important as the destination, if not more so. This is one of the reasons that the CLADE V theme started with "following Jesus on the path of life" and one of the FTL pioneers, Orlando Costas, often stressed doing theology *en el camino* (on the road). See Allen Yeh, *Se hace camino al andar: Periphery and Center in the Missiology of Orlando E. Costas* (DPhil diss., University of Oxford, 2008).

[63]Padilla DeBorst, "Who Sets the Table for Whom?," 122.

It continues to use the Internet and its webpage (www.ftl-al.org) as an ongoing resource for people. And it will keep holding meetings of the regional FTL chapters, smaller national conferences and, eventually, about once a decade the large international CLADE congress.

Today the general secretary of the FTL is Marcelo Vargas Adrián of Bolivia, the sixth to hold that office. He was elected in 2012, and the handoff was made at CLADE V in front of all attendees. He will carry on the work of the FTL and CLADE into the future, perhaps even organizing CLADE VI. He will continue to cooperate with other organizations such as COMIBAM (Cooperación Misionera Iberoamericana), which, in addition to Latin America, works in Spain.[64] COMIBAM differs from the FTL in that it is a missionary-sending organization to Spanish-speaking countries, rather than a theologizing entity.

Given the fact that this congress was held in Spanish rather than English, that does make worldwide impact a bit more difficult. English is dominant in international discourse as well as publishing power. English has the advantage, unlike Chinese and Spanish, which are the next two most-spoken languages on earth, of being more widespread (some people on every continent know English), whereas Chinese and Spanish are more concentrated in certain geographical areas on earth. Of course the natural solution is translation, both live via headsets at conferences and written in books. CLADE V did have headset translations into English, and the FTL also produces an English-language journal, *The Journal of Latin American Theology: Christian Reflections from the Latino South*,[65] to make accessible their most important documents to the English-speaking world. Will there come a day when Chinese or Spanish becomes the lingua franca of the world?[66]

---

[64]The FTL, it must be noted, also does have a Spain chapter, even if its focus is primarily in Latin America.

[65]Publication began in 2006 with two issues per year.

[66]It has been predicted for some time now that Chinese would surpass English as the language of the Internet (Conrad Quilty-Harper, "Chinese Internet Users to Overtake English Language Users by 2015," *The Telegraph*, September 26, 2012, www.telegraph.co.uk/technology/broadband/9567934/Chinese-internet-users-to-overtake-English-language-users-by-2015.html). This prediction from the UN Broadband Commission in 2012 was almost accurate. In November 2015 there were 872.9 million English-language Internet users, compared to 704.5 million Chinese-language Internet users. It is just a matter of time until Chinese will overtake English (www.internetworldstats.com/stats7.htm). The short-lived but immensely popular science fiction TV show *Firefly* (2002) shows

CREATION CARE DECLARATION AND CLADE V PASTORAL LETTER

All the 2010 conferences, with the exception of 2010Boston, produced final theological documents. Each of the 2010 conferences, with the exception of Tokyo 2010, produced a book compiling all the plenary speakers' talks. Though CLADE V did not do the latter, it did do the former. In the series of Latin American missiological conferences, Curitiba '76 produced the *Curitiba Covenant*, and each of the CLADEs wrote one as well: CLADE I produced the *Evangelical Declaration of Bogotá*;[67] CLADE II produced something different in the form of the "Letter to the Evangelical People of Latin America,"[68] which essentially affirmed both the *Declaration of Bogotá* and the *Lausanne Covenant*; CLADE III produced the *Quito Declaration*;[69] and CLADE IV ended not with a document but with a series of books published by Ediciones Kairós called the CLADE IV series, similar to Regnum's Edinburgh 2010 Centenary Series.

CLADE V's final documents were on a smaller scale and written by consultations and forums at the congress. For example, CLADE V's forum on creation care issued a "Declaration: Christian Commitment in Light of the Environmental Crisis and Its Victims in Latin America and the Caribbean"[70] and addressed a crucial and neglected issue that was hardly present at any of the 2010 conferences. Though Latinos are by no means the only ones to be conscious of creation care,[71] they have particular interest in it because Latin America (both Central America and the Amazon rainforest) has the largest biodiversity in the world, and even the current pope, Francis, is

---

a future where, due to the dominance of the United States and China in space, everyone is bilingual in English and Chinese.

[67]The declaration as well as all the other papers given at CLADE I can be found in *Acción en Cristo para un continente en crisis* (Miami: Caribe, 1970).

[68]*Carta de CLADE II*, as well as all the other papers given at that congress, can be found in *América Latina y la Evangelización en los Años 80* (Lima, 1979).

[69]This can be found in *CLADE III: Todo el evangelio para todos los pueblos desde América Latina* (Quito: FTL, 1992).

[70]*Journal of Latin American Theology* 8, no. 1 (2013): 71-74.

[71]Some good books on the topic include treatments by a Latin American, a US American and a European: Leonardo Boff, *Cry of the Earth, Cry of the Poor* (Maryknoll, NY: Orbis, 1997); Francis A. Schaeffer, *Pollution and the Death of Man* (Wheaton, IL: Crossway, 1970); Richard Bauckham, *The Bible and Ecology: Rediscovering the Community of Creation* (Waco, TX: Baylor University Press, 2010).

named after a saint who was famous for creation care.[72] The youth consultation at CLADE V produced a pastoral letter to address their concerns.[73] And CLADE V as a whole had a final pastoral letter.

Both pastoral letters of CLADE V were short documents but contained important and practical injunctions for the future of Latin America. The youth letter stressed that "the majority of the population in our countries is young (under 30) and this is clearly reflected in our faith communities."[74] This is true not only of Latin America, but of most of the Two-Thirds World: the average age is young, unlike in developed countries (like Europe and Japan) where the population is aging. But unfortunately, an "*adult-centered* perspective has not only held young people back from shouldering the responsibility of their leading role in the Church and Society; instead, their lack of recognition as essential to the Body of Christ has been an obstacle to other young people getting to know Jesus and the proposal of His Kingdom."[75] Some missiologists have developed the concept of the 4/14 Window[76] (not to be confused with the 10/40 Window, which is a geographic designation) to designate the ages between which most people make lifelong decisions for Christ.[77] If this is true, then youth ought to be a major focus of twenty-first-century missiology. But the youth pastoral letter also empowered youth to be active agents of change, not just passive recipients of other people's ministries and actions, and to aim to work intergenerationally. This is why it was organized by the CLADE V consultation called "Youth, Actors for Transformation."

The pastoral letter that represented the entire congress was framed around CLADE V's trinitarian theme, recognition of certain unacceptable Christian status quos toward each person of the Trinity, and recommendations for local FTL chapters to engage with each of these in biblical-

---

[72]Francis is the first pope to ever address creation care so fully. His first solo-authored encyclical was *Laudato si': On Care for Our Common Home* (May 24, 2015), taking its name from a phrase in St. Francis of Assisi's poem/prayer "Canticle of the Sun." Pope Francis also instituted the first World Day of Prayer for the Care of Creation, to be celebrated annually on September 1 starting in 2015.

[73]The full text of the "Pastoral Letter for the 'Youth, Actors for Transformation' Consultation at CLADE V" can be accessed at https://jovenescladev.files.wordpress.com/2012/07/carta-pastoral-de-la-consulta-de-jovenes-ingles.pdf.

[74]Ibid., 2.

[75]Ibid., 2-3.

[76]See www.4to14window.com.

[77]George Barna, *Transforming Children into Spiritual Champions* (Ventura, CA: Regal, 2003).

theological-contextual ways. This shows the FTL's evangelical roots (biblical) as well as keeping together both theology and context; the theory and praxis must work together. The Spanish word *evangélico* is perhaps better encapsulated by the English phrase "radical evangelical." It is not the Bible over context (evangelical) nor context over the Bible (liberation theology), but both. This is the holistic mission (*misión integral*) that influenced John Stott and the production of the *Lausanne Covenant*. And the *Lausanne Covenant*'s heir, the *Cape Town Commitment*, was disseminated at CLADE V, the FTL's child—thus it all came full circle. CLADE V's pastoral letter was not a long document, but it was clear and incisive at points where we need to critically address the realities of where Christians are falling short with regard to God. It is a prophetic, self-assessing statement, but one that moves missiologically out of that into hope for the world.

QUESTIONS

1. Should CLADE V be included in this book? Does it seem like the natural fifth conference in the 2010 series, or does it seem more like an attempt at reparation, similar to Panamá 1916, which was to redress a lack of representation in 1910? In other words, is CLADE V the Panamá 1916 of the twenty-first century, or is it its own thing?

2. Now that the "golden age" of Latin American theology of the 1970s[78] is over, is *misión integral* a subject that is no longer relevant? Has it lost its prophetic voice now that the world is already "on board" with it? Was anything new about *misión integral* said at CLADE V?

3. Just because the FTL is good about racial and international diversity does not mean it is necessarily good at gender diversity—just look at the list of the original twenty-five members of the FTL as well as the "old lions" on stage, all of whom were men. Perhaps some of this comes from the *machismo* inherent in many Latin American cultures (though certainly patriarchal tendencies are not limited to Latin America). This is often a criticism of multiethnic organizations: they can be excellent at one kind of diversity while oddly being insensitive about another. The

---

[78]As exemplified by the title of Daniel Salinas's book *Latin American Evangelical Theology in the 1970's: The Golden Decade* (Leiden: Brill, 2009).

election of Ruth Padilla DeBorst to the General Secretary office of the FTL was a good sign, as was the changing of the English name from Latin American Theological *Fraternity* to *Fellowship*. Considering that neither the West nor many cultures in the Majority World have achieved full gender equality and inclusion, do you think that the heart of the issue lies in theology or culture?

4. Should worldwide missionary conferences be operating more on the Pilgrim Principle than the Indigenizing Principle? Did CLADE V lean too much on the latter (in other words, was it too Latino and not global enough) to be effective and impactful for the whole church? Does offering the *CTC* in Spanish show unity of spirit with Christians on other continents, or would it have been better to have more of the fourth self, self-theologizing?

5. Does a conference need to be held in English in order to attract an international constituency? How does one negotiate between cultural imperialism and international accessibility? The three most-spoken languages in the world are English, Chinese and Spanish, in that order. If major international missionary conferences can be held in English, shouldn't that legitimate this one in Spanish? Shouldn't there eventually be one in Chinese as well?

6. What do you think about the creation care declaration and the youth pastoral letter from CLADE V? Should CLADE continue to focus on contextual issues such as these, or would producing a comprehensive missiological document be a better use of its efforts?

7. What future missiological subjects need to be addressed by the Latin American church? What issues do you think CLADE VI should discuss?

8. Did CLADE V bring the CLADE movement back to prominence in the same way that Cape Town 2010 did with the Lausanne movement?

9. What is the future of evangelicalism in Latin America? *Evangélicos* are only 17 percent of the Latin American population, and three-quarters of them are Pentecostals. Should CLADE fully embrace Pentecostalism as its future and/or partner more with Catholics, or is there a place for Protestants?

CONCLUSION

MANY PEOPLE THINK of multiethnicity, multiculturalism and polycentrism as ideals for Christianity but not as absolutely necessary. However, diversity was a mark of the early church, not just at Pentecost (Acts 2), where there were Jews from many nations, but at Antioch (Acts 11), which was the first multiethnic church in history and also the first time the believers are called "Christian." This is no coincidence, because the two go together. Without multiethnicity, the people of God are still Jewish and thus remain Israel. With multiethnicity and the ushering in of the Gentiles, it becomes the church. This is why Peter was so flabbergasted in Acts 10 with the vision of the sheet being let down from heaven three times—it didn't just mean that he no longer had to obey kosher dietary laws (hello bacon cheeseburgers!), but more fully it meant that Gentiles were included in the faith.

Christianity is also unique because it is the only religion in the world in which the Scriptures are not written in the language of its founder (Jesus spoke Aramaic, and the New Testament was written in *koine* Greek, which was the commercial language of the eastern Roman Empire) in order for it to spread to as many people as possible. And Christianity is the only religion in the world that has no one majority racial or ethnic group, and no geographical center—we have no Mecca or Varanasi or Jerusalem or Salt Lake City because the temple of the Holy Spirit is God's people. Even the early church exhibited this polycentric approach by having multiple patriarchates consisting of five ancient metropolitan centers (the so-called Pentarchy): one was in Africa (Alexandria), two were in Asia (Jerusalem and Antioch), one was in Europe (Rome), and one straddled both Europe and Asia (Constantinople).

Kenneth Scott Latourette famously dubbed the nineteenth century "the Great Century of Missions." The twentieth century ended up being "the Great Century of Ecumenism" (or, if one were to be negative, "the Great Reversal" or "the Great Century of Secularism"). But the twenty-first century is shaping up to become known as "the Great Century of World Christianity" or "the Great Century of Partnership,"[1] as Christianity has regained its status as a truly global religion with Two-Thirds World churches exploding in number (quantity) and developing in maturity (quality). This is why the four selfs are needed: self-propagating and self-sustaining contribute to their quantity; self-governing and self-theologizing are necessary for their quality.

Five conferences on five continents—why do we need such a multiplicity? What does each of these bring to the table? These were the questions this book was trying to answer. And, dare we ask, which does the best job of being a successor to Edinburgh 1910? The answer: all of them. In 1910, missions was "From the West to the Rest." In the twenty-first century, missions is "From Everyone to Everywhere" (hence the subtitle of this book) because, instead of being unidirectional, it is polycentric and polydirectional. World Christianity is not just a momentary trend; it looks like it is here to stay. This includes *every* continent on earth, where every Christian can be mobilized to be a missionary to any land. This necessitates that we do mission differently, as the demographics of the world have changed drastically. We now live in an age of *partnership*, not *paternalism*, and V. S. Azariah's cry of "Give us friends!" from a century ago resounds in our ears and hearts as the Two-Thirds World churches have now come into their own.

Let us also not forget the infamous omission of Latin America from Edinburgh 1910—have we really improved upon our predecessors that much in one hundred years as history has somewhat repeated itself with no Latin American conference in 2010? Latin Americans convened Panamá 1916 to

---

[1]Or "The Unexpected Christian Century," as dubbed by Scott Sunquist. See Sunquist, *The Unexpected Christian Century: The Reversal and Transformation of Global Christianity, 1900–2000* (Grand Rapids: Baker Academic, 2015).

address their exclusion, just as Costa Rica 2012 addressed the lack of a Latin American conference in 2010. This book, hopefully, will seal CLADE V in the annals of history as a full participant and voice in evangelicalism, ecumenism and mission in the twenty-first century. However, it was China, not Latin America, that seemed to be excluded from 2010. Sub-Saharan Africa and China are the two heartlands of world Christianity today, and though the former was well represented (even hosting the largest of the five conferences), the latter was practically missing. Perhaps China will eventually be the host of a major international missions conference! No one would have thought it possible, even twenty years ago, where China would stand today in terms of its explosion of Christianity. China has the ability to not only *be* Christian in vast numbers but to *lead* Christianity in missions. Anything is possible with our God!

It is worth reminding ourselves that, while we have improved on many things from previous generations (and have definitely done some things worse!), we still have a long ways to go and are reliant on future generations to take up the torch and keep pressing forward. Thus we are connected with the saints of old, that "great cloud of witnesses," as well as with those Christians yet to come.[2] Brian Stanley said it well at 2010Boston:

> I have a suspicion that if the proceedings of the various centennial mission conferences held in 2010, in Edinburgh, Tokyo, Cape Town, and Boston, were to be subjected in one hundred years' time to critical dissection by scholars in the light of the course that world Christianity has actually taken in the twenty-first century, the diagnoses and policy prescriptions advanced in these conferences of our own generation will prove to be no less flawed, partial in perception, and ideologically conditioned than those of our predecessors a century ago. Ultimately our responses to the pronouncements made in 1910 will depend on our own theological and philosophical commitments. For all of their Western cultural biases, the delegates at Edinburgh 1910 shared a common conviction that the Christian gospel was good news for all human beings without exception, and was not, therefore, to be confined within the frontiers of European or American Christendom. This

---

[2]As mentioned earlier, the tapestries in the Cathedral of Our Lady of the Angels in Los Angeles show this reality beautifully, depicting biblical characters, historical saints, contemporary people and imagined future generations all woven together by artist John Nava. See www.olacathedral.org/cathedral/art/tapestries.html.

theological absolutism, so uncongenial to many palates today, was in fact the foundation for the construction of Christianity as a multi-cultural world religion.[3]

May history prove it to be so—flexible in culture but unyieldingly devoted in our worship of the triune God. Hallelujah!

---

[3]Brian Stanley, "Discerning the Future of World Christianity: Vision and Blindness at the World Missionary Conference, Edinburgh 1910," in Todd Johnson et al., *2010Boston: The Changing Contours of World Mission and Christianity* (Eugene, OR: Pickwick, 2012), 63.

APPENDIX A

CONFERENCE PROGRAM SCHEDULES AND PLENARY SPEAKERS FROM THE FIVE CONFERENCES

Tokyo 2010

Wednesday, May 12

"Kingdom Mission: DNA of the Missionary Task," Dr. David Cho

"The New Renewal Missionary Movement," Dr. Obed Alvarez

"State of the Unfinished Task," Dr. Paul Eshleman

"The Biblical Foundation for Discipling Every People," Dr. Marv Newell

Thursday, May 13

"Making Disciples: A Way Forward in Missions," Rev. Gbile Akanni

"Japanese Challenges: Buddhism, Shintoism, Others," Dr. Minoru Okuyama

"Beyond Christianity," Rev. Kevin Higgins

"Indian Religions: Challenges and Outreach," Rev. Susanta Patra

Friday, May 14

"Rationale for Mission Structures," Dr. Sung Sam Kang

"Reaching the Secular Peoples of Europe," Dr. Stefan Gustavsson

"Islam Global Outreach," Dr. Hisham Kamel

"Global Peoples and Diaspora Missiology," Dr. Enoch Wan

Edinburgh 2010

Thursday, June 3

Plenary 1: "Missions in Long Perspective," Dr. Dana L. Robert

Friday, June 4

Plenary 2: "Missions Worldwide," Rev. Dr. Lee Young-Hoon, Dr. Tony Kireopoulos, Dr. Teresa Francesca Rossi, Dr. Fidon Mwombeki

Saturday, June 5

Plenary 3: "Towards a Common Call"

Cape Town 2010 (Lausanne III)

Monday, October 18

Plenary 1: "Celebration of the Bible," Ajith Fernando (Ephesians 1)

Plenary 2: "Making the Case for the Truth of Christ in a Pluralistic, Globalized World," Carver Yu, Michael Herbst, Os Guinness, Shirinai Dossoua

Plenary 3: "God at Work in the World Through His Church"

Regional Focus: Asia

Global Issues: the suffering church and religious freedom

Tuesday, October 19

Plenary 1: "Celebration of the Bible," Ruth Padilla DeBorst (Ephesians 2)

Plenary 2: "Building the Peace of Christ in Our Divided and Broken World," Antoine Rutayisire, Joseph D'souza, Pranitha Timothy, Christine MacMilan

Plenary 3: "God at Work in the World Through His Church"

Regional Focus: Middle East

Global Issues: HIV/AIDS and human trafficking

Wednesday, October 20

Plenary 1: "Celebration of the Bible," John Piper (Ephesians 3)

Plenary 2: "Bearing Witness to the Love of Christ with People of Other Faiths," Michael Ramsden, Archbishop Benjamin Kwashi

Plenary 3: "God at Work in the World Through His Church"

Regional Focus: Latin America and Caribbean

Global Issues: diaspora; megacities—Tim Keller

Friday, October 22

Plenary 1: "Celebration of the Bible," Vaughan Roberts (Ephesians 4:1-16)

Plenary 2: "Discerning the Will of Christ for 21st-Century World Evangelization," Paul Eshleman, David Yoo

Plenary 3: "God at Work in the World Through His Church"

Regional Focus: Africa

Global Issues: next generation, children and youth

Saturday, October 23

Plenary 1: "Celebration of the Bible," Calisto Odede (Ephesians 4:17–6:9)

Plenary 2: "Calling the Church of Christ Back to Humility, Integrity, and Simplicity," Chris Wright, Femi Adeleye, Elke Werner

Plenary 3: "God at Work in the World Through His Church"

Our Personal Stand Before God: Responding to God in Worship and Prayer

Regional Focus: Eurasia and the Western World

Sunday, October 24

Plenary 1: "Celebration of the Bible," Ramez and Rebecca Atallah (Ephesians 6:10-24)

Plenary 2: "Partnering in the Body of Christ Toward a New Global Equilibrium," Patrick Fung, David Ruiz, Leslie and Chad Segraves

Closing Ceremony

2010Boston

Wednesday, November 3

Pre-conference debriefing: "Mission of the Triune God, Mission of the Church, Mission of the World," Dr. Peter Phan

Thursday, November 4

"The Significance of Edinburgh, 1910–2010: An Overview," an Edinburgh 2010
    debriefing and discussion with Professors Dana Robert and Norm Thomas

First keynote: "Boston, Students, and Missions from 1810 to 2010,"
    Dana Robert

Friday, November 5

Second keynote: "Discerning the Future of World Christianity: Vision and
    Blindness at the World Missionary Conference, Edinburgh 1910,"
    Brian Stanley

"Reports from Edinburgh, Tokyo, and Cape Town," moderated and with
    comment/reflection by Episcopal Bishop Ian Douglas
    Allen Yeh (Tokyo)
    LouAnn Stropoli (Cape Town)
    John Kaoma (Edinburgh)

Third keynote: "Theological Education and Mission: A Non-Western Re-
    flection," Daniel Jeyaraj

Fourth keynote: "Journey to the Center of Gravity: Christian Mission One
    Century After Edinburgh 1910," Athanasios N. Papathanasiou (*Synaxis*,
    Greek Orthodox theological journal)

Saturday, November 6

Fifth keynote: "Wooden Boxes and Latticed Windows: Christian Witness
    and the Post-Colonizing, Post-Colonized Church," Ruth Padilla De-
    Borst (Latin American Theological Fraternity)

Sixth keynote: "Christianity and the Wider Ecumenism: 'Mission and Inter-
    religious Dialogue: Edinburgh, Vatican II, and Beyond,'" Peter Phan
    (Georgetown University)

Seventh keynote: "From Boston to the Whole World: 20th-Century North
    American Roman Catholic Missions and the 'Antioch Agenda,'" An-
    gelyn Dries (St. Louis University)

Eighth keynote: "Christian Mission and Peace-Making: Discerning Our
    Secret Non-Weapon," Brian McLaren

Sunday, November 7

Ninth keynote: "Who Is Jesus and What Does He Mean to Those Who Put
    Their Trust in Him?," Part 1—"God's Mission Is Performative"

Costa Rica 2012 (CLADE V)

Lunes, 9 de Julio
"Apertura de CLADE V: Recordar (Buscar a Jesús)"

Martes, 10 de Julio
"Plenaria Seguimiento de Jesús: Agradecer (Descubrir a Jesús)"
Región Brasil; Secretario Regional: Wilson Costa
Región Mesoamérica y Caribe; Secretario Regional: Edesio Sánchez Cetina

Miércoles, 11 de Julio
"Plenaria El Reino de la Vida: Escuchar (Duda y Misterio)"
Región Andina; Secretario Regional: Evita Morales
Región Norteamérica; Secretario Regional: Juan Martínez

Jueves, 12 de Julio
"Plenaria El Espíritu de la Vida: Responder (La Paz)"
Región Cono Sur; Secretario Regional: Juan José Barreda Toscano
Plenaria Foro Teológico, Dr. Juan José Tamayo

Viernes, 13 de Julio
"Comunidad Trinitaria: Celebrar (Desayuno de la Resurrección)"

APPENDIX B

FAMILY TREE OF 2010 CONFERENCES, FROM WILLIAM CAREY TO PRESENT

Proposed
CAPE TOWN 1810
WORLD MISSION CONFERENCE
WILLIAM CAREY

EDINBURGH 1910
WORLD MISSION CONFERENCE
JOHN MOTT

ECUMENICAL STREAM

EVANGELICAL STREAM

1928 JERUSALEM

1938 MADRAS

1948 AMSTERDAM

BILLY GRAHAM

RALPH WINTER

1961 DELHI

1974 *LAUSANNE I*

1980 MELBOURNE

1980 PATTAYA

1980 EDINBURGH

1989 MANILA
LAUSANNE II

1989 SINGAPORE
GCOWE

1995 SEOL
GCOWE

1989 PRETORIA, S.A.
GCOWE

2004 PATTAYA
FORUM FOR WE

EDINBURGH 2010
BOSTON 2010

CAPE TOWN 2010
LAUSANNE III

TOKYO 2010

Source: Marv Newell, "Family Tree of Global Mission Conferences," *Connections: The Journal of the WEA Mission Commission* 10, no. 1 (April 2012): 14.

APPENDIX C

CONFERENCE DOCUMENTS

Tokyo 2010 Declaration

MAKING DISCIPLES OF EVERY PEOPLE IN OUR GENERATION[1]

Preamble

We affirm that mission is the central theme of Scripture, through which God reveals Himself to be a God who communicates and works through us by action and word in a world estranged from Him. Furthermore, we recognize that fulfilling and bringing completion to Jesus' Great Commission (Mt. 28:18-20; Mk. 16:15; Lk. 24:44-49; Jn. 20:21; Acts 1:8) has been the ongoing responsibility of the Church for 2000 years.

In this era of missions, we of the Tokyo 2010 Global Mission Consultation value and commemorate the 1910 Edinburgh World Missionary Conference, a hallmark event which stands out as an inspiration and impetus to the modern global mission movement. We celebrate a legacy of 100 years of mission that has transpired since that first world missionary conference.

However, the world has dramatically changed since that conference was convened a century ago. Missions is no longer the predominant domain of Western Christianity. Rather, the preponderance of mission activity today is

---

[1]Beth Snodderly and A. Scott Moreau, eds., *Evangelical and Frontier Mission: Perspectives on the Global Progress of the Gospel* (Oxford: Regnum, 2011), 207-12; or online at www.ggcn.org/pdf /Tokyo_2010_Declaration.pdf.

being engaged by Majority World Christians outside of the West. Christ's ambassadors are coming from everywhere around the world and going to anywhere and everywhere in the world. We rejoice that today's mission force is global in composition, bearing a diversity of thought, practice and resources that enriches and energizes Christ's global Cause as never before.

Yet, the corresponding reality is that the present day mission task is so large and complex that no one church, agency, national missions movement, or regional mission block can take it on alone or independently. Also, the understanding of the essence of what is entailed in the remaining task has altered considerably in recent years.

Declaration

We, representatives of evangelical global mission structures, being intent on fulfilling the ultimate objective of the Great Commission, have gathered in Tokyo May 11–14, 2010 at this Global Mission Consultation to make the following declaration. We set forth this declaration in obedience to Christ's final command, as a means of calling Christ-followers everywhere to wholeheartedly embrace and earnestly engage in "making disciples of every people in our generation."

Mankind's Need

We affirm that all people are lost apart from faith in Christ. The clear statements of Scripture reveal that every individual, without exception, is a sinner by nature, choice and practice (Rom. 3:9-18, 23). As such, all are under God's wrath and condemnation (Jn. 3:18) because their sin is an affront to the perfect and holy nature of God (Rom. 1:18; 2:2-5). The tragic result of sin is man's alienation from God, leading to everlasting death (Rom. 6:23), and creation's bondage to corruption, subjecting it to futility (Rom. 8:18-21).

God's Remedy

We further affirm that out of love, God sent His only Son, Jesus Christ (Jn. 3:16), to reconcile the world to Himself, so that mankind's sin will not be counted against them (2 Cor. 5:19). God's justice for the penalty of sin was satisfied by the atoning death of Christ as a sacrifice on man's behalf. Through Jesus' vicarious death and victorious resurrection, mankind is brought into a restored relationship with God. God offers forgiveness and salvation to all who, through faith, repent of their sin and believe solely in the redemptive work of Christ on the cross on their behalf (Rom. 1:5, 16, 17; 3:21-26; Eph. 1:7; 2:8-10). Therefore the message of the Great Commission is that "repentance and forgiveness of sins will be preached in His name to all peoples" (Lk. 24:47). Salvation is found in none other (Acts 4:12), nor in any other way (Jn. 14:6).

Our Responsibility

Because of the reality of mankind's dire need and God's gracious remedy, Jesus left with His followers the missional priority of making disciples of every people (Mt. 28:18-20). By this mandate we acknowledge both the breadth of the unfinished task—all peoples—and the depth of the task—making disciples, as its focus.

We recognize the breadth of our task as geographical, by going "into all the world" (Mk 16:15); as ethnical, by engaging "all peoples" (Mt. 28:19; Lk. 24:49); and as individual by proclaiming the gospel to "every creature" (Mk. 16:15).

Furthermore, we recognize that the depth of the task contains three essentials that comprise aspects in discipling peoples (Mt. 28:19-20):

Penetration ("go"): making a priority of going to those who have had little or no exposure to the gospel. Messengers go and encounter non-believers by way of personal encounters, broadcasts, podcasts, printed material, recordings, electronic communications, or any other innovative means used as a channel of penetrating witness. Thus, the importance of the ministry of evangelizing.

Consolidation ("baptizing"): gathering new believers into a relationship with Jesus and other believers, which is evidenced by the identifying rite of baptism. To conserve the fruit of evangelism and then be able to systematically disciple believers takes a local body of believers living in corporate harmony. Thus, the importance of the ministry of establishing churches.

Transformation ("teaching to obey"): teaching Christ-followers to observe His commands with the outcome of transformed lives. The new believer's worldview must be adjusted to a biblical worldview; his lifestyle changed to increasingly conform to the image of Christ; and his ethical conduct progressively marked by biblical morals. Ideally, this results in individuals applying the gospel of the kingdom to every sphere and pursuit of life—from government to economics, from education to health, and from science to creation care. As a consequence whole communities, cultures and countries benefit from the transforming power of the gospel. Thus, the importance of the ministry of teaching.

Finishing the Task

Although none dare predict when the task of making disciples will be brought to completion, we leave Tokyo cognizant of two realities:

1) We are closer now to finishing the task than at any time in modern history.

2) God has entrusted this generation with more opportunities and resources to complete the task than any previous one. We have more mission-minded churches, more sending structures and bases, more missionaries, more material resources, more funding, more and better technology, more information and data, a deeper understanding of the task, and a clearer focus of our responsibility than previous generations. God will require much of our generation.

However, we caution that all these advantages must be matched with a corresponding will to serve and sacrifice, coupled with genuine reliance upon the Holy Spirit. We acknowledge that we are engaged in spiritual warfare in which the presence and empowering of the Holy Spirit is essential (Acts 1:8). We give evidence of our reliance on God and His Spirit through frequent and fervent prayer on behalf of the world, the work and the workers (Jn. 17:20-21; Col. 4:3-4; 1 Th. 5:17).

Our Pledge

Therefore, as representatives of this generation's global mission community, we pledge to obey the Great Commission. We covenant together to use all that God has entrusted to us in this obedience. We will seek to know where people are unreached, overlooked, ignored, or forgotten. We will pray for the Holy Spirit to give strength and guidance as we join with others in changing that neglect, to love and make disciples in the way of the Cross.

We confess that we have not always valued each other or each other's work. We repent of those wrongs and will endeavor to bring an end to competition where it exists, and reconcile where there is hurt, misunderstanding and mistrust. Furthermore, we will endeavor to recognize that each part of the Body has its very own purpose, whether risking their very lives to show God's passion for the salvation of others, or supporting those who lead us forward, or caring for those who quietly support, or fervently pray that His will be done throughout the whole earth. We will respect all mission-engaging individuals and groups as special vessels for God's glory, each endowed with abilities that extend His Kingdom in multiple ways.

Finally, we recognize that finishing the task will demand effective cooperative efforts of the entire global body of believers. To facilitate cooperation and on-going coordination between mission structures worldwide, we agree to the necessity of a global network of mission structures. With this in mind, we leave Tokyo pledging cooperation with one another, and all others of like faith, with the singular goal of "making disciples of every people in our generation."

Edinburgh 2010

COMMON CALL[2]

As we gather for the centenary of the World Missionary Conference of Edinburgh 1910, we believe the church, as a sign and symbol of the reign of God, is called to witness to Christ today by sharing in God's mission of love through the transforming power of the Holy Spirit.

1. Trusting in the Triune God and with a renewed sense of urgency, we are called to incarnate and proclaim the good news of salvation, of forgiveness of sin, of life in abundance, and of liberation for all poor and oppressed. We are challenged to witness and evangelism in such a way that we are a living demonstration of the love, righteousness and justice that God intends for the whole world.

2. Remembering Christ's sacrifice on the Cross and his resurrection for the world's salvation, and empowered by the Holy Spirit, we are called to authentic dialogue, respectful engagement and humble witness among people of other faiths—and no faith—to the uniqueness of Christ. Our

---

[2]Available online at www.edinburgh2010.org/fileadmin/Edinburgh_2010_Common_Call_with_ Explanation.pdf.

approach is marked with bold confidence in the gospel message; it builds friendship, seeks reconciliation and practices hospitality.

3. Knowing the Holy Spirit who blows over the world at will, reconnecting creation and bringing authentic life, we are called to become communities of compassion and healing, where young people are actively participating in mission, and women and men share power and responsibilities fairly, where there is a new zeal for justice, peace and the protection of the environment, and renewed liturgy reflecting the beauties of the Creator and creation.

4. Disturbed by the asymmetries and imbalances of power that divide and trouble us in church and world, we are called to repentance, to critical reflection on systems of power, and to accountable use of power structures. We are called to find practical ways to live as members of One Body in full awareness that God resists the proud, Christ welcomes and empowers the poor and afflicted, and the power of the Holy Spirit is manifested in our vulnerability.

5. Affirming the importance of the biblical foundations of our missional engagement and valuing the witness of the Apostles and martyrs, we are called to rejoice in the expressions of the gospel in many nations all over the world. We celebrate the renewal experienced through movements of migration and mission in all directions, the way all are equipped for mission by the gifts of the Holy Spirit, and God's continual calling of children and young people to further the gospel.

6. Recognising the need to shape a new generation of leaders with authenticity for mission in a world of diversities in the twenty-first century, we are called to work together in new forms of theological education. Because we are all made in the image of God, these will draw on one another's unique charisms, challenge each other to grow in faith and understanding, share resources equitably worldwide, involve the entire human being and the whole family of God, and respect the wisdom of our elders while also fostering the participation of children.

7. Hearing the call of Jesus to make disciples of all people—poor, wealthy, marginalised, ignored, powerful, living with disability, young, and old—we are called as communities of faith to mission from everywhere to everywhere. In joy we hear the call to receive from one another in our witness by

word and action, in streets, fields, offices, homes, and schools, offering reconciliation, showing love, demonstrating grace and speaking out truth.

8. Recalling Christ, the host at the banquet, and committed to that unity for which he lived and prayed, we are called to ongoing co-operation, to deal with controversial issues and to work towards a common vision. We are challenged to welcome one another in our diversity, affirm our membership through baptism in the One Body of Christ, and recognise our need for mutuality, partnership, collaboration and networking in mission, so that the world might believe.

9. Remembering Jesus' way of witness and service, we believe we are called by God to follow this way joyfully, inspired, anointed, sent and empowered by the Holy Spirit, and nurtured by Christian disciplines in community. As we look to Christ's coming in glory and judgment, we experience his presence with us in the Holy Spirit, and we invite all to join with us as we participate in God's transforming and reconciling mission of love to the whole creation.

The Edinburgh 2010 Common Call emerged from the Edinburgh 2010 study process and conference to mark the centenary of the World Missionary Conference, Edinburgh 1910. The Common Call was affirmed in the Church of Scotland Assembly Hall in Edinburgh on 6 June 2010 by representatives of world Christianity, including Catholic, Evangelical, Orthodox, Pentecostal, and Protestant churches.

For further information, see www.edinburgh2010.org.

The Cape Town Commitment

[Due to the extensive length of his document, it is not printed in its entirety here, but rather the official summary is reproduced.][3]

The Cape Town Commitment (CTC) is a masterful and comprehensive document, faithfully reflecting the proceedings of The Third Lausanne Congress on World Evangelization, which took place in Cape Town, South Africa (October 2010). It is impossible to capture the spirit of Lausanne III in a three-page summary, so this synopsis should be read in conjunction with the full CTC.

---

[3] Available online at www.lausanne.org/content/summary-of-the-cape-town-commitment.

The CTC is rooted in the conviction that "we must respond in Christian mission to the realities of our own generation." The mission of the Church must take seriously both the unchanging nature of God's word and the changing realities of our world. The CTC reflects the Lausanne call for the whole Church to take the whole gospel to the whole world; it is framed in the language of love—love for the whole gospel, the whole Church, and the whole world. The Commitment has two parts: a confession of faith and a call to action.

PART I—*For the Lord we love: The Cape Town Confession of Faith*

The opening sentences set the framework, "The mission of God flows from the love of God. The mission of God's people flows from our love for God and for all that God loves."

The first five points deal with our love for God himself. We love the living God, above all rivals and with a passion for his glory. We love the triune God: Father, Son, and Holy Spirit. With respect to the Father, the CTC calls for a renewed appreciation of God's fatherhood. Concerning the Son, it highlights our duty to trust, obey, and proclaim Christ. Of the Spirit, it says, "Our engagement in mission, then, is pointless and fruitless without the presence, guidance and power of the Holy Spirit. . . . There is no true or whole gospel, and no authentic biblical mission, without the Person, work and power of the Holy Spirit."

The last five points cover our love for God's Word, world, gospel, people, and missions. (a) We reaffirm our submission to the Bible as God's final revelation, and affirm our love for the Person it reveals, the story it tells, the truth it teaches, and the life it requires (while admitting we often confess to love the Bible without loving the life it teaches, a life of costly practical discipleship). (b) We love God's world, all that he has made and loves. This includes caring for creation, loving all peoples and valuing ethnic diversity, longing to see the gospel embedded in all cultures, loving the world's poor and suffering people, and loving our neighbours as we love ourselves. It does not mean loving or being like "the world" (i.e. world-liness). (c) We love the gospel—the story it tells, the assurance it gives, and the transformation it produces. (d) We love all God's people, recognising that such love calls for unity, honesty, and solidarity. (e) We love the mission of God. "We are committed to world mission, because it is central to our understanding of God, the Bible, the Church, human history and the ultimate future. . . . The Church exists to worship and glorify God for all eternity and to participate in the transforming mission of God within history. Our mission is wholly derived from God's mission, addresses the whole of God's creation, and is grounded at its centre in the redeeming victory of the cross." We are called to *integral mission*, which is the proclamation *and* demonstration of the gospel.

PART II—For the world we serve: The Cape Town Call to Action

The call to action uses the six Congress themes, which are linked to the six expositions of Ephesians.

A. *Bearing witness to the truth of Christ in a pluralistic, globalized world.* The Congress affirmed belief in absolute truth, and particularly in Jesus Christ as *the Truth*. Christians, therefore, are called to be people of truth, to live and proclaim the truth. We must face the threat of postmodern relativistic pluralism with robust apologetics. We must promote truth in the workplace and the global media. We must harness the arts for mission, promote authentically-Christian responses to emerging technologies, and actively engage the public arenas of government, business, and academia with biblical truth.

B. *Building the peace of Christ in our divided and broken world.* Christ has reconciled believers to God and to one another; the unity of God's people is both a fact and a mandate. The Church, therefore, has a responsibility to live out its reconciliation and to engage in biblical peace-making in the name of Christ. This includes bringing Christ's truth and peace to bear on racism and ethnic diversity, slavery and human trafficking, poverty, and minority groups such as people with disabilities. It also means our missional calling includes responsible stewardship of God's creation and its resources.

C. *Living the love of Christ among people of other faiths.* Our "neighbours" include people of other faiths. We must learn to see them as neighbours and be neighbours to them. We seek to share the good news in *ethical evangelism*, and we reject unworthy proselytizing. We accept that our commission includes a willingness to suffer and die for Christ in reaching out to people of other faiths. We are called to embody and commend the gospel of grace in loving action, in all cultures. We need to respect "diversity in discipleship," and encourage one another to exercise cultural discernment. We recognise global diaspora as strategic for evangelization: scattered peoples can be both recipients and agents of Christ's mission. While being willing to sacrifice our own rights for the sake of Christ, we commit to uphold and defend the human rights of others, including the right to religious freedom.

D. *Discerning the will of Christ for world evangelization.* Six key areas are identified as strategically important for the next decade: (a) unreached and unengaged people groups; (b) oral cultures; (c) Christ-centred leaders; (d) cities; (e) children; all with (f) prayer. The focus on Christian leaders is to prioritize discipleship and address the problems that arise from "generations of reductionist evangelism." Within this, key priorities are Bible translation, the preparation of oral story Bibles and other oral methodologies, as well as eradicating biblical illiteracy in the Church. Cities are home to four strategic groups: future leaders, migrant unreached peoples, culture shapers, and the poorest of the poor. All children are at risk; children represent both a mission field and a mission force.

E. *Calling the Church of Christ back to humility, integrity and simplicity.* The integrity of our mission in the world depends on our own integrity. The Congress called Christ-followers back to humble, sacrificial discipleship, simple living, and moral integrity. We need to be separate and distinct from the world (morally). Four "idolatries" were singled out: disordered sexuality, power, success, and greed. Disciples of Christ must reject these. (The prosperity gospel is rejected under the banner of "greed.")

F. *Partnering in the body of Christ for unity in mission.* Paul teaches us that Christian unity is a creation of God, based on our reconciliation with God and with one another. We lament the divisiveness of our churches and organizations, because a divided Church has no message for a divided world. Our failure to live in reconciled unity is a major obstacle to authenticity and effectiveness in mission. We commit to *partnership* in global mission. No one ethnic group, nation or continent can claim the exclusive privilege of being the ones to complete the Great Commission. Two specific aspects of unity in mission are the partnership of women and men and the recognition of the missional nature of theological education.

Prepared by Kevin Smith from the South African Theological Seminary.
This summary document is saturated with the actual language of the CTC, for

which reason quotation marks are not used for every phrase lifted from the CTC. Only longer quotations and key phrases are marked by quotation marks. This document serves as a précis of the CTC. To read the full CTC, please go to www.lausanne.org/ctcommitment.

THE SEOUL COMMITMENT[4]

We commit ourselves to loving the gospel of Christ. We are determined to humbly learn the vision of evangelization of the Lausanne Movement, to walk in the light of the gospel, to proclaim the gospel in Chinese society, and to advance the evangelical movement.

We commit ourselves to maintaining the unity of the Spirit in the bond of peace. We are determined to receive one another, to strive for the unity exemplified in the Lausanne Movement and to live out a loving covenant community, so that we can bring praise to His glory as a spectacle to angels and men.

We commit ourselves to joining hands with the global church in world missions. We are determined to take the vision of world mission of the Lausanne Movement, to pray faithfully for world missions, and to take action in mission mobilization, mission education and missionary sending.

We commit ourselves to raising up younger leaders of the next generation. We are determined to respond to the challenges and opportunities of our era in the spirit of Lausanne Movement, pass the vision of evangelization onto the younger generation and proclaim the salvation message of the old rugged cross with creative methods.

Forum on Creation Care, CLADE V

DECLARATION: CHRISTIAN COMMITMENT IN LIGHT OF THE ENVIRONMENTAL CRISIS AND ITS VICTIMS IN LATIN AMERICA AND THE CARIBBEAN[5]

The environmental crisis is a determinative factor for the survival of the entire creation, and it is directly connected to the themes analyzed in all

---

[4]Available online at www.lausanne.org/content/statement/the-seoul-commitment-china.
[5]"Declaration: Christian Commitment in Light of the Environmental Crisis and Its Victims in Latin America and the Caribbean," *Journal of Latin American Theology* 8, no. 1 (2013): 71-74.

the other consultations in CLADE V. In spite of its relevance, it would appear that most people within our churches are either asleep or indifferent to this reality. We sincerely desire to produce real commitments that lead to action and not repeat what occurred in the recent United Nations Conference on Sustainable Development (RIO+20) which did not lead to any significant results.

Expressions of Death

Creation groans . . . Do we hear it? Each time its groans are louder, even in our Latin American contexts, with expressions of death like the destruction of our forests and the continual advance of agricultural boundaries, the contamination and scarcity of water, soil degradation, the loss of food sovereignty, and the acquisition of the most fertile lands by a wealthy minority. All of these expressions, and many more, relate to favoring economic interests over the interest of creation's well-being. The poorest and most vulnerable people groups, including indigenous populations, bear the most negative impacts of these problems, which also transcend the present and will harm future generations throughout the entire creation.

We acknowledge that the theology in the majority of our churches today is insufficient to respond adequately to these expressions of death. Our eschatological teaching is all too often tied in to the destruction of the earth. Our anthropocentric and self-centered spirituality has limited our relationships with the rest of creation and therefore has also distorted the exercise of our role as responsible stewards.

Expressions of Life

In spite of our being surrounded by these expressions of death, the Holy Spirit is inspiring and calling the church to wake up from our lethargy. And some Christians are hearing and responding:

- Pastors throughout the entire region are beginning processes of reflection about our call to care for creation.

- Churches in Nicaragua are carrying out massive reforestation projects.

- Churches in Peru are educating youth and children in order to foster a greater appreciation for creation and for our call to protect it.

- Brazilian churches are working together to defend environmental rights and to mobilize others.

Although the Lord has made creation with an amazing ability to restore itself, it is important that we fulfill our vocation as co-creators.

Confessions

We confess that we have not paid attention to the leading of the Holy Spirit regarding our relationship with the rest of creation: we have ignored our responsibility as stewards, we have been accomplices in the destruction of creation and in the negative impacts on the most vulnerable people through our unsustainable lifestyles of ever-increasing consumerism.

We confess that, as a church, we have not demonstrated a response in solidarity regarding the devastating environmental situation in various parts of our region, especially in Haiti. Due to our greed and indifference, we have contributed to the reality of the forced migration and persecution that thousands of our peasant and indigenous brothers and sisters are suffering.

We confess our selfishness and our arrogance because we have lived as if we were the only important forms of life on this earth.

> *Forgive us, Lord, for our lack of creativity to teach our families and churches to love and take care of your creation. Forgive us, Lord, and guide us, Holy Spirit, to become transformed into instruments of peace and reconciliation with your whole creation.*

Call to Commitment:

In the same way that God saves and calls the church to evangelize, he will make a new heaven and a new earth, and he calls us to participate in this mission. As followers of Jesus Christ we are called to:

- develop a holistic theology from the perspective of the New Creation and to teach it in our churches.

- become involved and to incarnate ourselves in an interactive dialogue with and in our local communities so that we might obtain from creation what it offers to bless humanity and supply us with what we need, without destroying creation.

- live individually, as families and as churches, with a lifestyle that respects creation and thereby gives witness to our commitment of faith.

- commit ourselves to the well-being of those that suffer most from the consequences of these expressions of death.

As in other areas of our faith, let us dare to be different in our care of creation! May God's will be done, here on earth, as it is in heaven. Amen.

CLADE V Pastoral Letter

Final Declaration of CLADE V

As Christian sisters and brothers we participated in the Fifth Latin American Congress on Evangelization (CLADE V), held in San José, Costa Rica, July 9-13, 2012, sponsored by the Fraternidad Teológica Latinoamericana (FTL, Latin American Theological Fellowship).[6] We are grateful to God for the opportunity to gather together around the theme "Following Jesus in God's Kingdom of Life. Guide us, Holy Spirit!," and we would like to share the following reflections.

Following Jesus in the Path of Life

Faced with false, commercialized, esoteric, and spiritualized images that allude to religious conceptions of Jesus, we recognize the urgent need to follow Jesus fully in his path of life. One of our urgent tasks is to rediscover the biblical Jesus and what it means to walk with him. This will lead us to consider our context, to transcend mere theory, and to actively identify with our communities. Our varied realities demand biblical answers to our human needs, answers that will produce a just transformation that will be inclusive regarding gender, ethnic origin, age, differing physical and mental abilities, and minority groups that have traditionally been marginalized, such as immigrant communities. Following Jesus means incarnating his call to transformative mission.

Recommendation

In light of CLADE V, we recommend that local chapters of the FTL in every region encourage dialogue and biblical-theological-contextual reflection, and the subsequent publication and dissemination of such, regarding the meanings and practice of following the biblical Jesus today in his path of life.

---

[6]"CLADE V Pastoral Letter," *Journal of Latin American Theology* 8, no. 1 (2013): 75-79.

The Kingdom of Life

Faced with reductionistic, commercialized, and mystical concepts of the kingdom of God, we recognize the lack of coherence between our verbal commitment with the mission of God's kingdom and our praxis. We urge an open exploration of this kingdom that takes into account diversity, a sense of community, and solidarity, as we make it part of our task of reflection. We need to promote spaces for dialogue and renewal that are inclusive and pluralistic and that connect the presence of God's kingdom with the social realities of our contexts. To achieve inclusivity, we propose taking seriously every human being with his or her unique diversity and creation as the places where this kingdom is manifested. We recognize that God's reign is also demonstrated in movements that struggle for life, for the care of creation, for equality of treatment of men and women of all ages, and for social justice. Therefore, as active agents of this kingdom, we need to involve ourselves in these struggles and, at the same time, to assume a prophetic role that promotes the values of God's kingdom.

Recommendation

In light of CLADE V, we recommend that local chapters of the FTL in every region encourage dialogue and biblical-theological-contextual reflection, and the subsequent publication and dissemination of such, regarding the meanings and practices of the kingdom of life today as we face so many manifestations of death.

The Spirit of Life

Faced with attempts by certain megalomaniac leaders to limit and appropriate the Spirit of life as their own personal property, we recognize that discriminatory and patriarchal practices grieve the Spirit of life. The moving of the Spirit goes beyond ministerial limits by working sovereignly throughout the entire world and inviting us to participate in the kingdom's signs of life. To that end, we need to assume our responsibility as agents of hope in all of the areas of death in our society. We need the Spirit of life to guide us to discern the times and to confront the powers that marginalize our people and that promote environmental destruction, fear, and death. The Spirit gives us power to, with a prophetic voice, denounce the many manifestations of darkness and announce the hope of the utopian[7] kingdom of God and God's injustice as revealed in Jesus Christ.

Recommendation

In light of CLADE V, we recommend that the local chapters of the FTL in every region encourage dialogue and biblical-theological-contextual reflection, and the subsequent publication and dissemination of such, regarding the meanings and practices of the Spirit of life's guidance today.

The Trinitarian Community

Faced with ecclesiastical models that are dominated by business or commercial models or have sold out to the culture of "show business" and that reproduce an individualistic spirituality isolated from our social realities of poverty, individualism, and despair, we recognize that we are frequently seduced to egotistical power that limits the possibility of life for others and promotes closed and apathetic communities. We reaffirm the model of the Trinitarian community that celebrates dialogue, encounter, interculturality, and the mission of God. Our communities should promote love instead of human domination, forgiveness instead of revenge, the justice of the kingdom instead of corruption, peace instead of violence, reconciliation instead of discrimination, the restoration of dreams and the utopia of God's kingdom instead of despair. We should promote communities that follow Jesus in his reign of life and that are passionate for the redemption of all creation by the resurrected Jesus. We urge all followers of Jesus to participate in communities of faith as equals where equality, justice, celebration, freedom, and mutual responsibility flourish as concrete evidence of transformed lives.

Conclusion

Faced with these challenges, we extend a call:

> Follow Jesus in his kingdom of life, with all that this entails, faced with the
> opposing reality, in total dependence on the guidance of the Spirit, even when
> this pursuit means that our Trinitarian communities go against the grain and

---

[7]Translator's note: The word "utopia" in Spanish does not mean a non-existent place as it might mean in English, akin to a pipe dream. Here it does not mean "unrealistic" but rather a powerful vision which, though not totally achievable in this life, does indeed inspire people to live out their lives here on earth with greater hope and at a higher ethical level.

that with our lives we challenge the expressions of death and darkness in our societies.

Jesus encourages us with the words: "As the Father has sent me, I am sending you" (John 20:21).

Recommendation

In light of CLADE V, we recommend that the local chapters of the FTL in every region encourage dialogue and biblical-theological-contextual reflection, and the subsequent publication and dissemination of such, regarding:

- The meanings and practices of following the biblical Jesus today in the path of life.
- The meanings and practices of the kingdom of life today when faced with so many manifestations of death.
- The meanings and practices of guidance by the Spirit of life today.
- The meanings and practices of being a community today modeled after the life of the Trinity.

Editorial Committee

Clemir Fernandes
Silvina Kosacki
Alejandra Ortiz
Daniel Salinas

WORLD COUNCIL OF CHURCHES TIMELINE

oikoumene

A timeline of the World Council of Churches

An Ecumenical Journey

1890

1895

1900

1905

1910

1915

1920

1925

1930

1935

1940

1945

1950

• World Student Christian Federation founded, 1895

EDINBURGH, 1910
WORLD MISSION CONFERENCE

• First proposal for a Week of Prayer for Christian Unity

• Edinburgh World Mission Conference, 1910

WORLD MISSION CONFERENCE

LAKE MOHONK, 1921

OXFORD, 1923

• The Ecumenical Synod of Constantinople calls for a "League of Churches," 1920

JERUSALEM, 1928

MADRAS, 1938

WORLD CONFERENCE ON FAITH AND ORDER

LAUSANNE, 1927

EDINBURGH, 1937

WORLD CONFERENCE ON LIFE AND WORK

STOCKHOLM, 1925

OXFORD, 1937

UTRECHT, 1938

AMSTERDAM, 1939
World Conference of Christian Youth

• Life and Work, Faith and Order agree to form World Council of Churches, 1937

WHITBY, 1947

WILLINGEN,

WORLD COUNCIL OF CHURCH

• Foundation of WCC's Ecumenical dispute at (near Geneva) and of the Commission on International Affairs (CCIA), 1946

LUND, 1952

ROME, 1907

WORLD COUNCIL OF CHRISTIAN EDUCATION (WCCE) CONFERENCES

STOCKHOLM, 1925

FRANKF

TORONTO, 1950

1st WCC ASSEMBLY
Amsterdam, The Netherlands • 22 August
Theme: "Man's Disorder and God's Design"
Delegates: 351 (147 member churches)

2nd WCC
Evanston, USA
Theme: "Chris
Delegates: 502

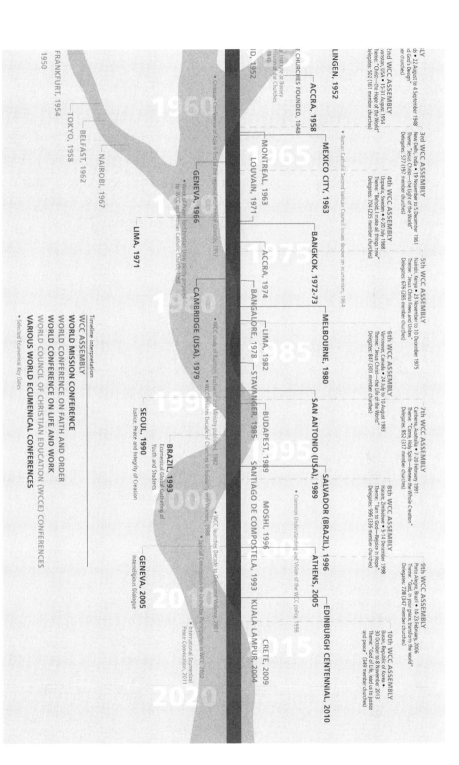

ILY
ds • 22 August to 4 September 1948
d God's Design
er churches)

3rd WCC ASSEMBLY
New Delhi, India • 19 November to 5 December 1961
Theme: "Jesus Christ—the Light of the World"
Delegates: 577 (197 member churches)

5th WCC ASSEMBLY
Nairobi, Kenya • 23 November to 10 December 1975
Theme: "Jesus Christ Frees and Unites"
Delegates: 676 (285 member churches)

7th WCC ASSEMBLY
Canberra, Australia • 7-20 February 1991
Theme: "Come, Holy Spirit—Renew the Whole Creation"
Delegates: 852 (317 member churches)

9th WCC ASSEMBLY
Porto Alegre, Brazil • 14-23 February, 2006
Theme: "God, in your grace, transform the world"
Delegates: 728 (347 member churches)

2nd WCC ASSEMBLY
Evanston, USA • 15-31 August 1954
Theme: "Christ—the Hope of the World"
Delegates: 502 (161 member churches)

4th WCC ASSEMBLY
Uppsala, Sweden • 4-20 July 1968
Theme: "Behold, I make all things new"
Delegates: 704 (235 member churches)

6th WCC ASSEMBLY
Vancouver, Canada • 24 July to 10 August 1983
Theme: "Jesus Christ—the Life of the World"
Delegates: 847 (301 member churches)

8th WCC ASSEMBLY
Harare, Zimbabwe • 3-14 December 1998
Theme: "Turn to God—Rejoice in Hope"
Delegates: 996 (336 member churches)

10th WCC ASSEMBLY
Busan, Republic of Korea •
30 October to 8 November 2013
Theme: "God of Life, lead us to justice
and peace" (349 member churches)

al Institute at Bossey
Mission of the Churches
1946

ID, 1952

LINGEN, 1952

• Christian Conference of Asia a field for the regional ecumenical councils, 1957

CHURCHES FOUNDED, 1948

ACCRA, 1958

MEXICO CITY, 1963

• Roman Catholic Second Vatican Council issues decree on ecumenism, 1964

MONTREAL, 1963

LOUVAIN, 1971

BANGKOK, 1972-73

MELBOURNE, 1980

SAN ANTONIO (USA), 1989

SALVADOR (BRAZIL), 1996

ATHENS, 2005

EDINBURGH CENTENNIAL, 2010

• Common Understanding and Vision of the WCC policy, 1998

GENEVA, 1966

ACCRA, 1974

BANGALORE, 1978

LIMA, 1982

STAVANGER, 1985

BUDAPEST, 1989

SANTIAGO DE COMPOSTELA, 1993

MOSHI, 1996

CRETE, 2009

KUALA LUMPUR, 2004

CAMBRIDGE (USA), 1979

• Week of Prayer for Christian Unity jointly prepared
by WCC and Roman Catholic Church, 1968

• WCC study of Baptism, Eucharist and Ministry published, 1982

• WCC celebrates Decade of Churches in Solidarity with Women, 1988

• WCC launches Decade to Overcome Violence, 2001

• Special Commission on Orthodox Perception within WCC, 1998

• International Ecumenical
Peace Convocation, 2011

LIMA, 1971

BRAZIL, 1993
Ecumenical Global Gathering of
Youth and Students

SEOUL, 1990
Justice, Peace and Integrity of Creation

GENEVA, 2005
Interreligious Dialogue

NAIROBI, 1967

BELFAST, 1962

TOKYO, 1958

FRANKFURT, 1954

1950

Timeline interpretation

WCC ASSEMBLY
WORLD MISSION CONFERENCE
WORLD CONFERENCE ON FAITH AND ORDER
WORLD CONFERENCE ON LIFE AND WORK
WORLD COUNCIL OF CHRISTIAN EDUCATION (WCCE) CONFERENCES
VARIOUS WORLD ECUMENICAL CONFERENCES

• Selected Ecumenical Key Dates

NAME INDEX

SUBJECT INDEX

SCRIPTURE INDEX